DEAT

WOL\

COLLECTION EDITOR: **JENNIFER GRÜNWALD**

ASSISTANT EDITOR: **SARAH BRUNSTAD**

ASSOCIATE MANAGING EDITOR: **ALEX STARBUCK**

EDITOR, SPECIAL PROJECTS: **MARK D. BEAZLEY**

SENIOR EDITOR, SPECIAL PROJECTS: **JEFF YOUNGQUIST**

SVP PRINT, SALES & MARKETING: **DAVID GABRIEL**

BOOK DESIGN: **JEFF POWELL**

DEATH OF WOLVERINE. Contains material originally published in magazine form as DEATH OF WOLVERINE #1-4. First printing 2015. ISBN# 978-0-7851-9351-7. Published by MARVEL WORLDWIDE, INC., a subsidiary of MARVEL ENTERTAINMENT, LLC. OFFICE OF PUBLICATION: 135 West 50th Street, New York, NY 10020. Copyright © and 2015 Marvel Characters, Inc. All rights reserved. All characters featured in this issue and the distinctive names and likenesses thereof, and all related indicia are trademarks of Marvel Characters, Inc. No similarity between any of the names, characters, persons, and/or institutions in this magazine with those of any living or dead person or institution is intended, and any such similarity which may exist is purely coincidental. **Printed in the U.S.A.** ALAN FINE, EVP - Office of the President, Marvel Worldwide, Inc. and EVP & CMO Marvel Characters B.V.; DAN BUCKLEY, Publisher & President - Print, Animation & Digital Divisions; JOE QUESADA, Chief Creative Officer; TOM BREVOORT, SVP of Publishing; DAVID BOGART, SVP of Operations & Procurement, Publishing; C.B. CEBULSKI, SVP of Creator & Content Development; DAVID GABRIEL, SVP Print, Sales & Marketing; JIM O'KEEFE, VP of Operations & Logistics; DAN CARR, Executive Director of Publishing Technology; SUSAN CRESPI, Editorial Operations Manager; ALEX MORALES, Publishing Operations Manager; STAN LEE, Chairman Emeritus. For information regarding advertising in Marvel Comics or on Marvel.com, please contact Niza Disla, Director of Marvel Partnerships, at ndisla@marvel.com. For Marvel subscription inquiries, please call 800-217-9158. **Manufactured between 10/31/2014 and 12/15/2014 by WORZALLA PUBLISHING CO., STEVENS POINT, WI, USA.**

10 9 8 7 6 5 4 3 2 1

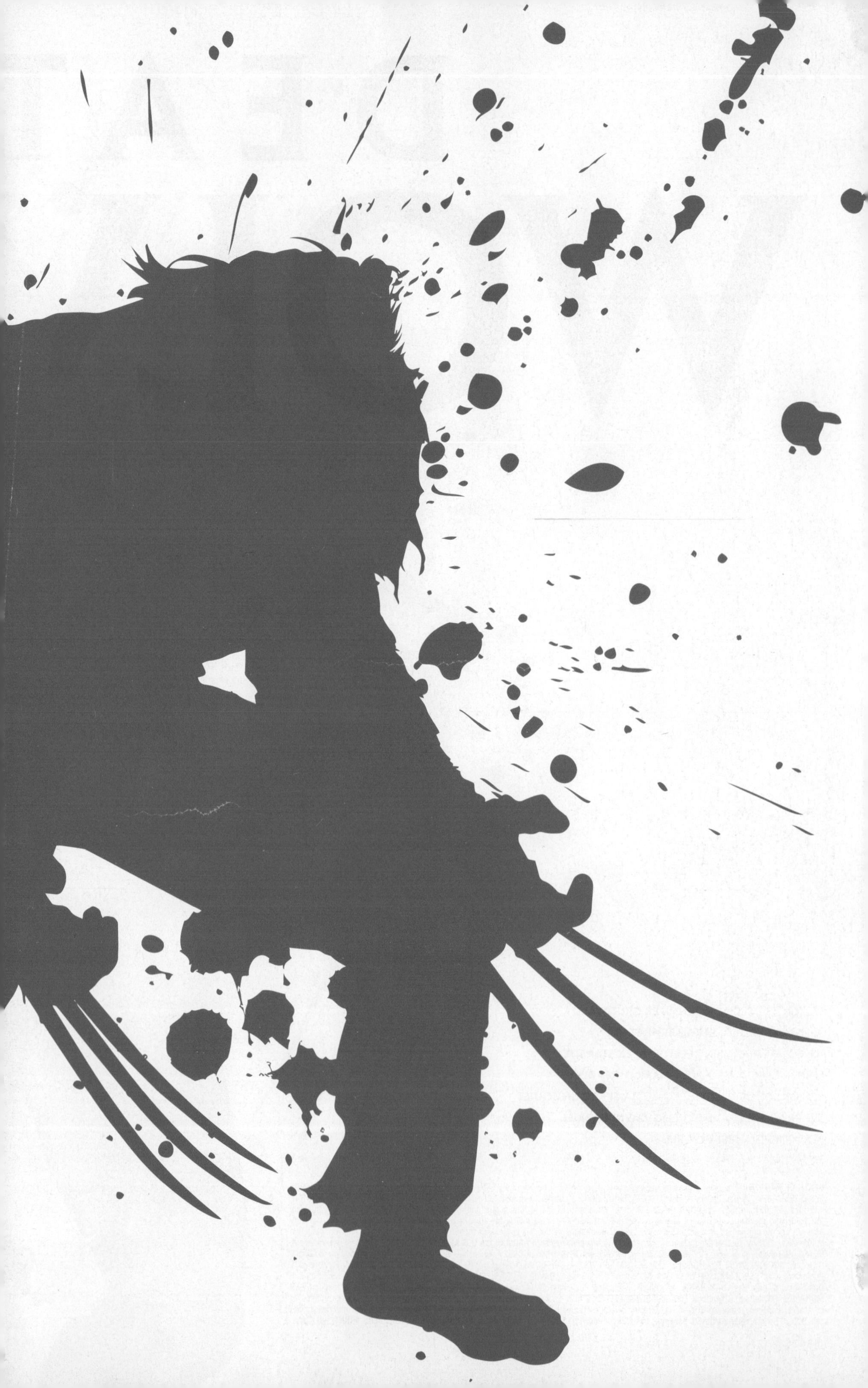

H OF
ERINE

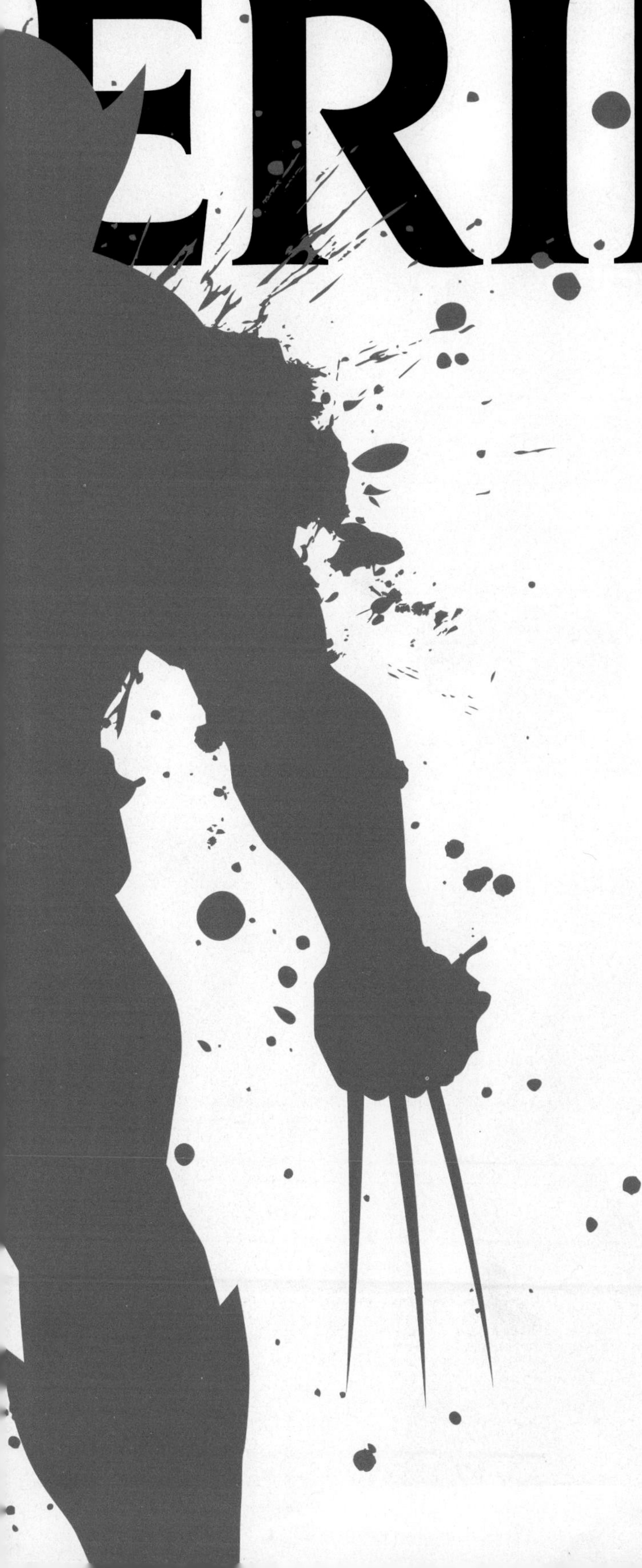

WRITER
CHARLES SOULE

PENCILER
STEVE McNIVEN

INKER
JAY LEISTEN

COLORIST
JUSTIN PONSOR

LETTERER
CHRIS ELIOPOULOS

COVER ART
STEVE McNIVEN,
JAY LEISTEN
& JUSTIN PONSOR

ASSISTANT EDITOR
XANDER JAROWEY

CONSULTING EDITOR
KATIE KUBERT

EDITOR
MIKE MARTS

1

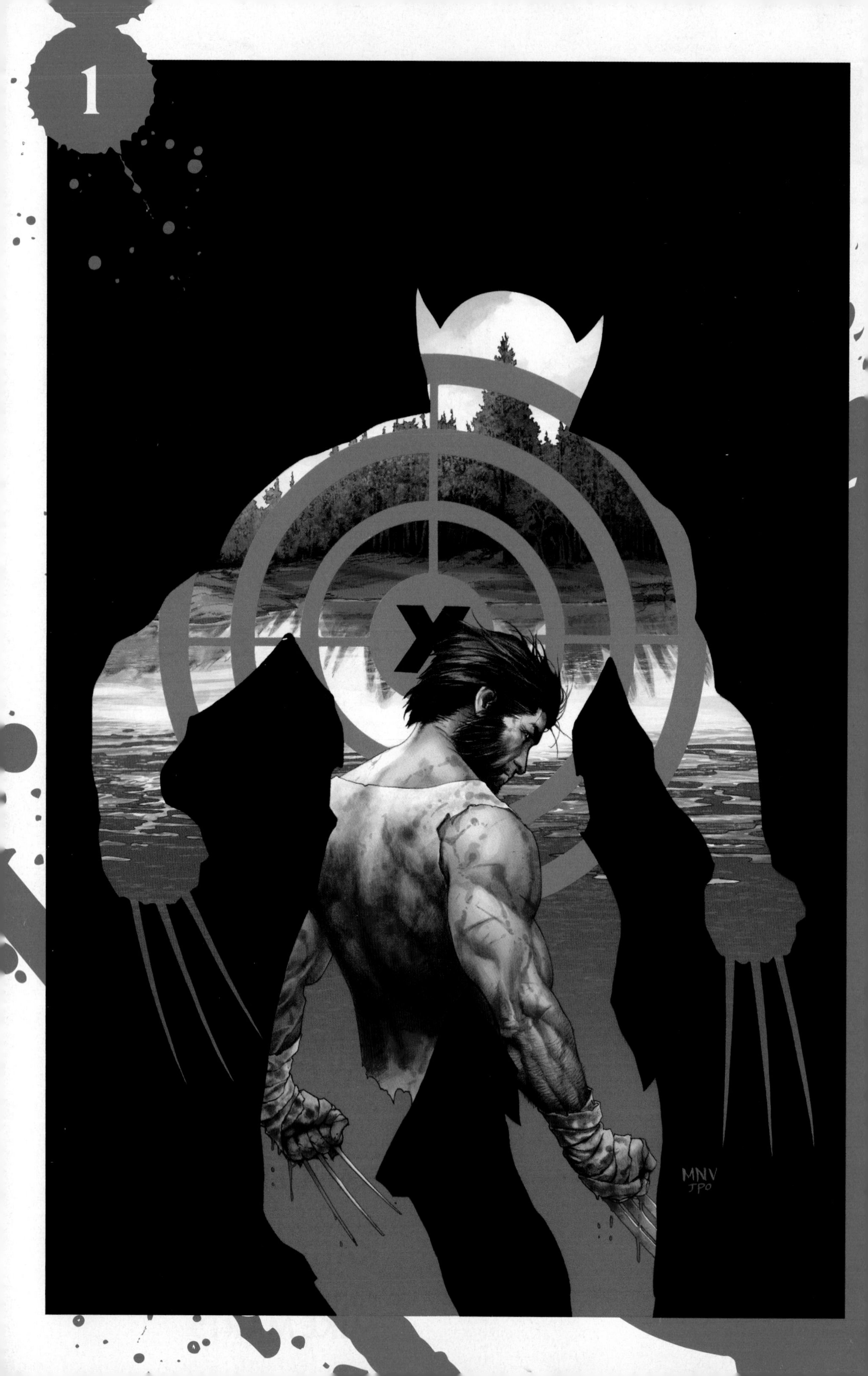
MNV
JPO

THE END

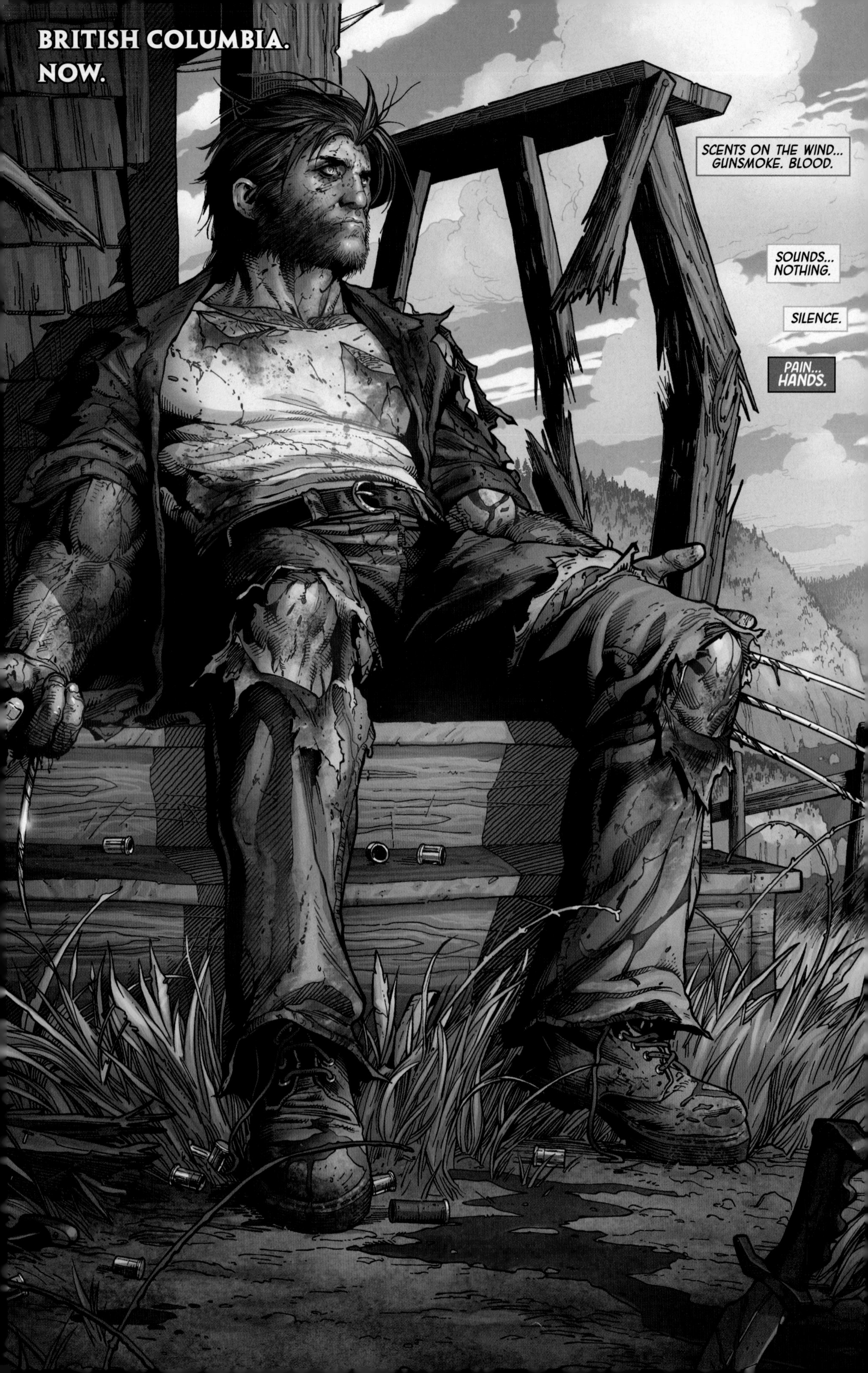
BRITISH COLUMBIA. NOW.
SCENTS ON THE WIND... GUNSMOKE. BLOOD.
SOUNDS... NOTHING.
SILENCE.
PAIN... HANDS.

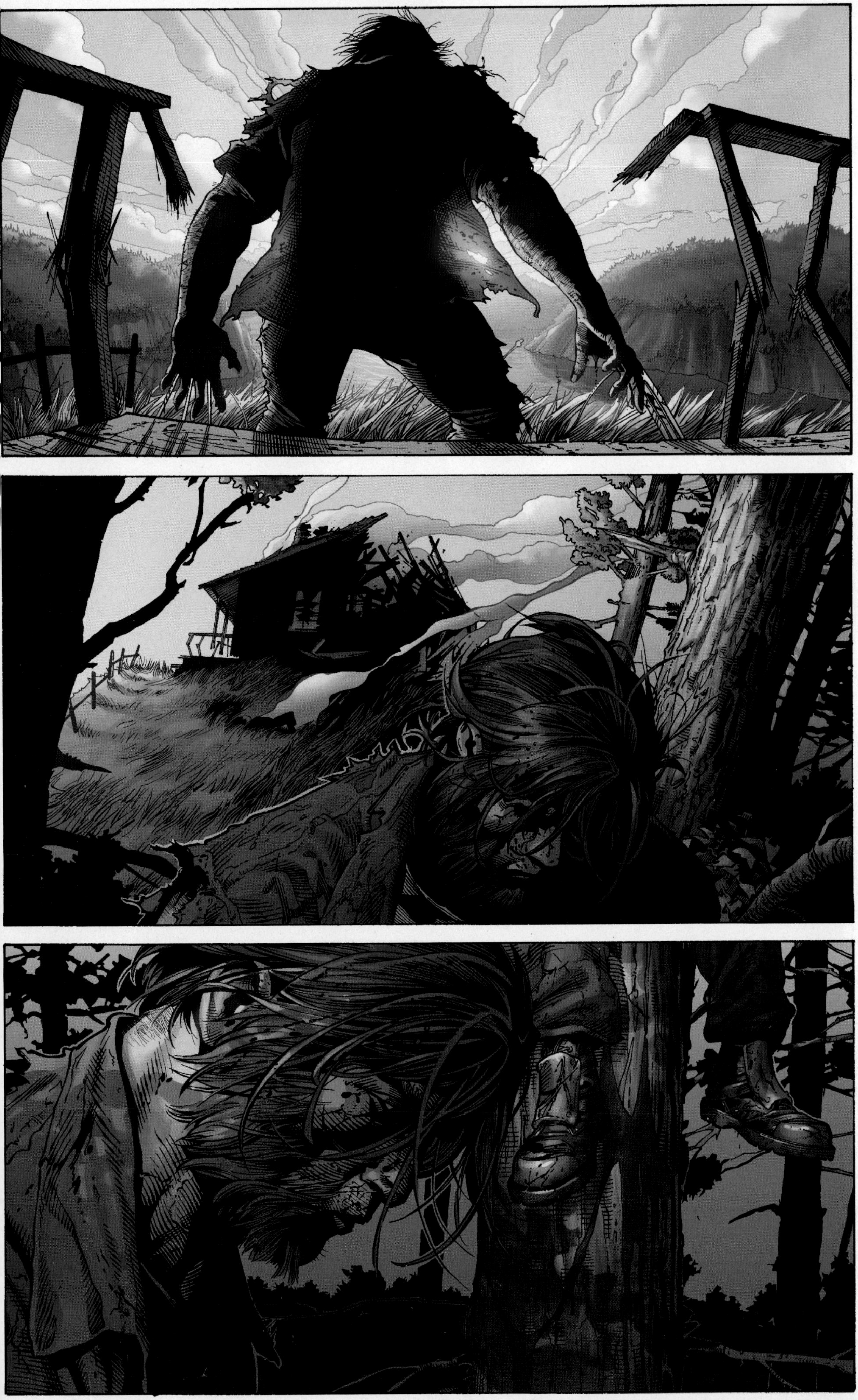

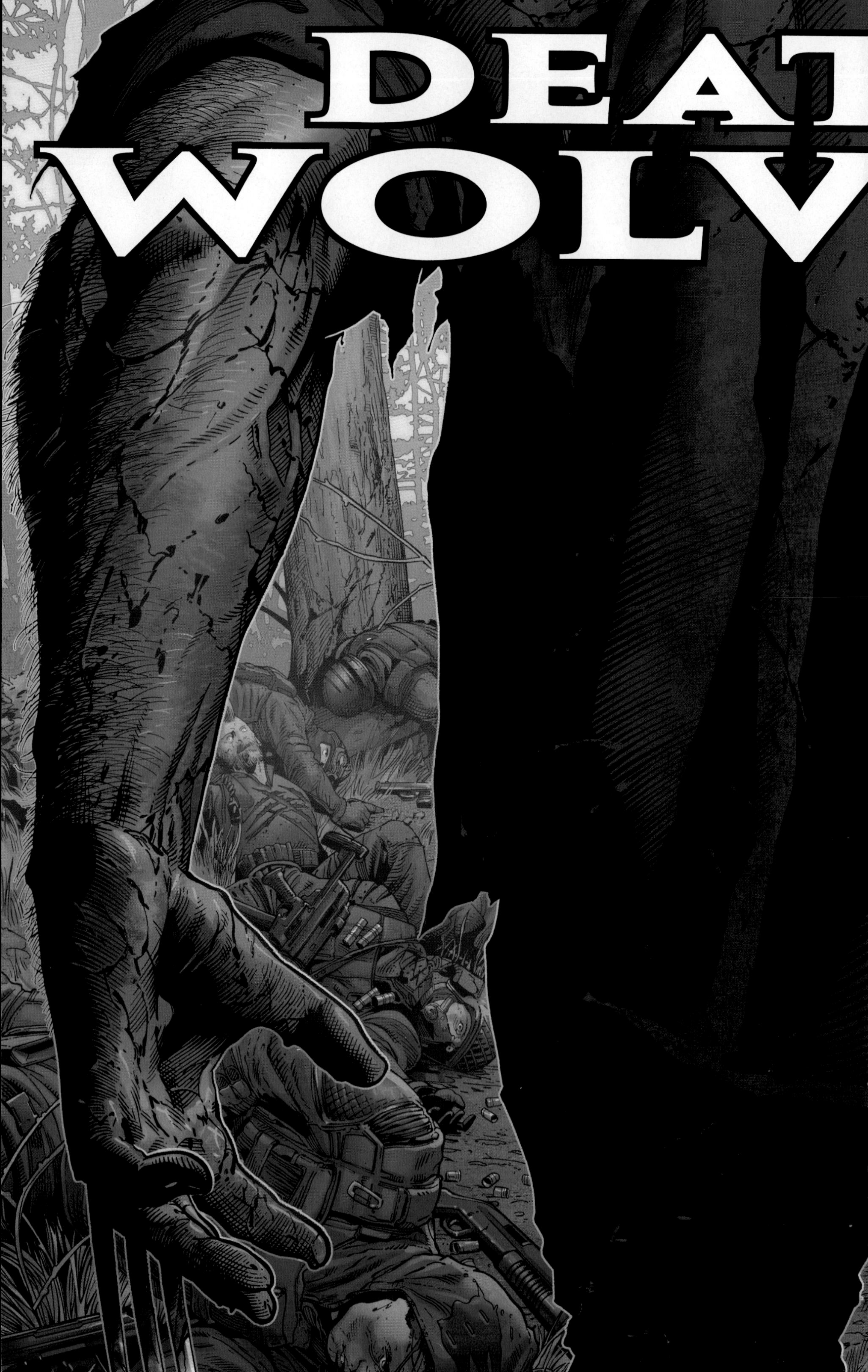
DEAT
WOLV

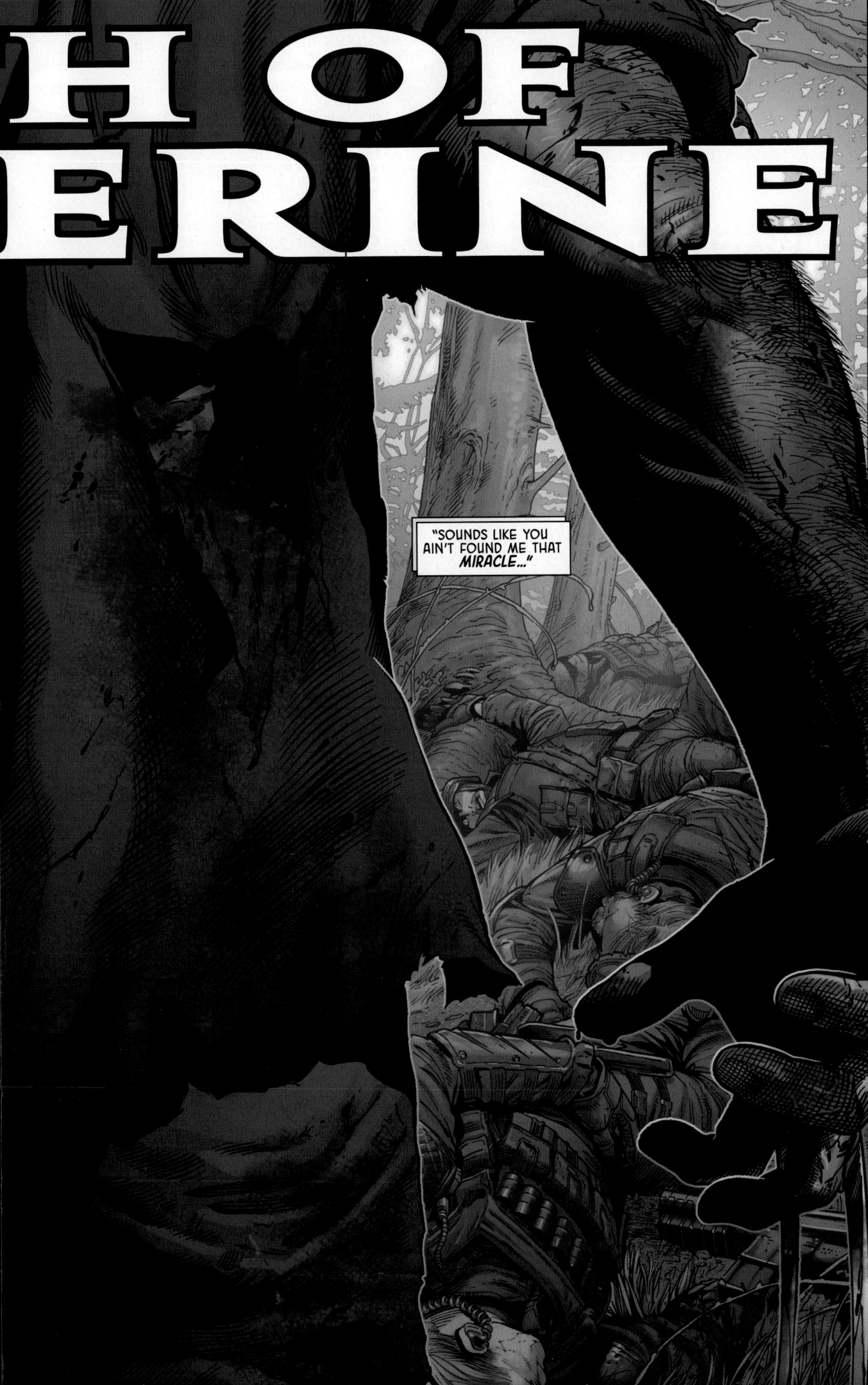
H OF
ERINE
"SOUNDS LIKE YOU AIN'T FOUND ME THAT *MIRACLE*..."

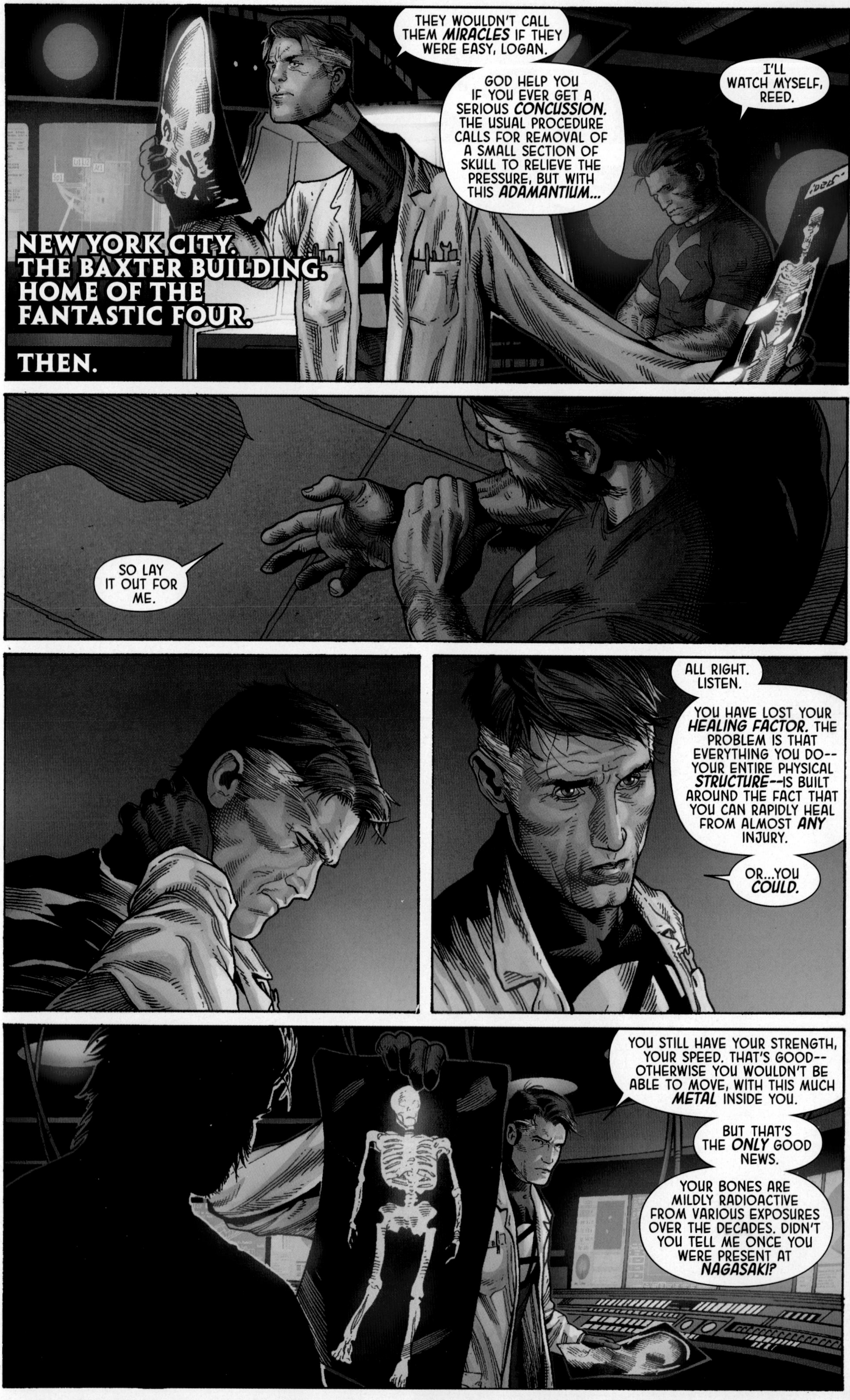
NEW YORK CITY. THE BAXTER BUILDING. HOME OF THE FANTASTIC FOUR.
THEN.
THEY WOULDN'T CALL THEM *MIRACLES* IF THEY WERE EASY, LOGAN.
GOD HELP YOU IF YOU EVER GET A SERIOUS *CONCUSSION.* THE USUAL PROCEDURE CALLS FOR REMOVAL OF A SMALL SECTION OF SKULL TO RELIEVE THE PRESSURE, BUT WITH THIS *ADAMANTIUM*...
I'LL WATCH MYSELF, REED.
SO LAY IT OUT FOR ME.
ALL RIGHT. LISTEN.
YOU HAVE LOST YOUR *HEALING FACTOR.* THE PROBLEM IS THAT EVERYTHING YOU DO--YOUR ENTIRE PHYSICAL *STRUCTURE*--IS BUILT AROUND THE FACT THAT YOU CAN RAPIDLY HEAL FROM ALMOST *ANY* INJURY.
OR...YOU *COULD.*
YOU STILL HAVE YOUR STRENGTH, YOUR SPEED. THAT'S GOOD--OTHERWISE YOU WOULDN'T BE ABLE TO MOVE, WITH THIS MUCH *METAL* INSIDE YOU.
BUT THAT'S THE *ONLY* GOOD NEWS.
YOUR BONES ARE MILDLY RADIOACTIVE FROM VARIOUS EXPOSURES OVER THE DECADES. DIDN'T YOU TELL ME ONCE YOU WERE PRESENT AT *NAGASAKI?*

YEAH.

YES, WELL. YOU'RE A PRIME CANDIDATE FOR HEAVY METAL-RELATED *LEUKEMIA.*

IF YOU DON'T GET ENDOCARDITIS FROM ALL THE BACTERIA YOU PULL INTO YOURSELF EVERY TIME YOU USE YOUR CLAWS.

I CAN SOLVE THIS FOR YOU. I CAN SPEAK WITH STARK, AND HANK McCOY... WE CAN--

ALREADY SEEN 'EM. YOU'RE THE LAST GENIUS ON MY LIST, STRETCH. NO OFFENSE.

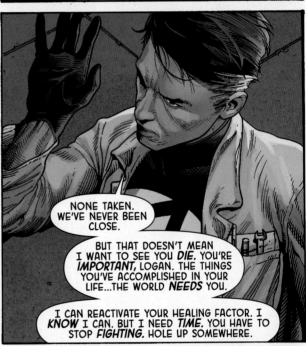

NONE TAKEN. WE'VE NEVER BEEN CLOSE.

BUT THAT DOESN'T MEAN I WANT TO SEE YOU *DIE.* YOU'RE *IMPORTANT,* LOGAN. THE THINGS YOU'VE ACCOMPLISHED IN YOUR LIFE...THE WORLD *NEEDS* YOU.

I CAN REACTIVATE YOUR HEALING FACTOR. I *KNOW* I CAN. BUT I NEED *TIME.* YOU HAVE TO STOP *FIGHTING.* HOLE UP SOMEWHERE.

YEAH, SEE, THAT'S THE PROBLEM. WORD'S GONNA GET OUT. DON'T KNOW *HOW,* DON'T KNOW *WHO,* BUT IT *WILL.*

AND THEN THEY'LL COME HUNTING. OPEN SEASON.

WELL, FINE. BUT YOU DON'T HAVE TO *INVITE* IT.

AND FOR GOD'S SAKE, LOGAN, PLEASE...

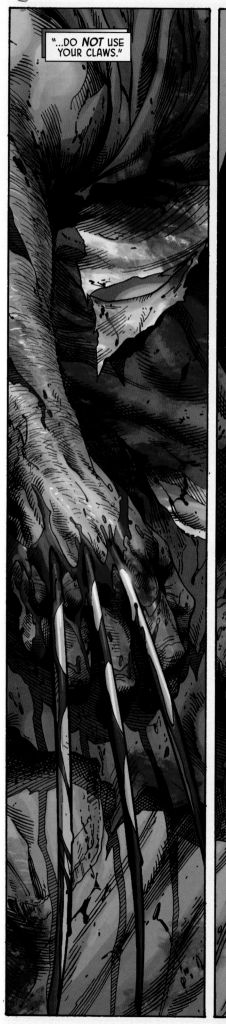

"...DO **NOT** USE YOUR CLAWS."

SHKK

HANDS

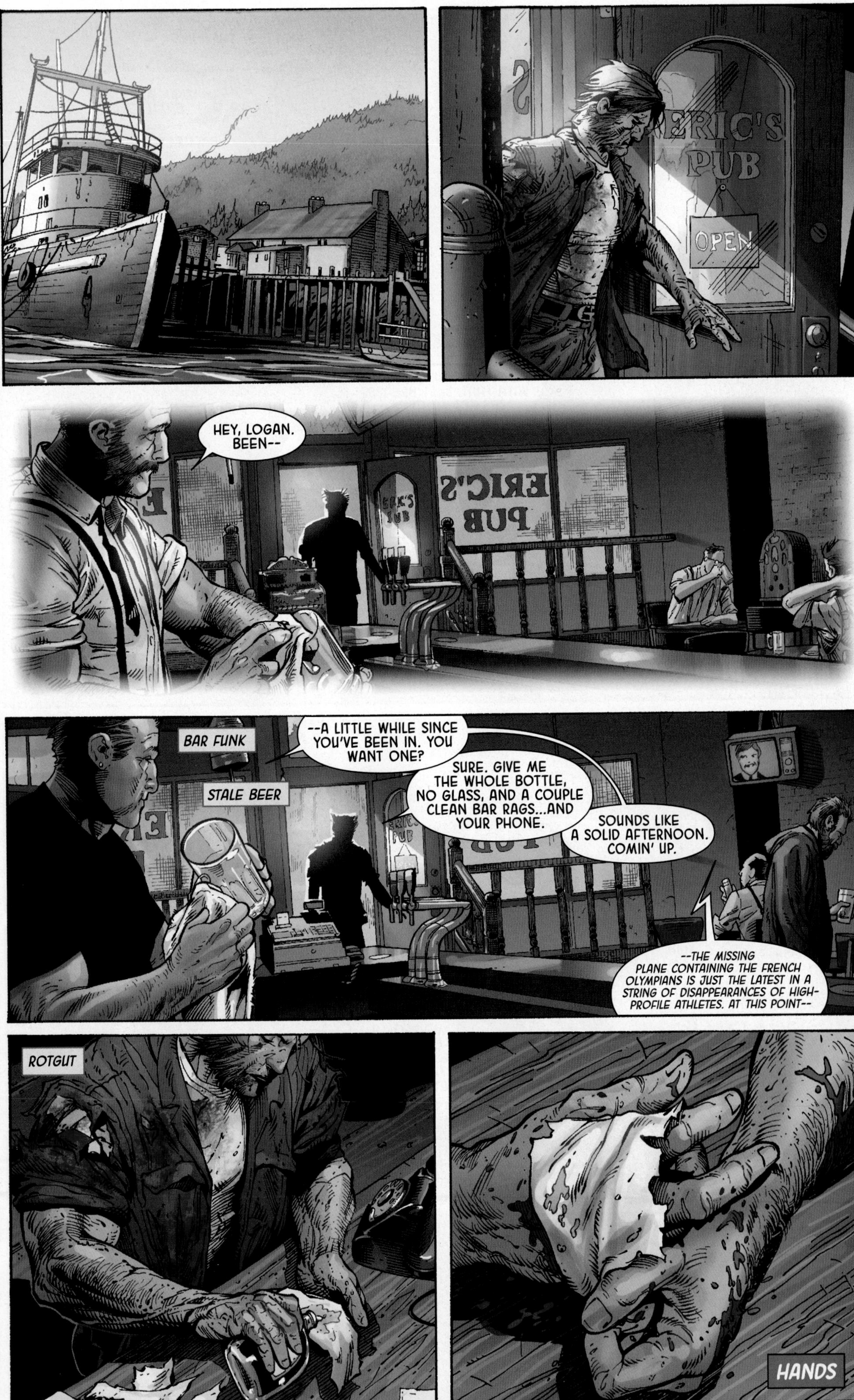

ERIC'S PUB
OPEN
HEY, LOGAN. BEEN--
BAR FUNK
STALE BEER
--A LITTLE WHILE SINCE YOU'VE BEEN IN. YOU WANT ONE?
SURE. GIVE ME THE WHOLE BOTTLE, NO GLASS, AND A COUPLE CLEAN BAR RAGS...AND YOUR PHONE.
SOUNDS LIKE A SOLID AFTERNOON. COMIN' UP.
--THE MISSING PLANE CONTAINING THE FRENCH OLYMPIANS IS JUST THE LATEST IN A STRING OF DISAPPEARANCES OF HIGH-PROFILE ATHLETES. AT THIS POINT--
ROTGUT
HANDS

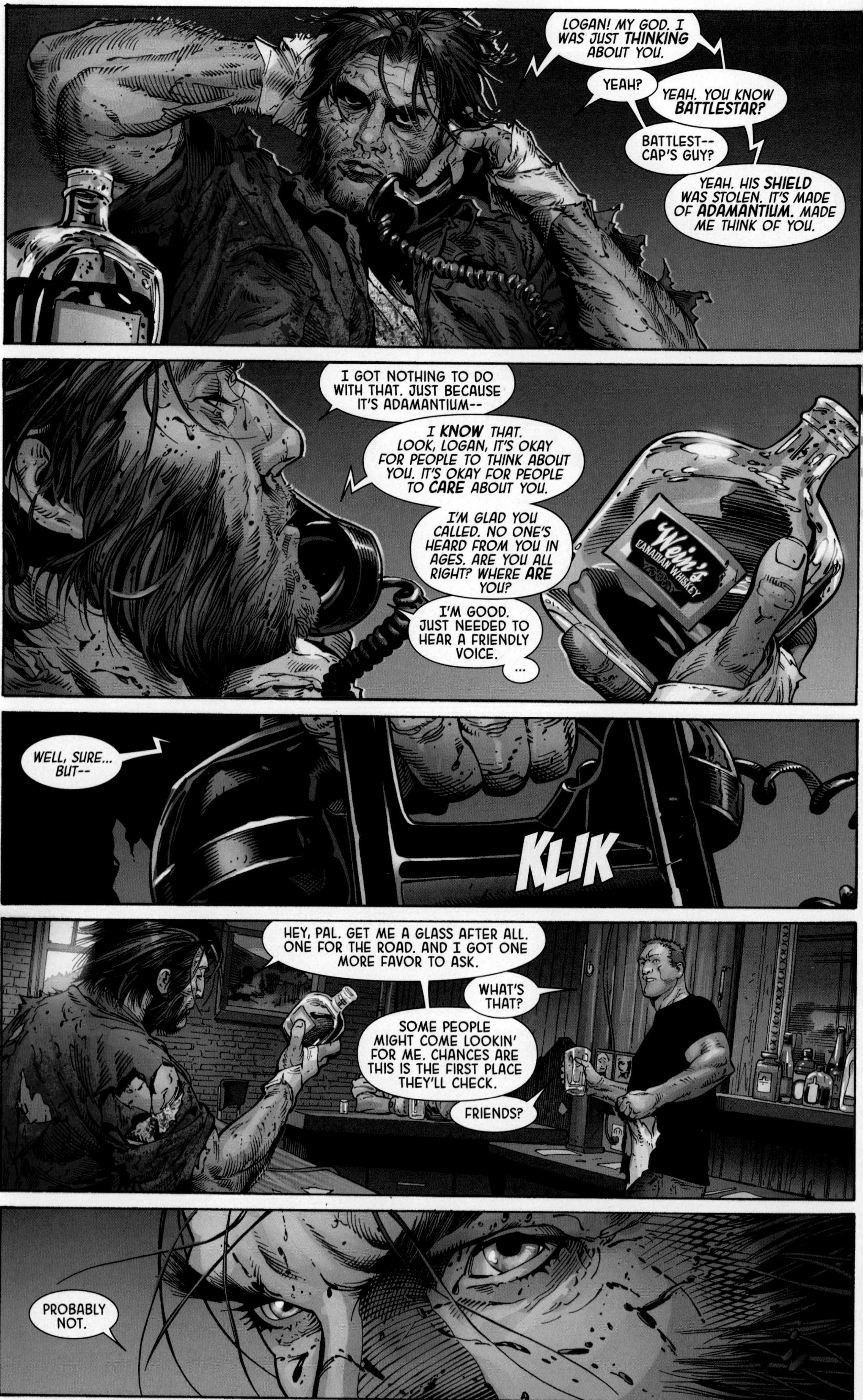
LOGAN! MY GOD. I WAS JUST THINKING ABOUT YOU.
YEAH?
YEAH. YOU KNOW BATTLESTAR?
BATTLEST-- CAP'S GUY?
YEAH. HIS SHIELD WAS STOLEN. IT'S MADE OF ADAMANTIUM. MADE ME THINK OF YOU.
I GOT NOTHING TO DO WITH THAT. JUST BECAUSE IT'S ADAMANTIUM--
I KNOW THAT. LOOK, LOGAN, IT'S OKAY FOR PEOPLE TO THINK ABOUT YOU. IT'S OKAY FOR PEOPLE TO CARE ABOUT YOU.
I'M GLAD YOU CALLED. NO ONE'S HEARD FROM YOU IN AGES. ARE YOU ALL RIGHT? WHERE ARE YOU?
Wein's CANADIAN WHISKEY
I'M GOOD. JUST NEEDED TO HEAR A FRIENDLY VOICE.
...
WELL, SURE... BUT--
KLIK
HEY, PAL. GET ME A GLASS AFTER ALL. ONE FOR THE ROAD. AND I GOT ONE MORE FAVOR TO ASK.
WHAT'S THAT?
SOME PEOPLE MIGHT COME LOOKIN' FOR ME. CHANCES ARE THIS IS THE FIRST PLACE THEY'LL CHECK.
FRIENDS?
PROBABLY NOT.

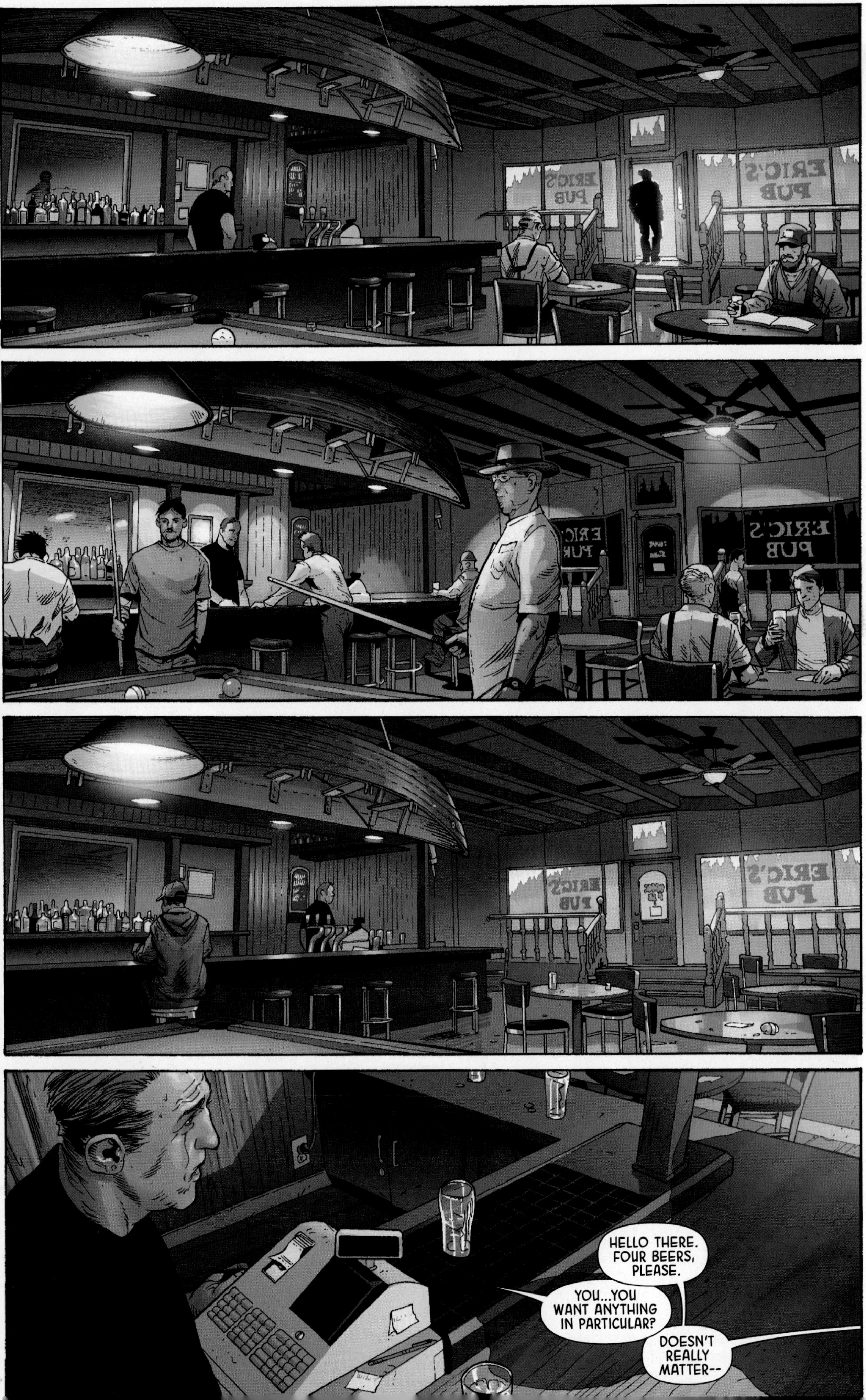
ERIC'S PUB
HELLO THERE. FOUR BEERS, PLEASE.
YOU...YOU WANT ANYTHING IN PARTICULAR?
DOESN'T REALLY MATTER--

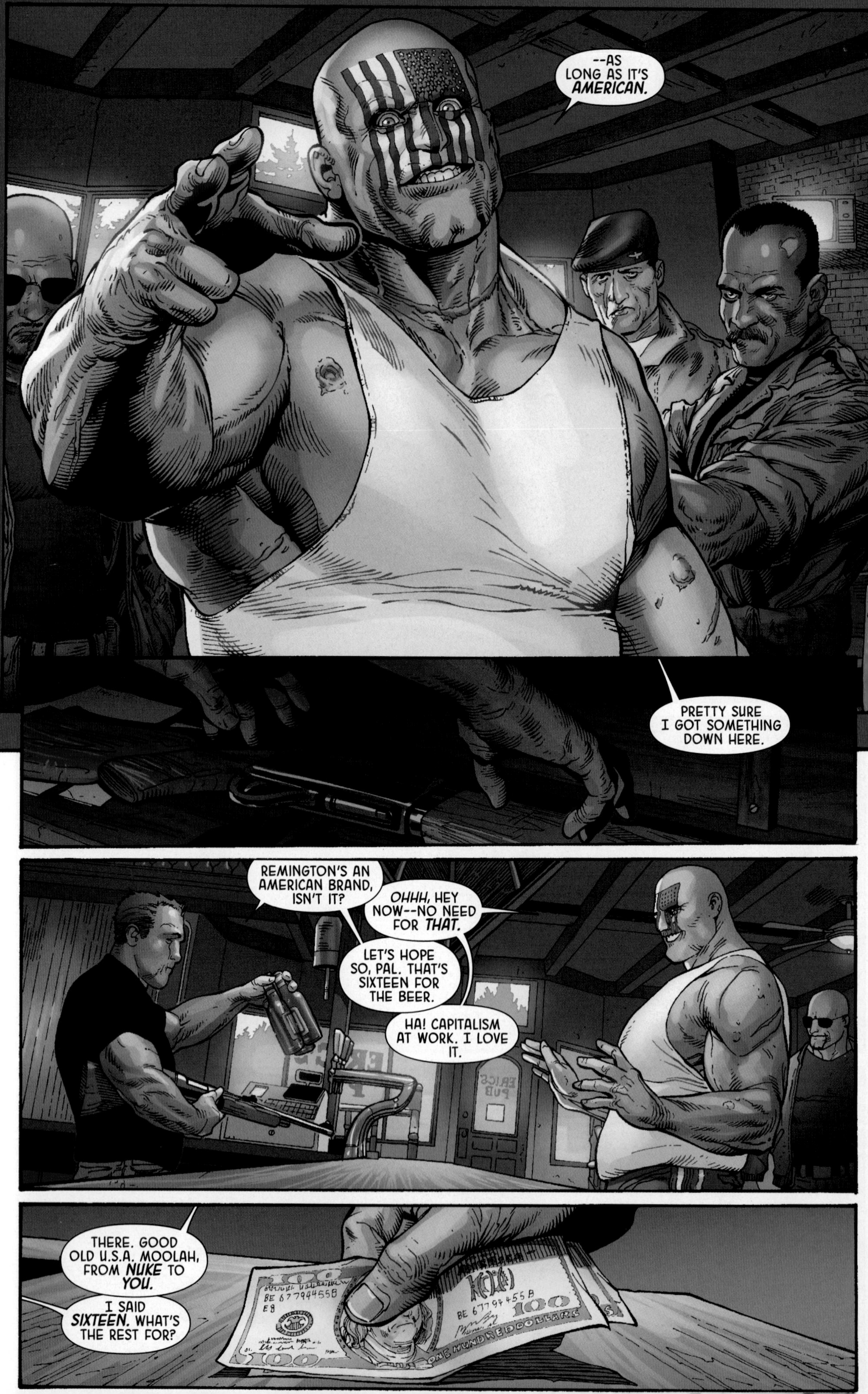

--AS LONG AS IT'S AMERICAN.
PRETTY SURE I GOT SOMETHING DOWN HERE.
REMINGTON'S AN AMERICAN BRAND, ISN'T IT?
OHHH, HEY NOW--NO NEED FOR THAT.
LET'S HOPE SO, PAL. THAT'S SIXTEEN FOR THE BEER.
HA! CAPITALISM AT WORK. I LOVE IT.
ERIC'S PUB
THERE. GOOD OLD U.S.A. MOOLAH, FROM NUKE TO YOU.
I SAID SIXTEEN. WHAT'S THE REST FOR?

KRRNCH

FOR *THIS.*

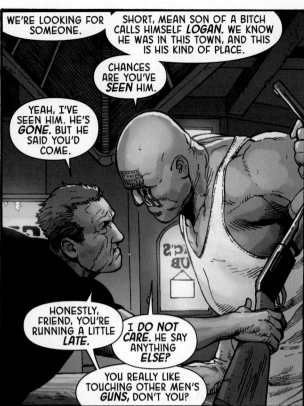

WE'RE LOOKING FOR SOMEONE.

SHORT, MEAN SON OF A BITCH CALLS HIMSELF *LOGAN.* WE KNOW HE WAS IN THIS TOWN, AND THIS IS HIS KIND OF PLACE.

CHANCES ARE YOU'VE *SEEN* HIM.

YEAH, I'VE SEEN HIM. HE'S *GONE.* BUT HE SAID YOU'D COME.

HONESTLY, FRIEND, YOU'RE RUNNING A LITTLE *LATE.*

I DO NOT CARE. HE SAY ANYTHING *ELSE?*

YOU REALLY LIKE TOUCHING OTHER MEN'S *GUNS,* DON'T YOU?

I'LL ASK ONE MORE TIME BEFORE I START TAKING FINGERS. *WHAT DID LOGAN SAY?*

HE DIDN'T *SAY* NOTHIN'.

HE JUST LEFT *THIS.*

COME ON THEN YOU COWARDS

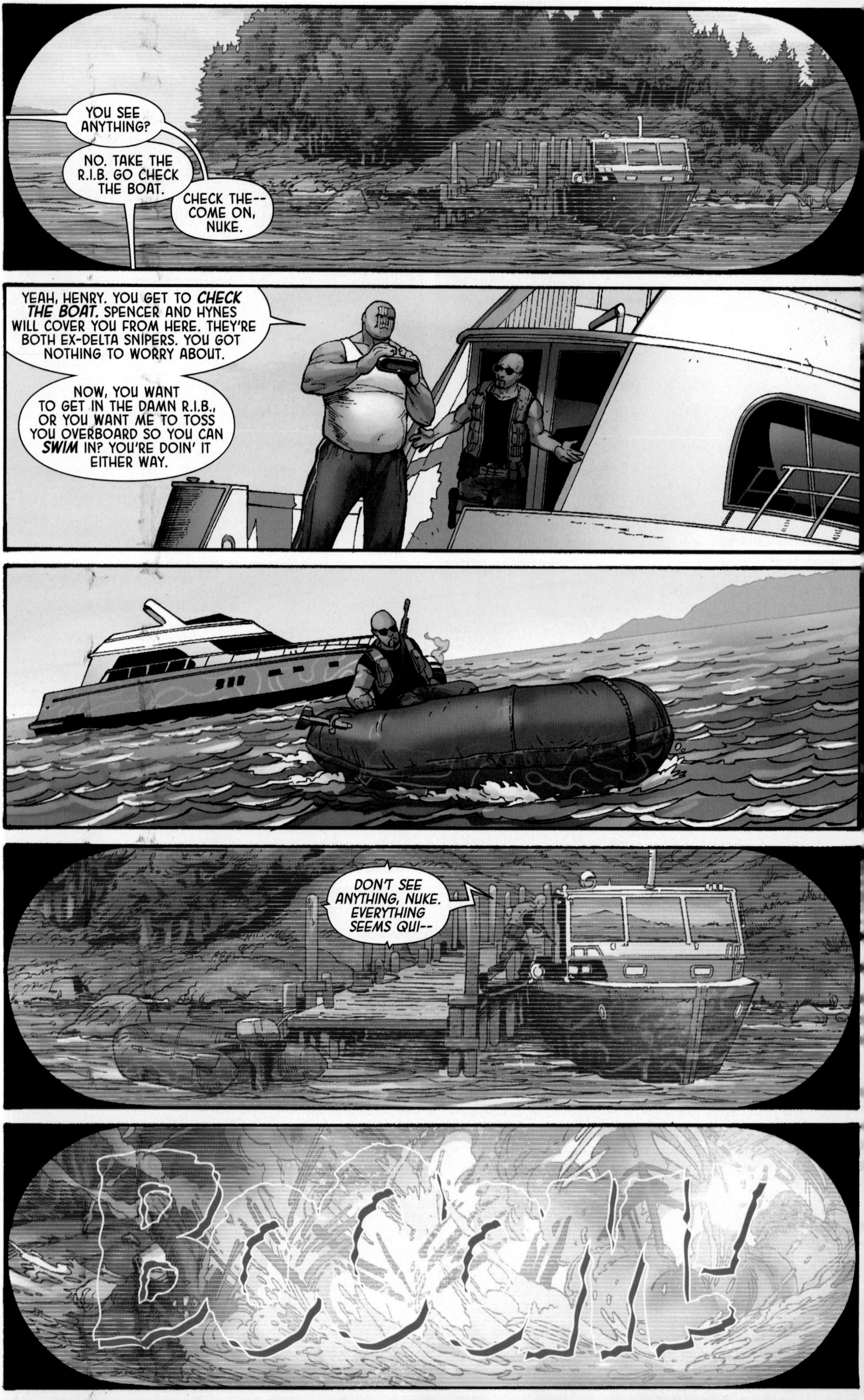
YOU SEE ANYTHING?
NO. TAKE THE R.I.B. GO CHECK THE BOAT.
CHECK THE-- COME ON, NUKE.
YEAH, HENRY. YOU GET TO *CHECK THE BOAT.* SPENCER AND HYNES WILL COVER YOU FROM HERE. THEY'RE BOTH EX-DELTA SNIPERS. YOU GOT NOTHING TO WORRY ABOUT.
NOW, YOU WANT TO GET IN THE DAMN R.I.B., OR YOU WANT ME TO TOSS YOU OVERBOARD SO YOU CAN *SWIM* IN? YOU'RE DOIN' IT EITHER WAY.
DON'T SEE ANYTHING, NUKE. EVERYTHING SEEMS QUI--
BOOM!

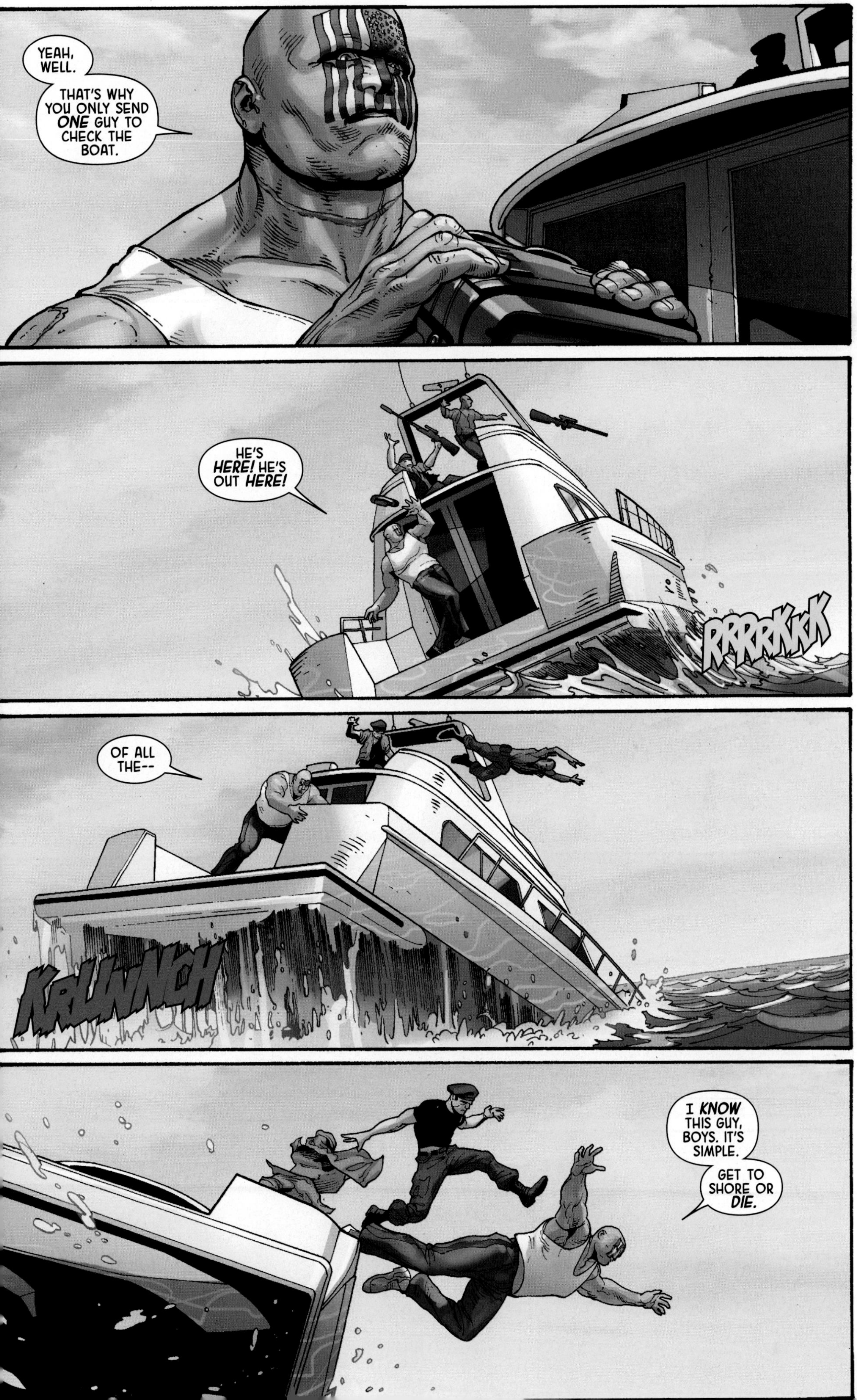

YEAH, WELL.
THAT'S WHY YOU ONLY SEND ONE GUY TO CHECK THE BOAT.
HE'S HERE! HE'S OUT HERE!
RRRRKKK
OF ALL THE--
KRUNCH
I KNOW THIS GUY, BOYS. IT'S SIMPLE.
GET TO SHORE OR DIE.

NNF!
OH...YOU SON OF A...PRETTY GOOD, LOGAN. THAT WAS...PRETTY GOOD.
OH NO.

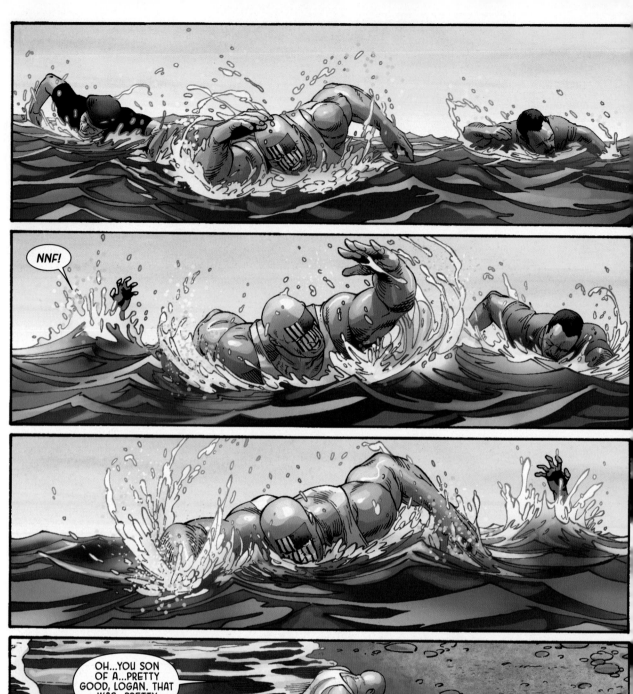

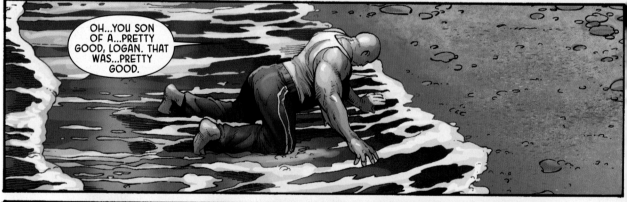

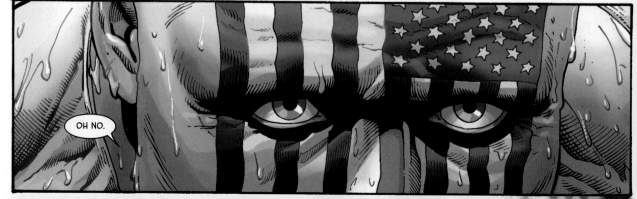

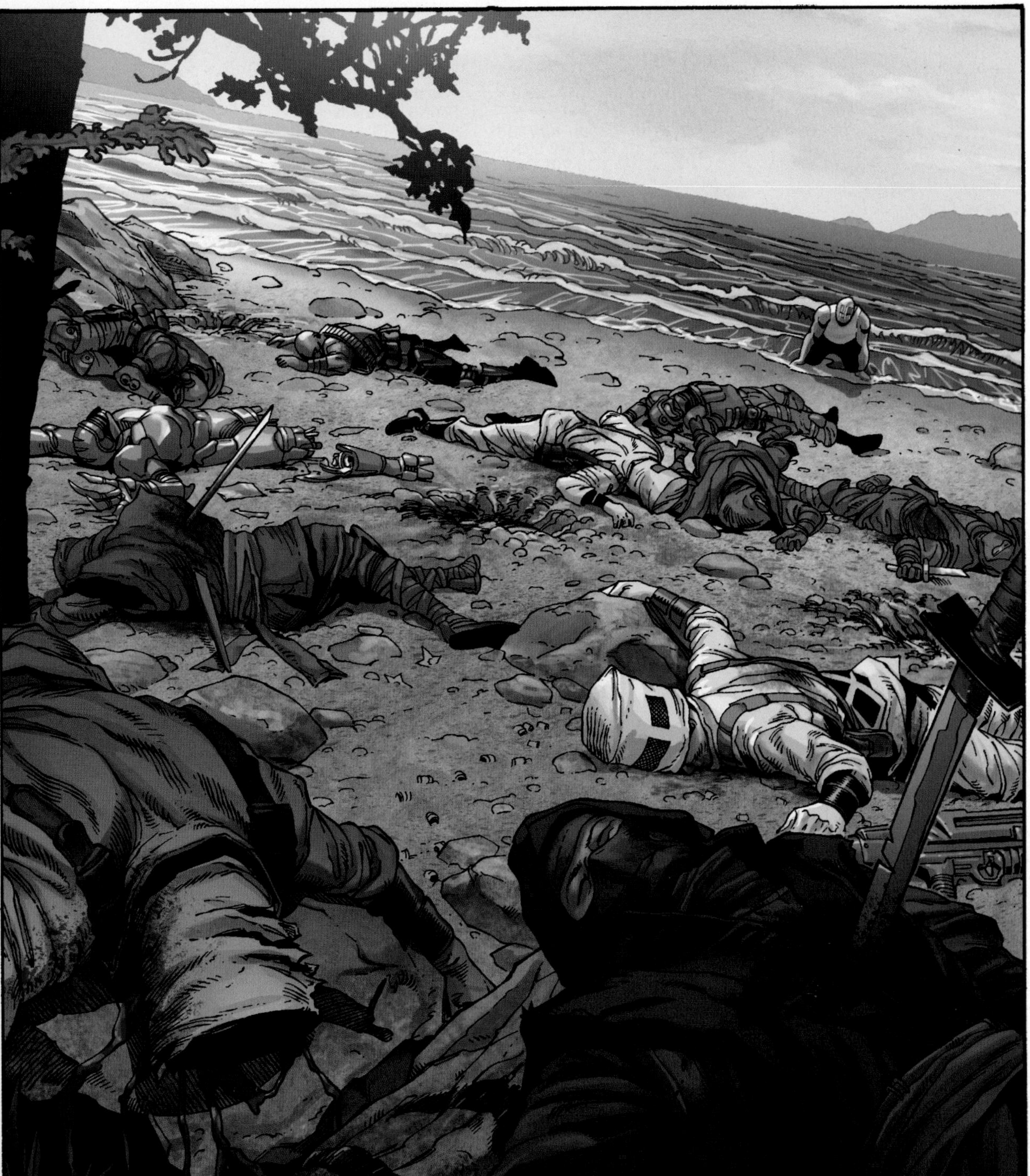

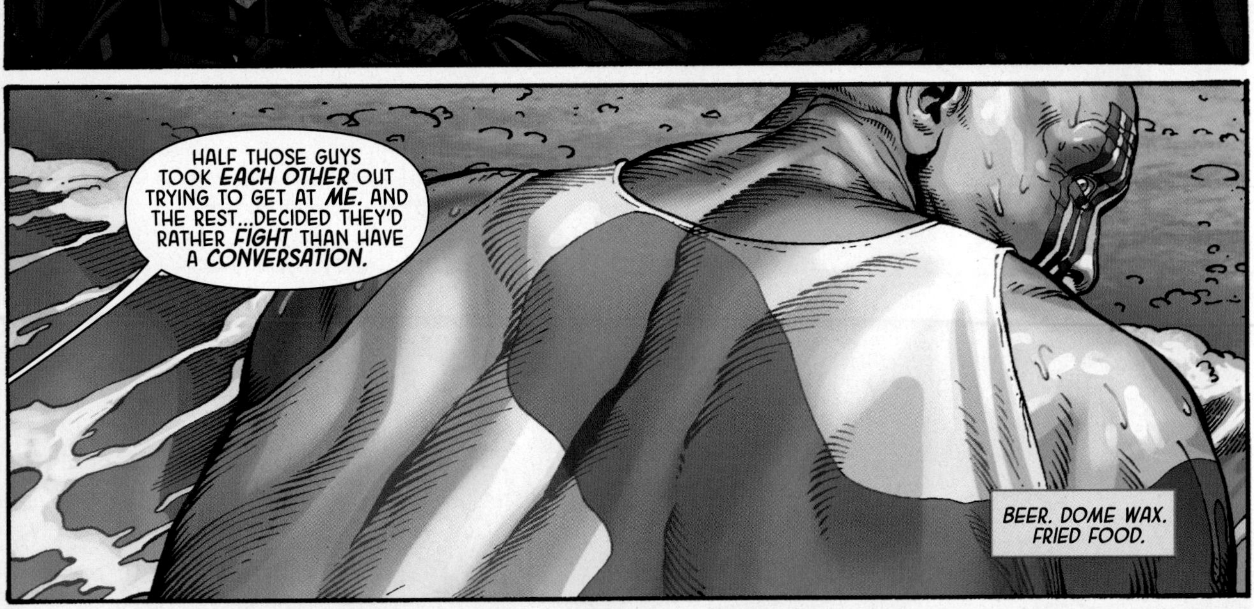
HALF THOSE GUYS TOOK EACH OTHER OUT TRYING TO GET AT ME. AND THE REST...DECIDED THEY'D RATHER FIGHT THAN HAVE A CONVERSATION.
BEER. DOME WAX. FRIED FOOD.

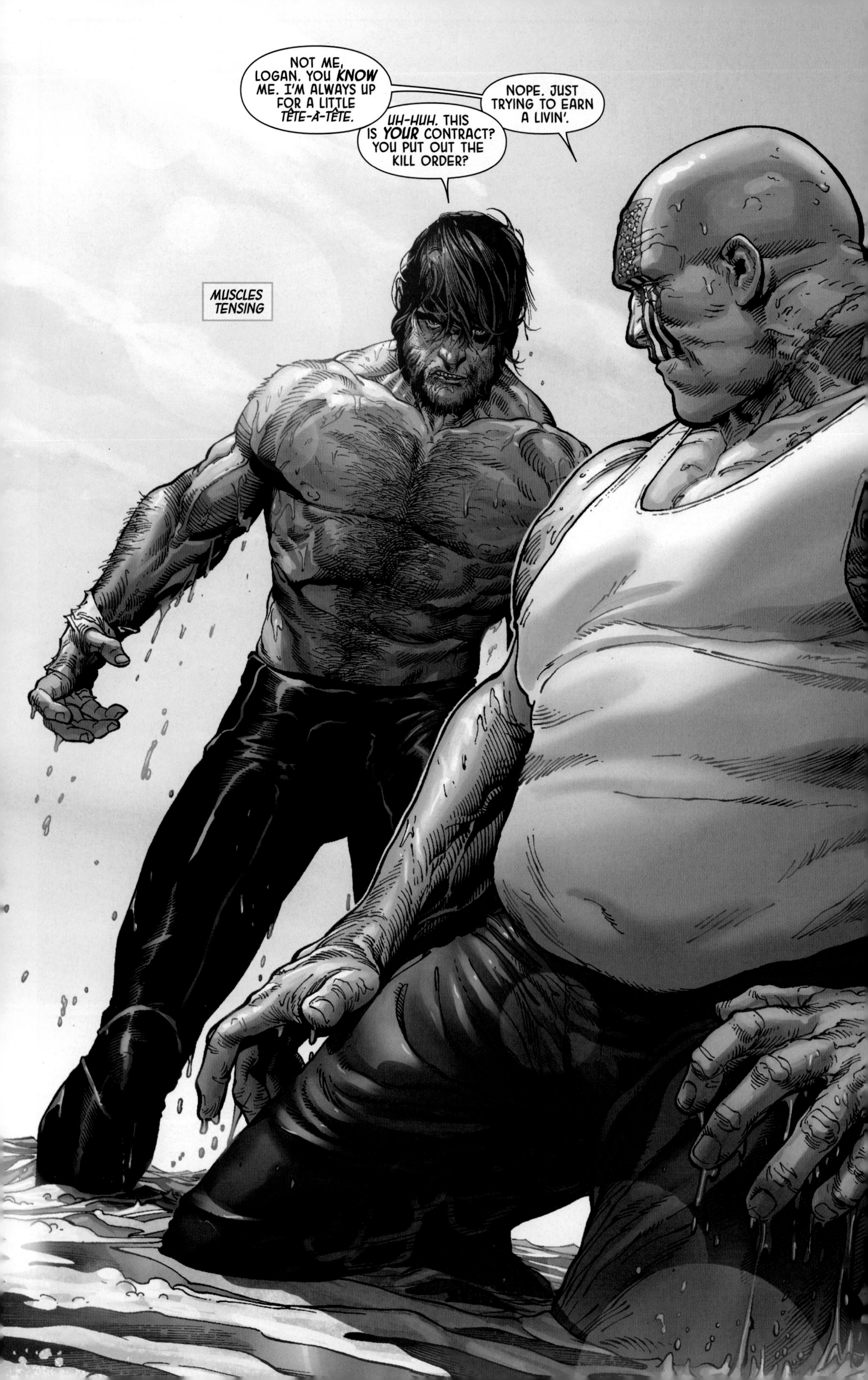
NOT ME, LOGAN. YOU KNOW ME. I'M ALWAYS UP FOR A LITTLE TÊTE-À-TÊTE.
UH-HUH. THIS IS YOUR CONTRACT? YOU PUT OUT THE KILL ORDER?
NOPE. JUST TRYING TO EARN A LIVIN'.
MUSCLES TENSING

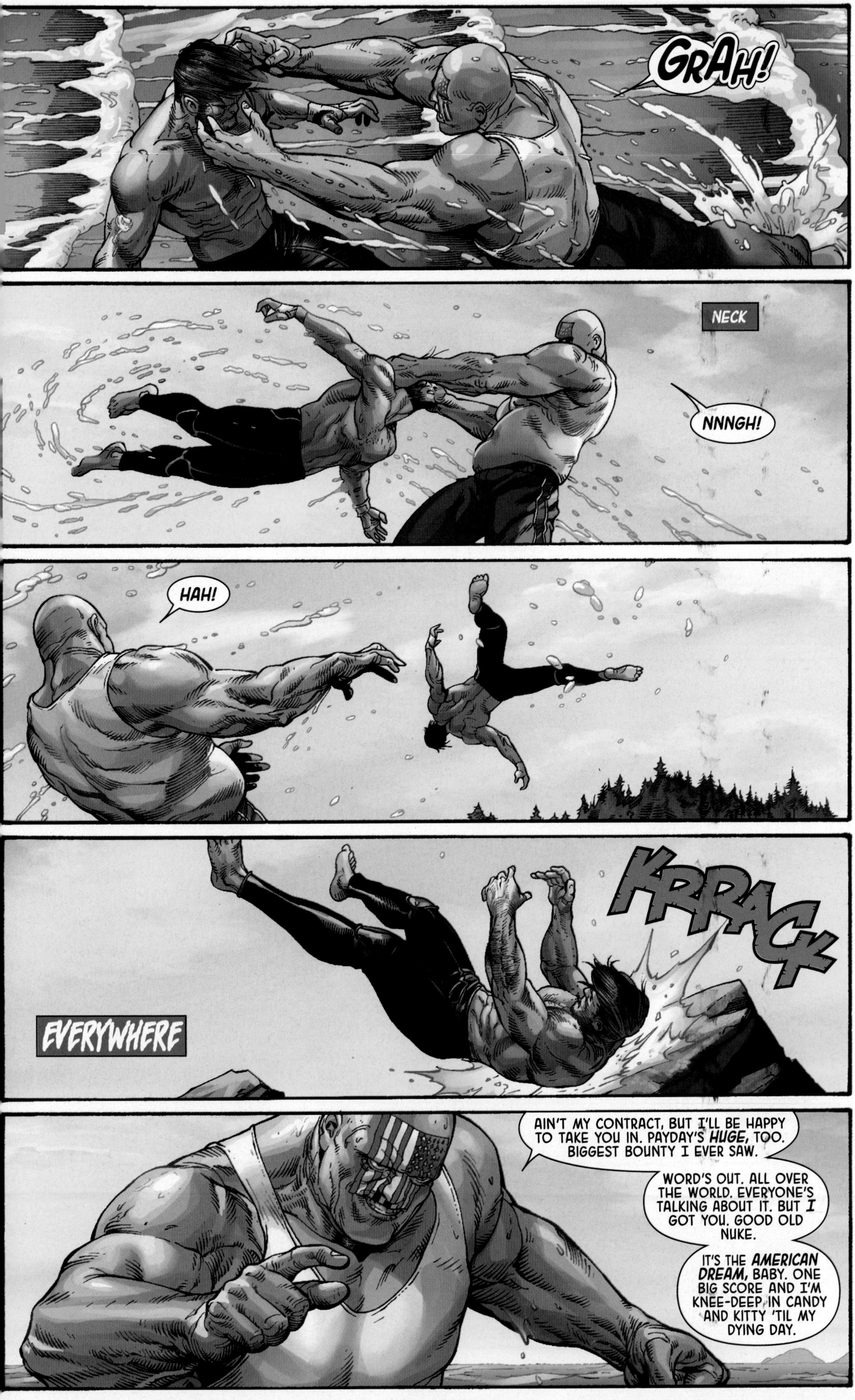
GRAH!
NECK
NNNGH!
HAH!
KRRACK
EVERYWHERE
AIN'T MY CONTRACT, BUT I'LL BE HAPPY TO TAKE YOU IN. PAYDAY'S HUGE, TOO. BIGGEST BOUNTY I EVER SAW.
WORD'S OUT. ALL OVER THE WORLD. EVERYONE'S TALKING ABOUT IT. BUT I GOT YOU. GOOD OLD NUKE.
IT'S THE AMERICAN DREAM, BABY. ONE BIG SCORE AND I'M KNEE-DEEP IN CANDY AND KITTY 'TIL MY DYING DAY.

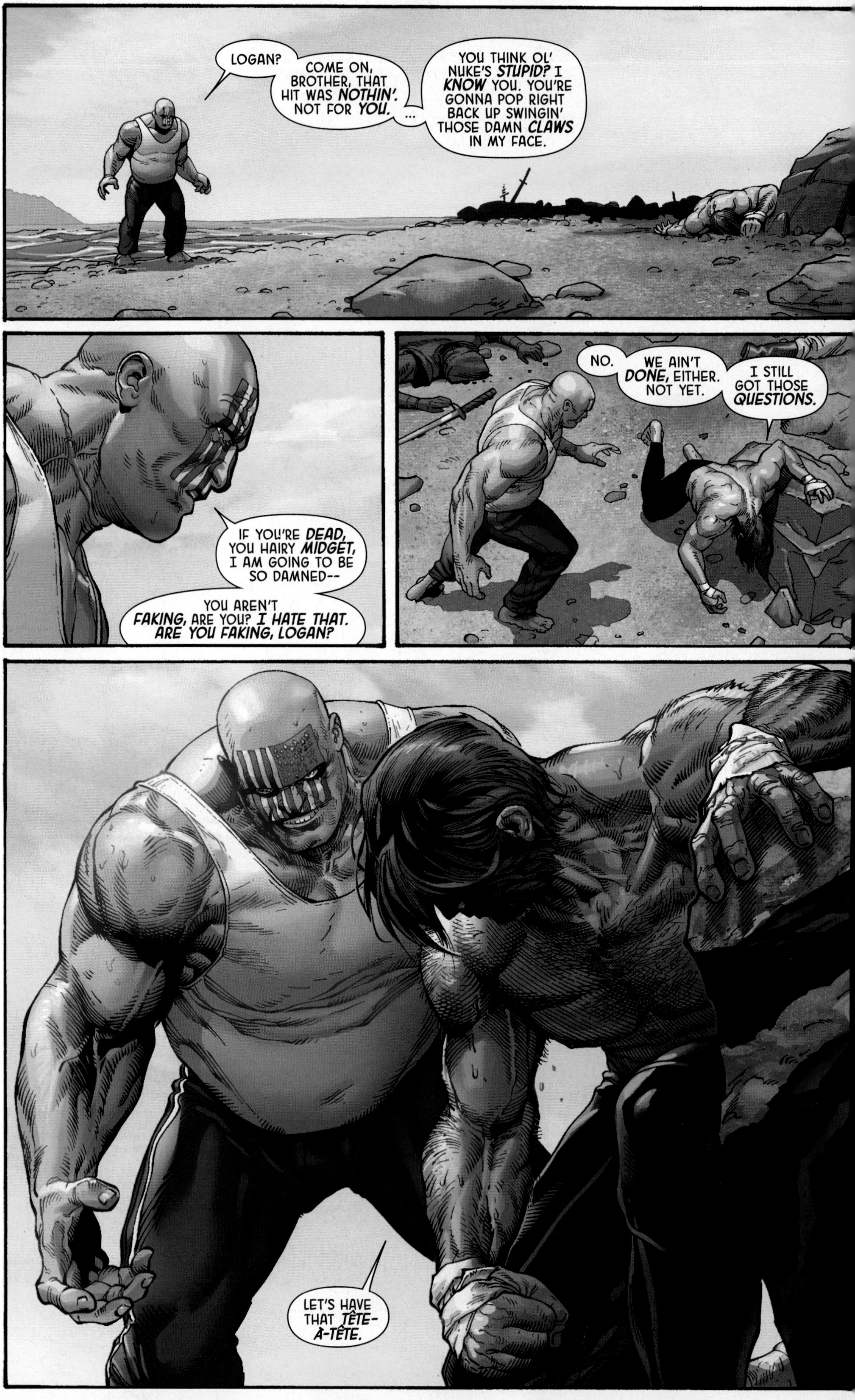
LOGAN?
COME ON, BROTHER, THAT HIT WAS NOTHIN'. NOT FOR YOU.
...
YOU THINK OL' NUKE'S STUPID? I KNOW YOU. YOU'RE GONNA POP RIGHT BACK UP SWINGIN' THOSE DAMN CLAWS IN MY FACE.
IF YOU'RE DEAD, YOU HAIRY MIDGET, I AM GOING TO BE SO DAMNED--
YOU AREN'T FAKING, ARE YOU? I HATE THAT. ARE YOU FAKING, LOGAN?
NO.
WE AIN'T DONE, EITHER. NOT YET.
I STILL GOT THOSE QUESTIONS.
LET'S HAVE THAT TÊTE-À-TÊTE.

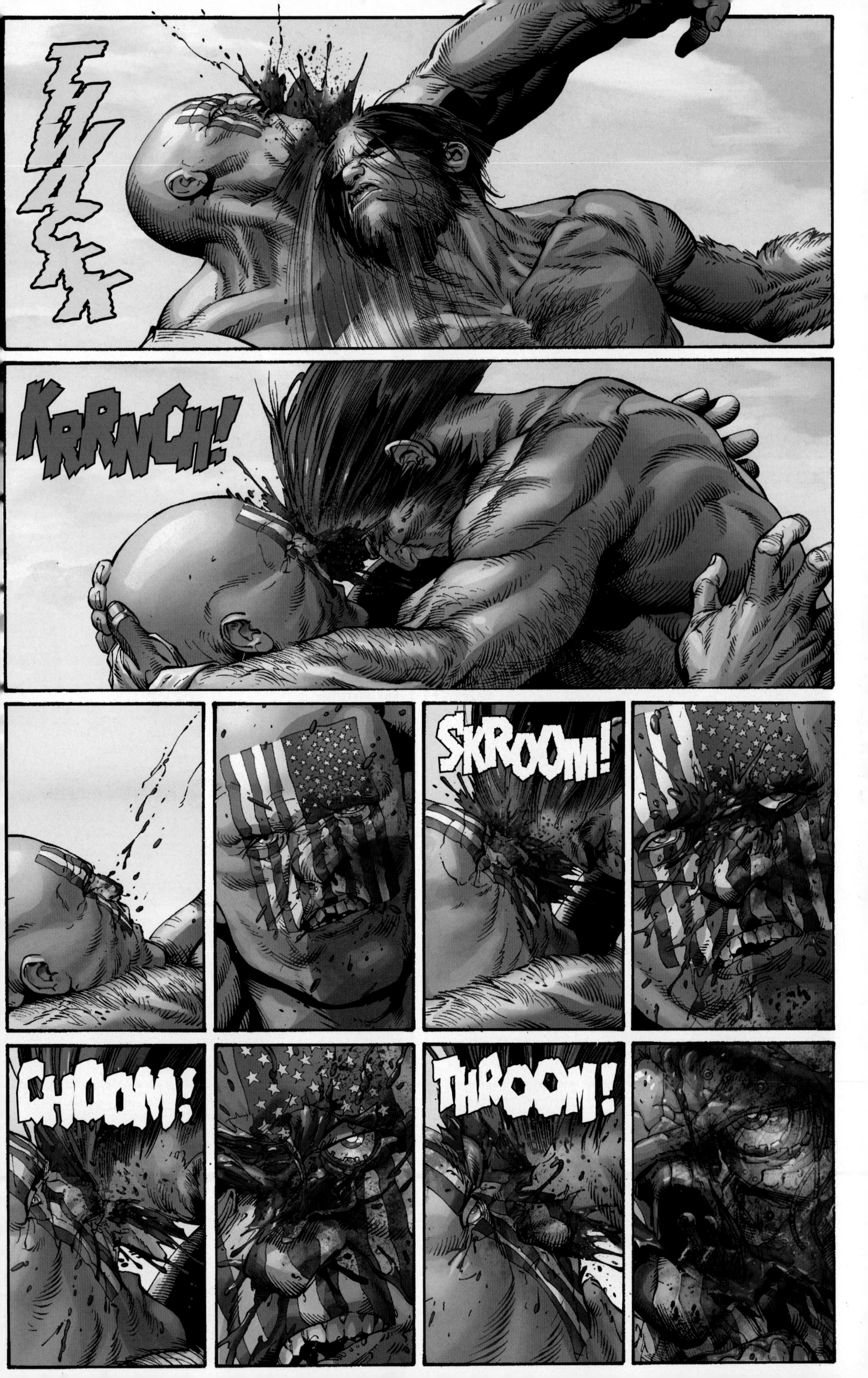
THWACK
KRRNCH!
SKROOM!
CHOOM!
THROOM!

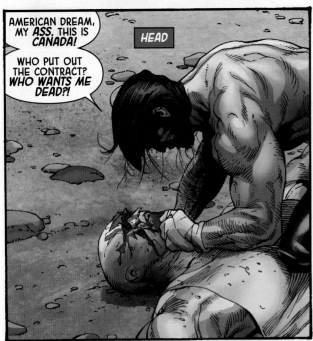

AMERICAN DREAM, MY *ASS*. THIS IS *CANADA*!

HEAD

WHO PUT OUT THE CONTRACT? *WHO WANTS ME DEAD*?!

N-NOT *DEAD*. ONLY PAYS OUT IF YOU'RE *ALIVE*.

C-CAPTURE, NOT KILL. YOU'RE *MONEY*. WALKING, TALKING *MONEY*. BUT THE BOUNTY GOES *DOWN* THE LONGER IT TAKES TO GET YOU. IT'S A *RACE*.

...

THEY'RE JUST GONNA KEEP COMIN'. ANYWHERE I GO...

GUYS LIKE *YOU*, NOT CARING WHO GETS IN THE WAY, WHO GETS HURT, WHO *DIES*.

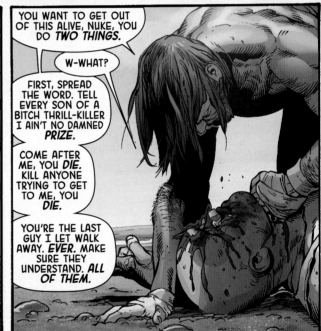

YOU WANT TO GET OUT OF THIS ALIVE, NUKE, YOU DO *TWO THINGS*.

W-WHAT?

FIRST, SPREAD THE WORD. TELL EVERY SON OF A BITCH THRILL-KILLER I AIN'T NO DAMNED *PRIZE*.

COME AFTER ME, YOU *DIE*. KILL ANYONE TRYING TO GET TO ME, YOU *DIE*.

YOU'RE THE LAST GUY I LET WALK AWAY. *EVER*. MAKE SURE THEY UNDERSTAND. *ALL OF THEM*.

SECOND THING. YOU TELL ME... *RIGHT NOW*. WHO?

C-CONTRACT CAME OUT OF... *MADRIPOOR*.

WHO?

LADY WHO RUNS THAT WHOLE *POISON CITY*. OWNS EVERYTHING, HAS EVERYTHING. DOESN'T NEED *NOTHIN'*-- EXCEPT THE WOLVERINE.

YOU KNOW HER NAME. THE *GREEN QUEEN*.

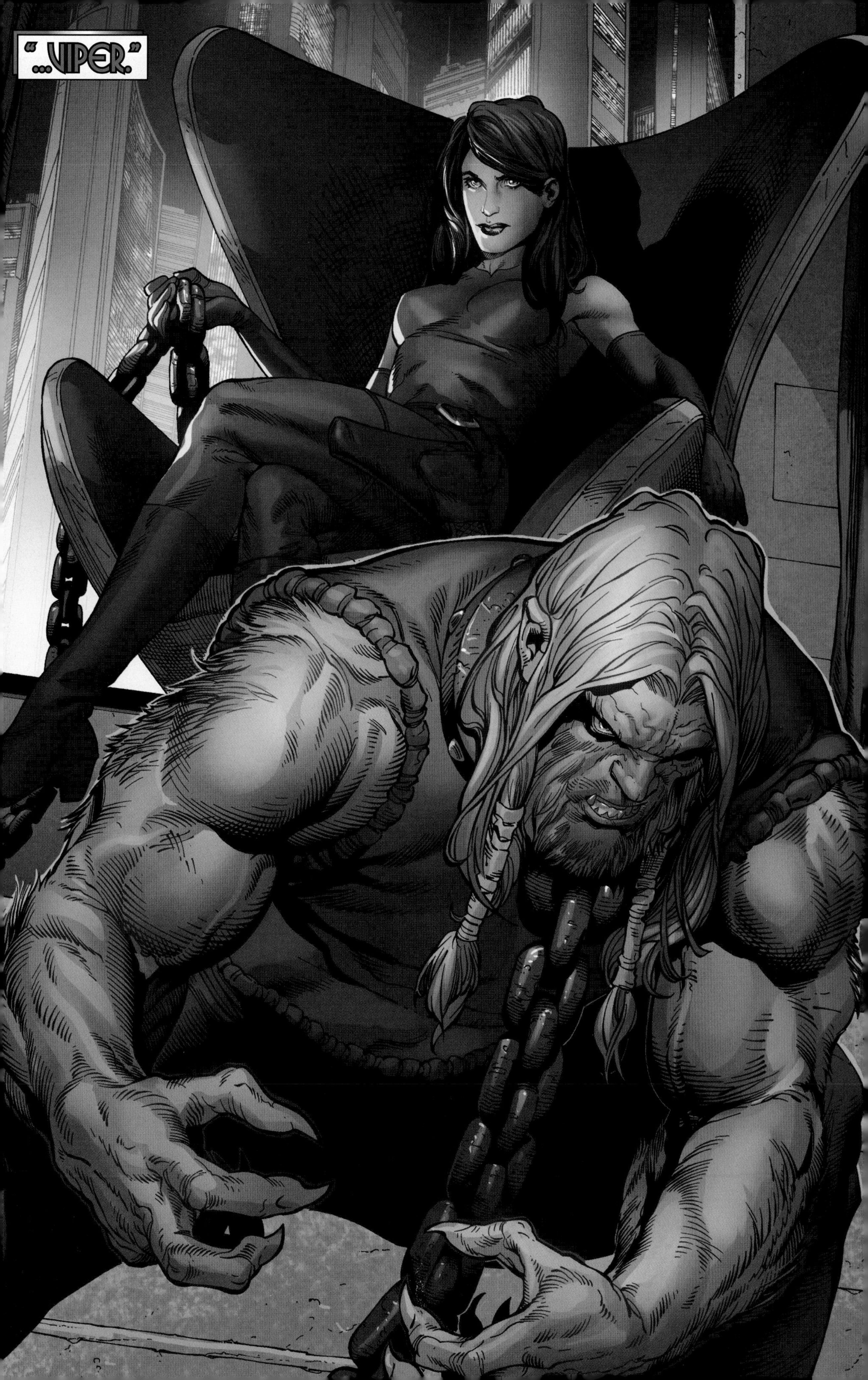
"...VIPER."

2

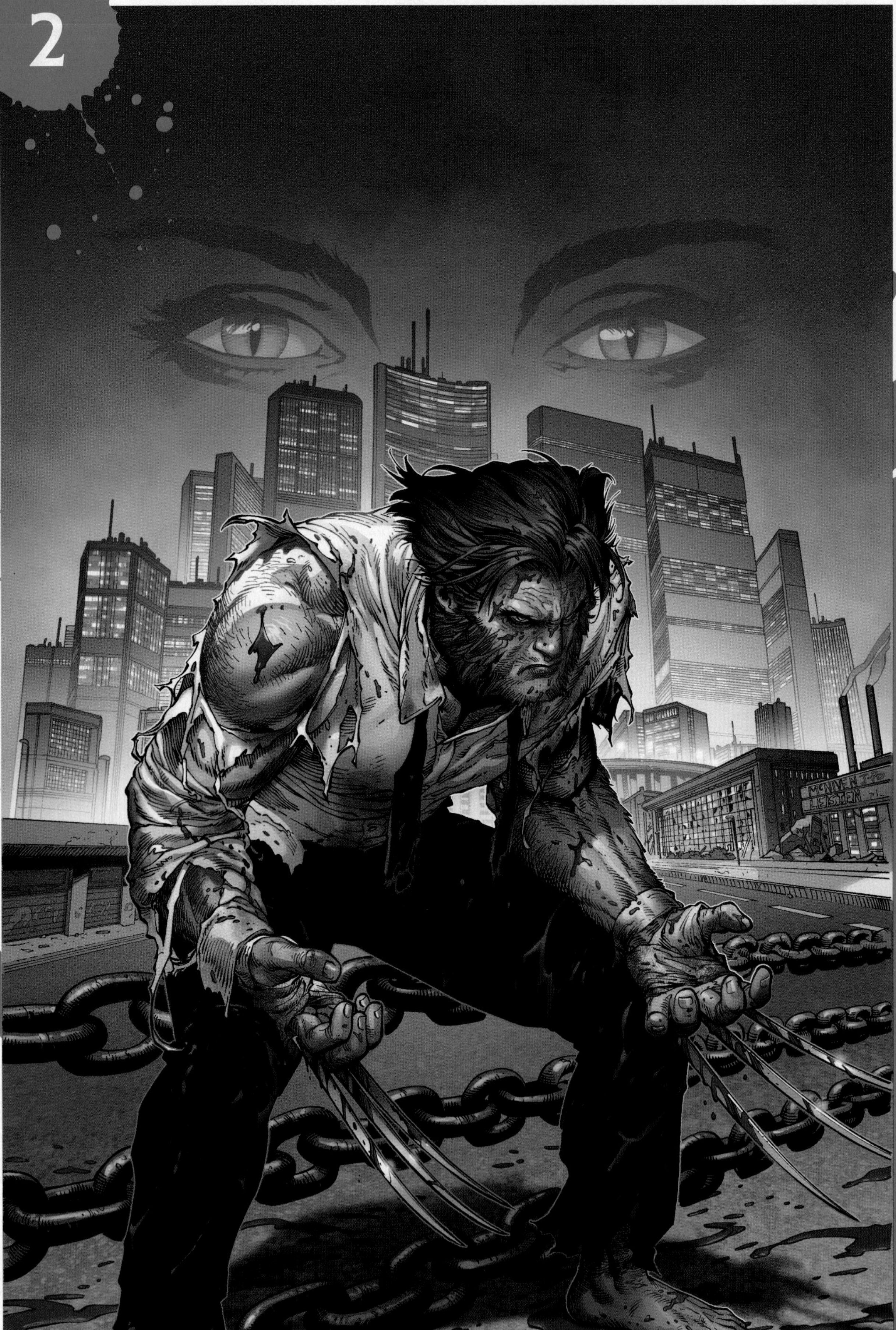

POISON

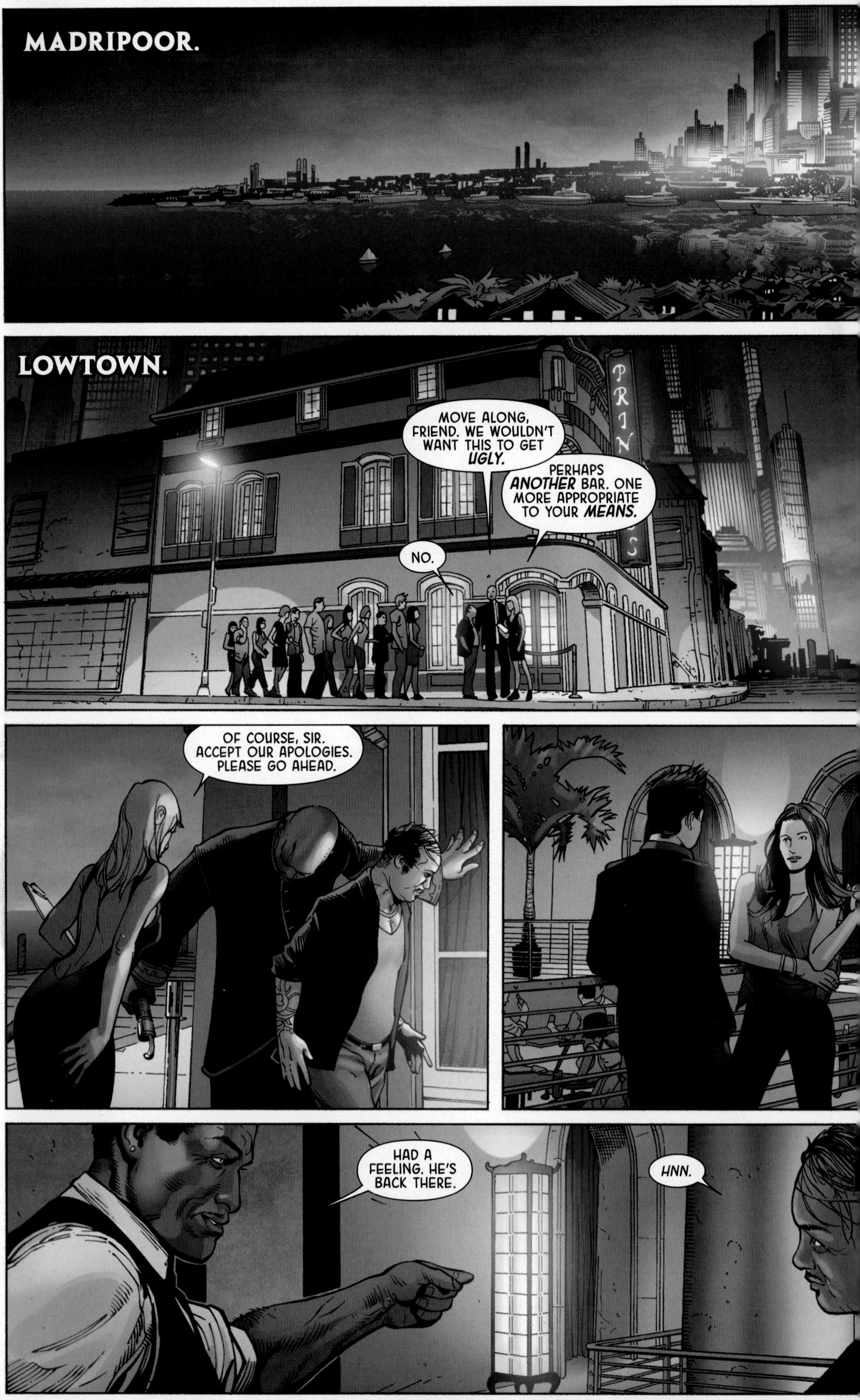
MADRIPOOR.
LOWTOWN.
PRIN
MOVE ALONG, FRIEND. WE WOULDN'T WANT THIS TO GET UGLY.
PERHAPS ANOTHER BAR. ONE MORE APPROPRIATE TO YOUR MEANS.
NO.
OF COURSE, SIR. ACCEPT OUR APOLOGIES. PLEASE GO AHEAD.
HAD A FEELING. HE'S BACK THERE.
HNN.

THIS IS THE RIGHT PLACE.

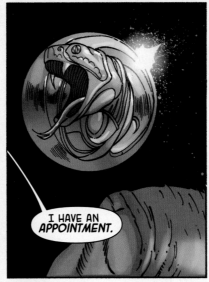

I HAVE AN *APPOINTMENT.*

V-- HUSH.

WHAT *HAPPENED* TO THIS PLACE? LAST TIME I WAS HERE, YOU COULD ACTUALLY AFFORD TO GET A *DRINK.*

YOU KNOW...*MADRIPOOR.* SOMEONE DECIDED THEY COULD MAKE A FEW RINGGITS CHARGING THE HIGHTOWN FOLKS AN ARM AND A LEG TO PRETEND THEY'RE HAVING A DANGEROUS NIGHT OUT DOWN BY THE DOCKS.

BUT *YOU* DON'T SEEM LIKE YOU'RE HERE FOR THAT.

NO. I'M MEETING SOMEONE.

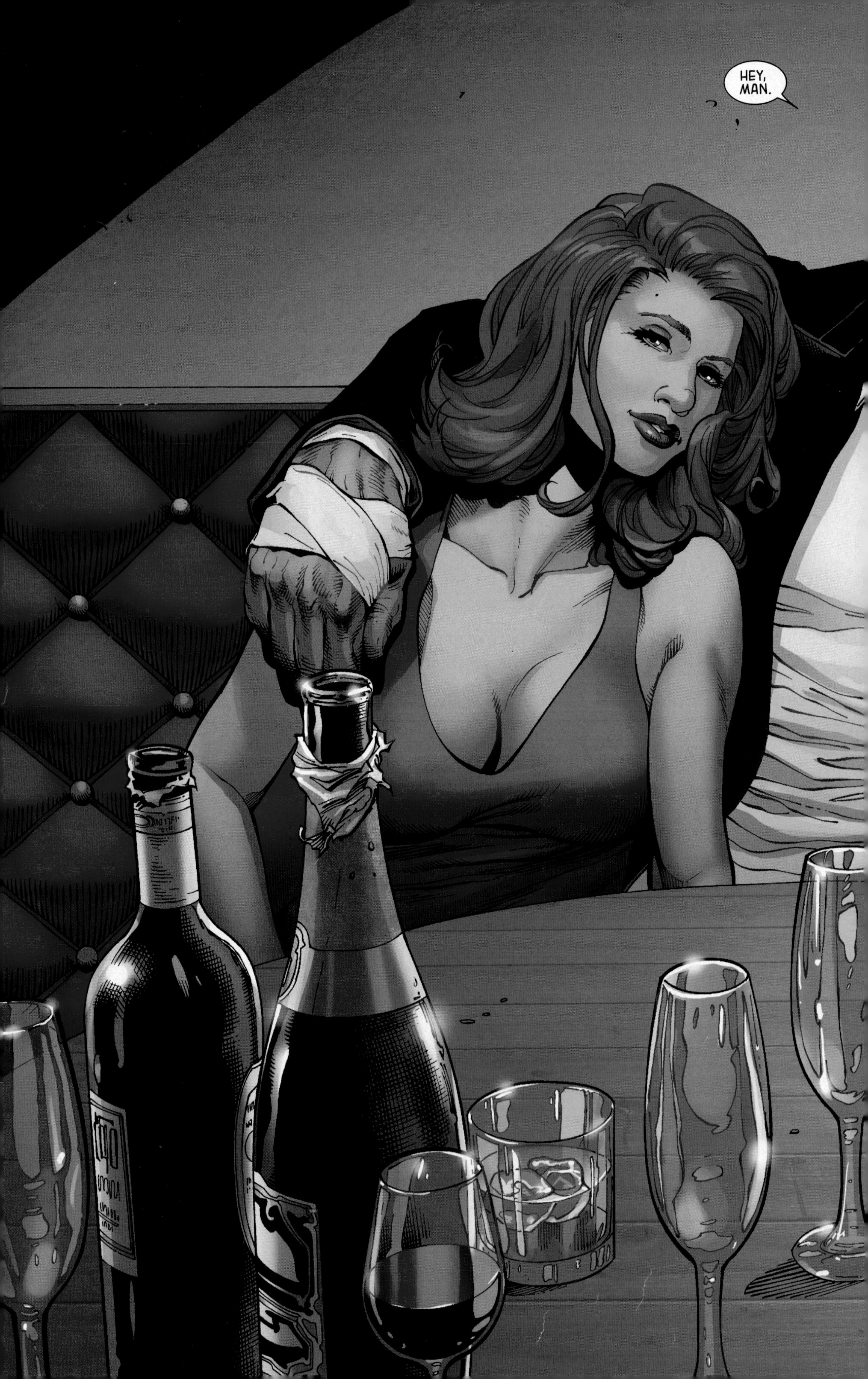
HEY, MAN.

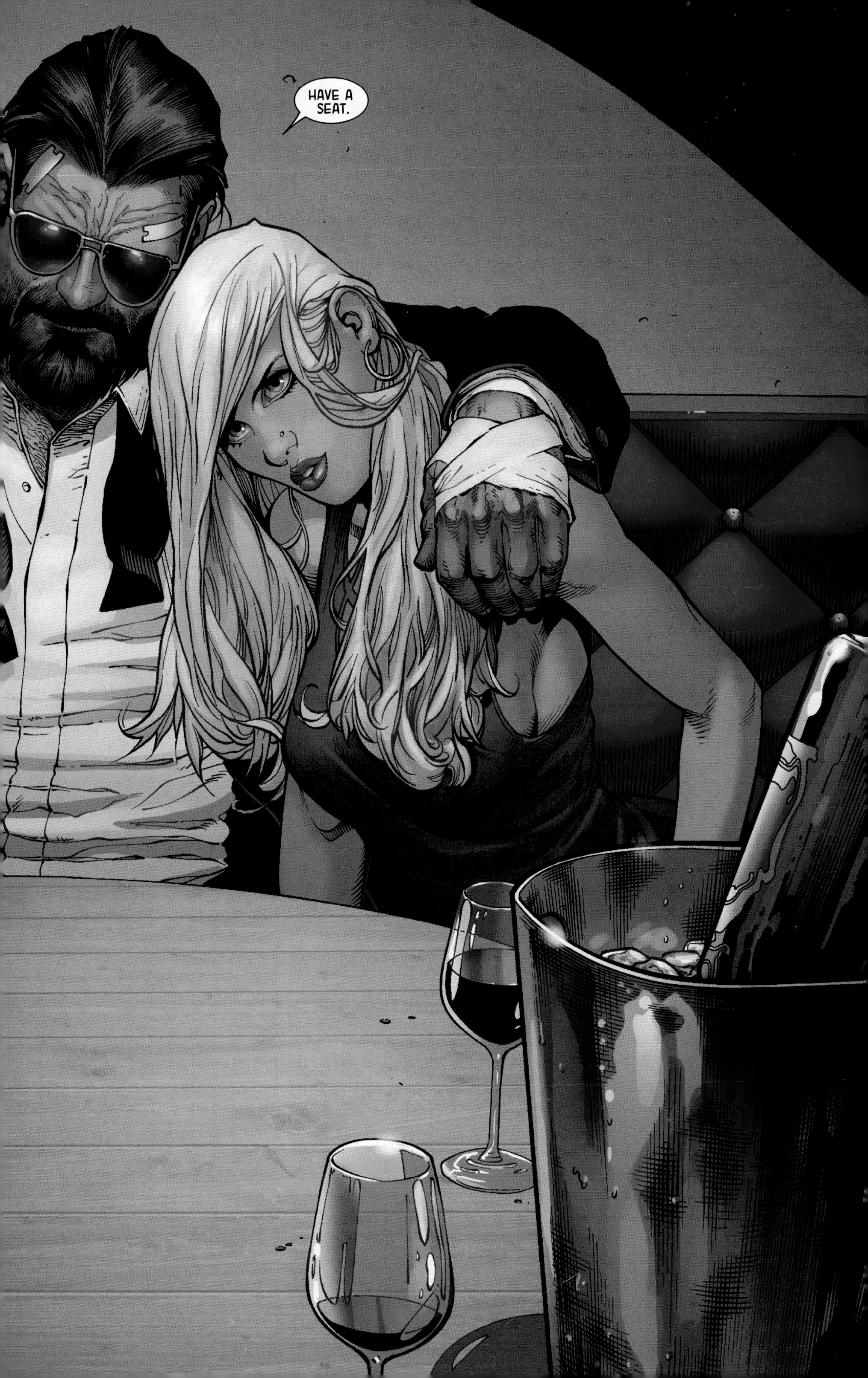
HAVE A SEAT.

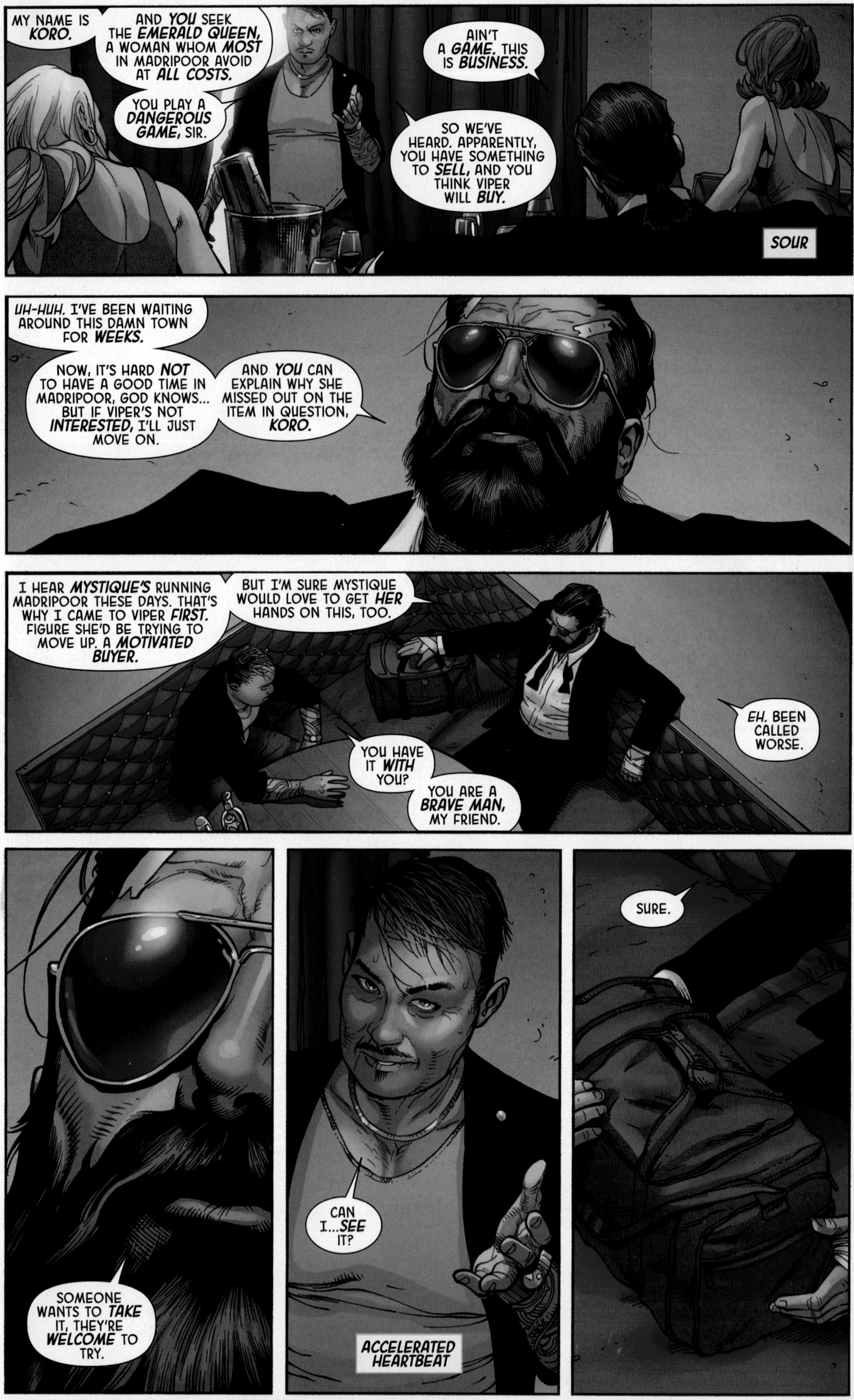

MY NAME IS KORO.
AND YOU SEEK THE EMERALD QUEEN, A WOMAN WHOM MOST IN MADRIPOOR AVOID AT ALL COSTS.
YOU PLAY A DANGEROUS GAME, SIR.
AIN'T A GAME. THIS IS BUSINESS.
SO WE'VE HEARD. APPARENTLY, YOU HAVE SOMETHING TO SELL, AND YOU THINK VIPER WILL BUY.
SOUR
UH-HUH. I'VE BEEN WAITING AROUND THIS DAMN TOWN FOR WEEKS.
NOW, IT'S HARD NOT TO HAVE A GOOD TIME IN MADRIPOOR, GOD KNOWS... BUT IF VIPER'S NOT INTERESTED, I'LL JUST MOVE ON.
AND YOU CAN EXPLAIN WHY SHE MISSED OUT ON THE ITEM IN QUESTION, KORO.
I HEAR MYSTIQUE'S RUNNING MADRIPOOR THESE DAYS. THAT'S WHY I CAME TO VIPER FIRST. FIGURE SHE'D BE TRYING TO MOVE UP. A MOTIVATED BUYER.
BUT I'M SURE MYSTIQUE WOULD LOVE TO GET HER HANDS ON THIS, TOO.
YOU HAVE IT WITH YOU?
YOU ARE A BRAVE MAN, MY FRIEND.
EH. BEEN CALLED WORSE.
SOMEONE WANTS TO TAKE IT, THEY'RE WELCOME TO TRY.
CAN I...SEE IT?
ACCELERATED HEARTBEAT
SURE.

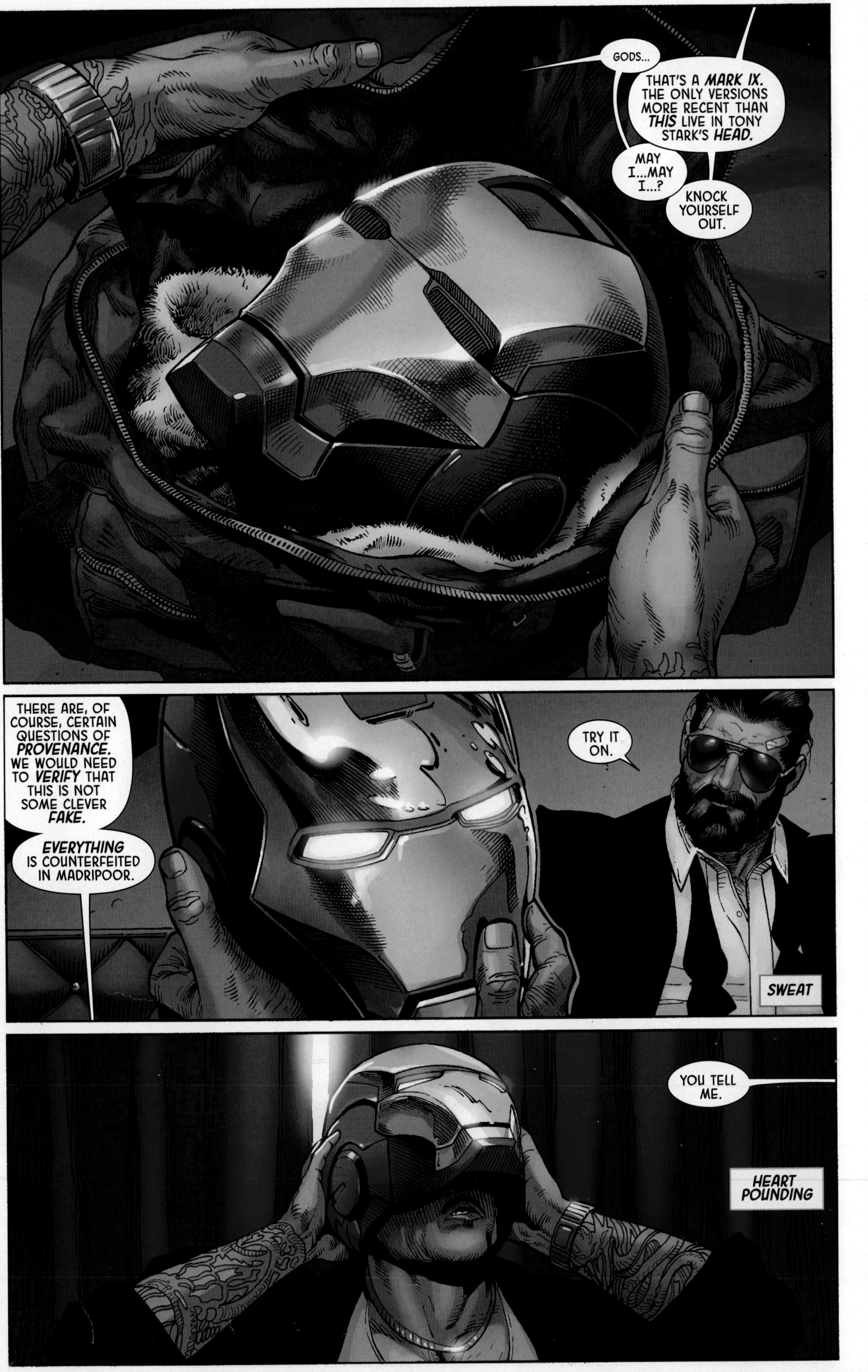
GODS...
THAT'S A MARK IX. THE ONLY VERSIONS MORE RECENT THAN THIS LIVE IN TONY STARK'S HEAD.
MAY I...MAY I...?
KNOCK YOURSELF OUT.
THERE ARE, OF COURSE, CERTAIN QUESTIONS OF PROVENANCE. WE WOULD NEED TO VERIFY THAT THIS IS NOT SOME CLEVER FAKE.
EVERYTHING IS COUNTERFEITED IN MADRIPOOR.
TRY IT ON.
SWEAT
YOU TELL ME.
HEART POUNDING

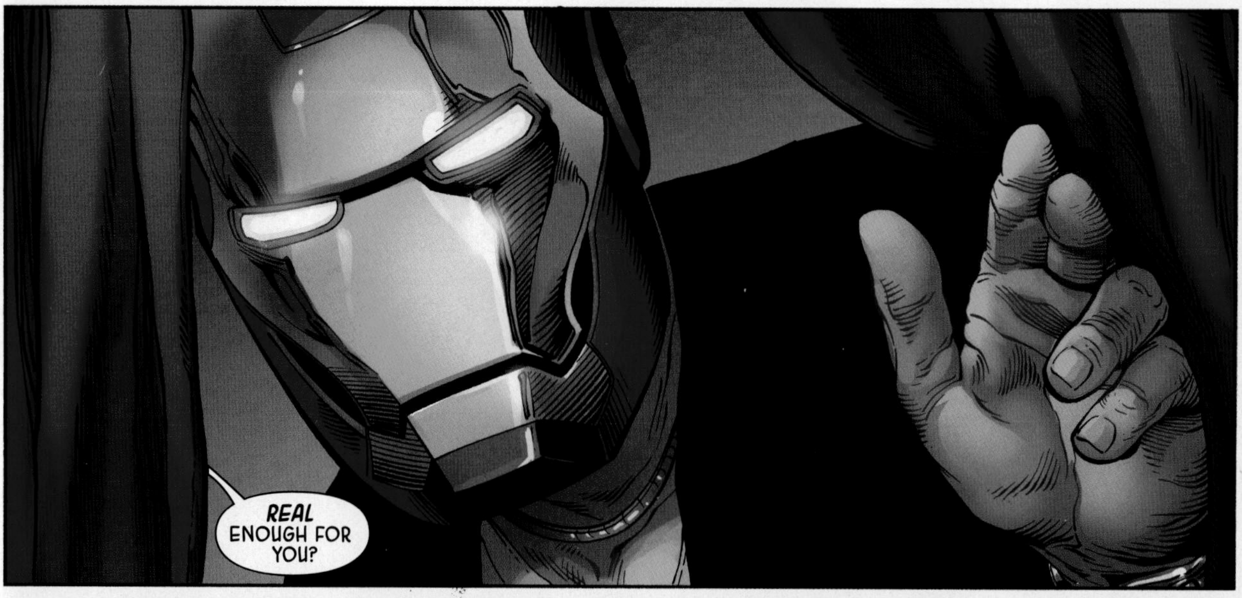
REAL ENOUGH FOR YOU?

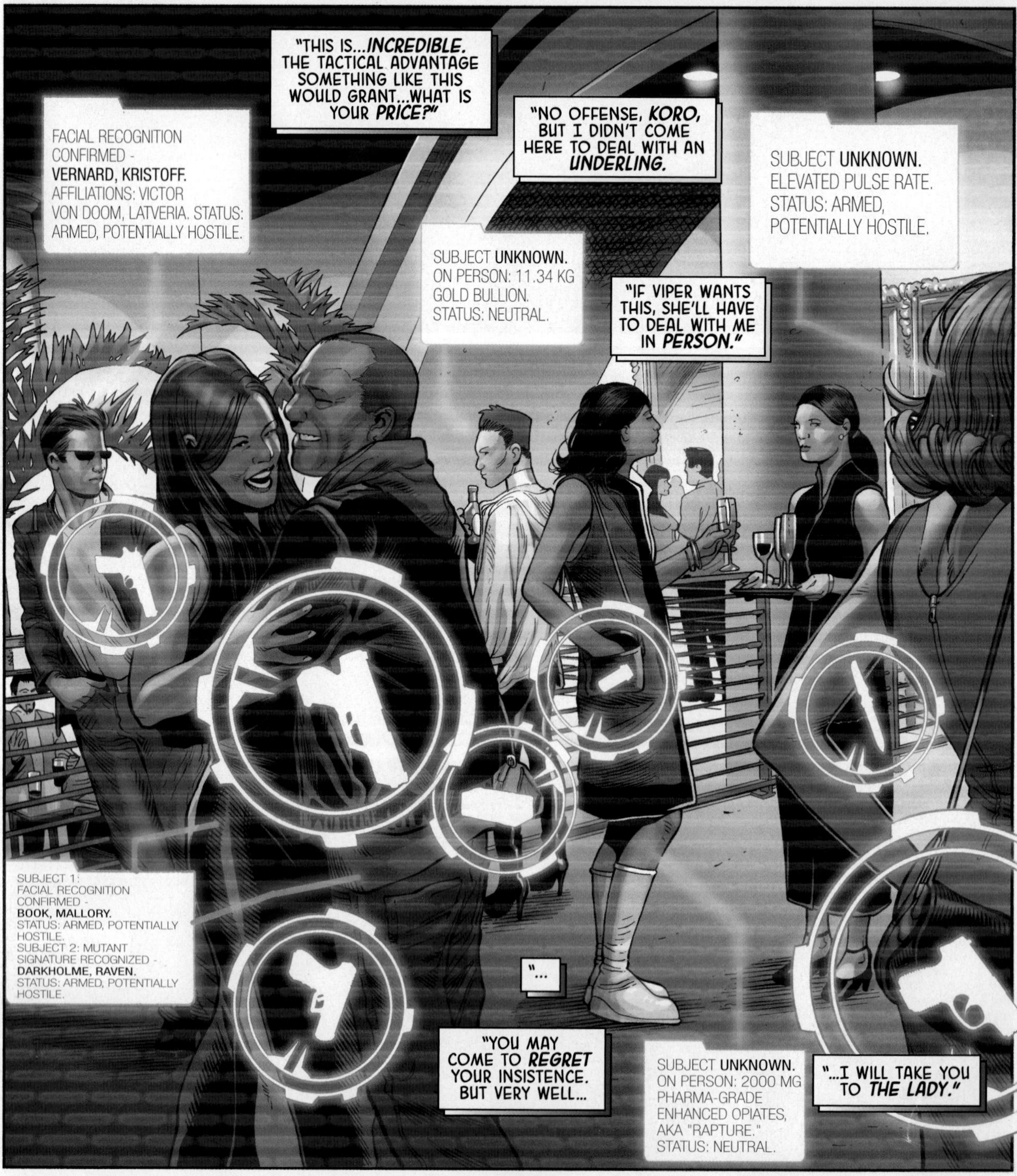
"THIS IS...INCREDIBLE. THE TACTICAL ADVANTAGE SOMETHING LIKE THIS WOULD GRANT...WHAT IS YOUR PRICE?"
FACIAL RECOGNITION CONFIRMED - VERNARD, KRISTOFF. AFFILIATIONS: VICTOR VON DOOM, LATVERIA. STATUS: ARMED, POTENTIALLY HOSTILE.
"NO OFFENSE, KORO, BUT I DIDN'T COME HERE TO DEAL WITH AN UNDERLING.
SUBJECT UNKNOWN. ELEVATED PULSE RATE. STATUS: ARMED, POTENTIALLY HOSTILE.
SUBJECT UNKNOWN. ON PERSON: 11.34 KG GOLD BULLION. STATUS: NEUTRAL.
"IF VIPER WANTS THIS, SHE'LL HAVE TO DEAL WITH ME IN PERSON."
SUBJECT 1: FACIAL RECOGNITION CONFIRMED - BOOK, MALLORY. STATUS: ARMED, POTENTIALLY HOSTILE. SUBJECT 2: MUTANT SIGNATURE RECOGNIZED - DARKHOLME, RAVEN. STATUS: ARMED, POTENTIALLY HOSTILE.
"...
"YOU MAY COME TO REGRET YOUR INSISTENCE. BUT VERY WELL...
SUBJECT UNKNOWN. ON PERSON: 2000 MG PHARMA-GRADE ENHANCED OPIATES, AKA "RAPTURE." STATUS: NEUTRAL.
"...I WILL TAKE YOU TO THE LADY."

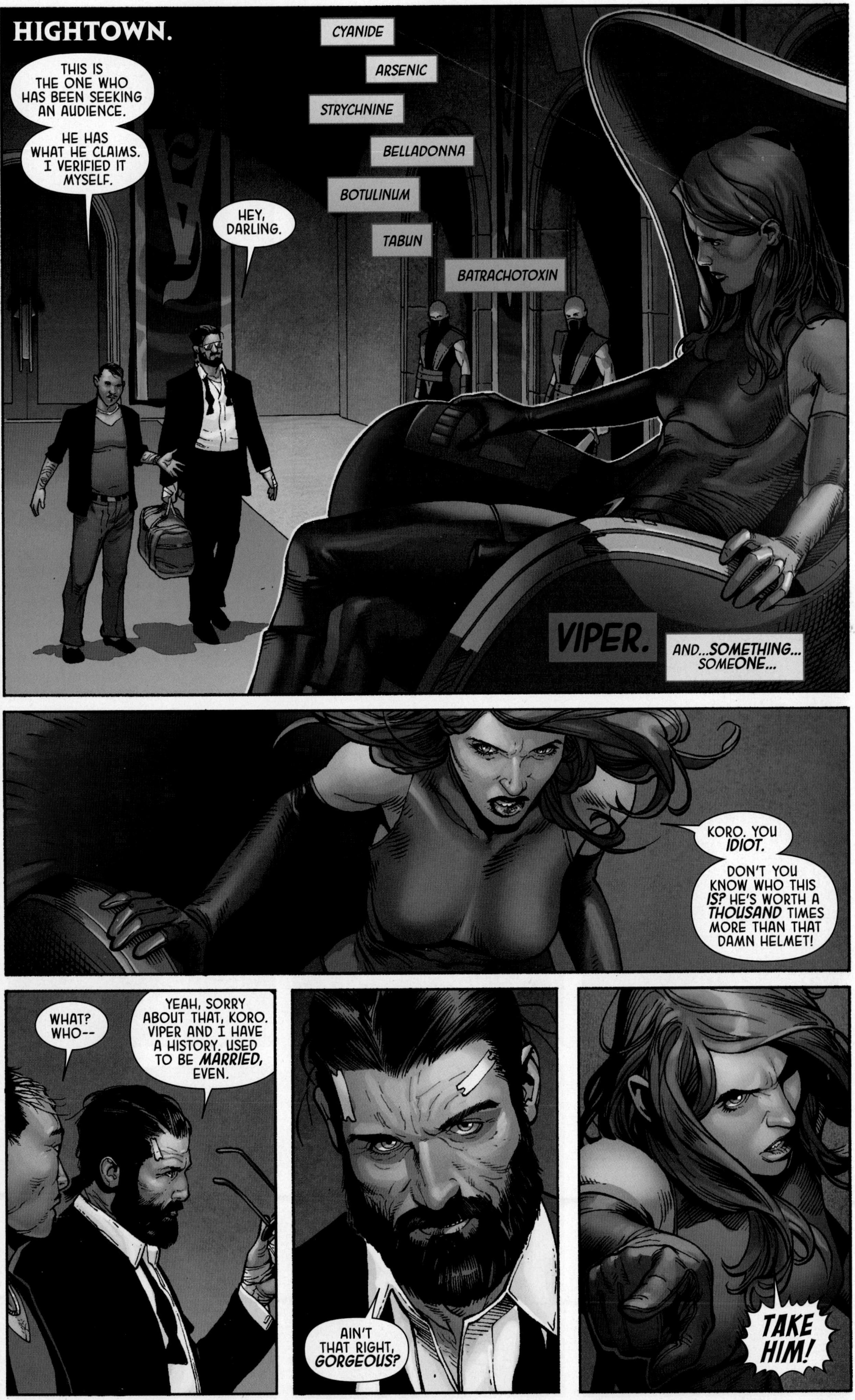
HIGHTOWN.
CYANIDE
ARSENIC
STRYCHNINE
BELLADONNA
BOTULINUM
TABUN
BATRACHOTOXIN
THIS IS THE ONE WHO HAS BEEN SEEKING AN AUDIENCE.
HE HAS WHAT HE CLAIMS. I VERIFIED IT MYSELF.
HEY, DARLING.
VIPER.
AND...SOMETHING... SOMEONE...
KORO. YOU IDIOT.
DON'T YOU KNOW WHO THIS IS? HE'S WORTH A THOUSAND TIMES MORE THAN THAT DAMN HELMET!
WHAT? WHO--
YEAH, SORRY ABOUT THAT, KORO. VIPER AND I HAVE A HISTORY. USED TO BE MARRIED, EVEN.
AIN'T THAT RIGHT, GORGEOUS?
TAKE HIM!

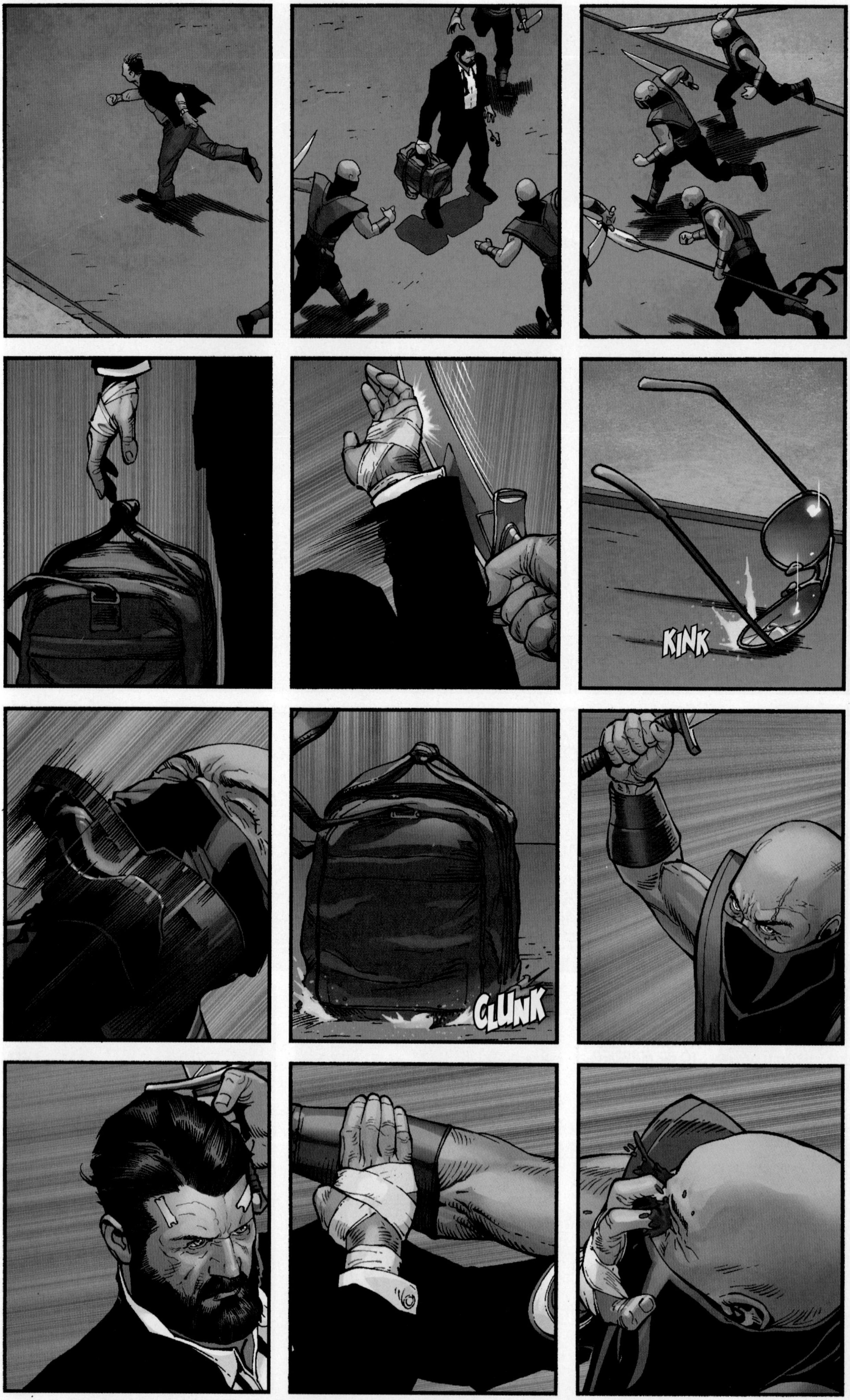
KINK
CLUNK

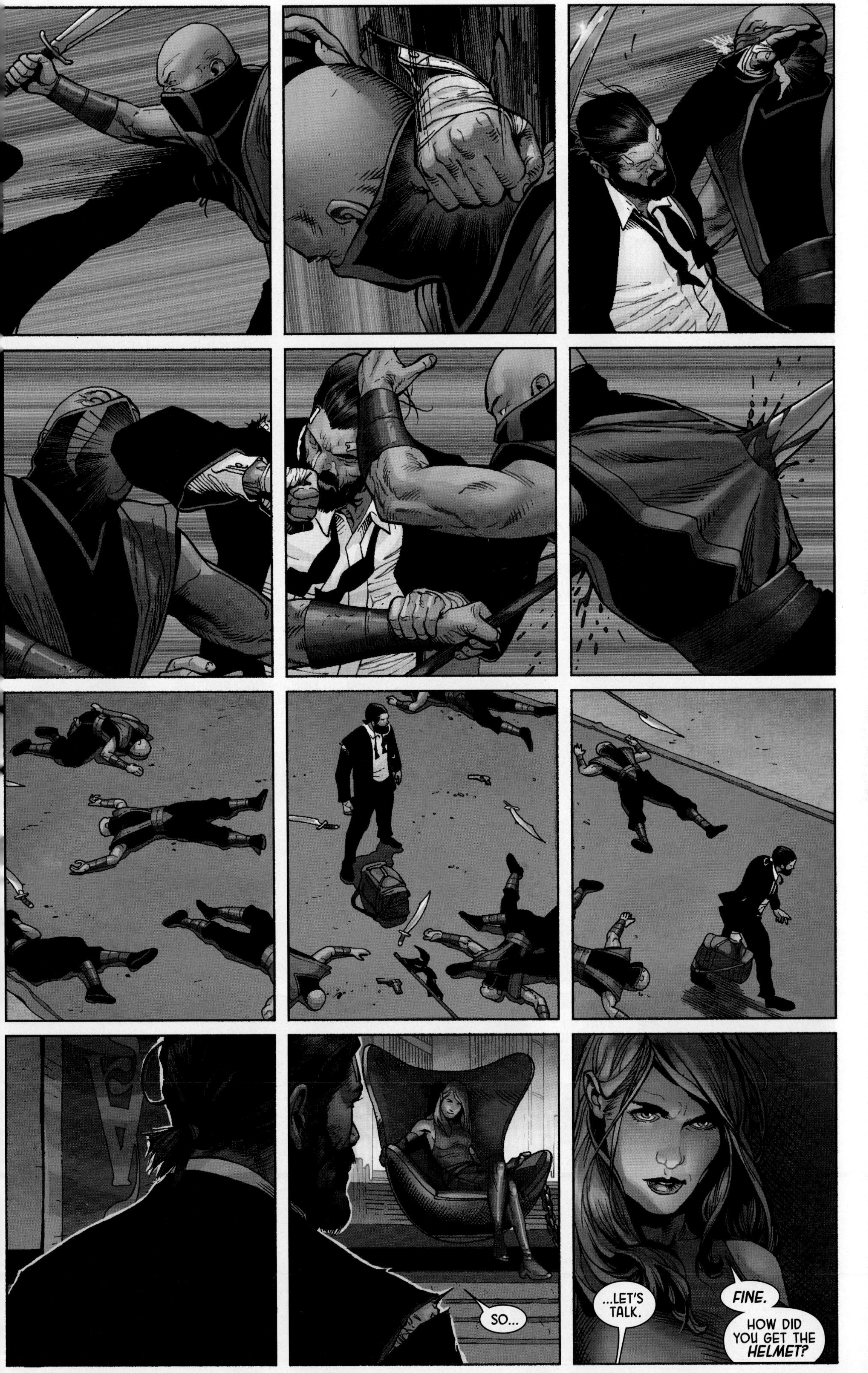
SO...
...LET'S TALK.
FINE.
HOW DID YOU GET THE HELMET?

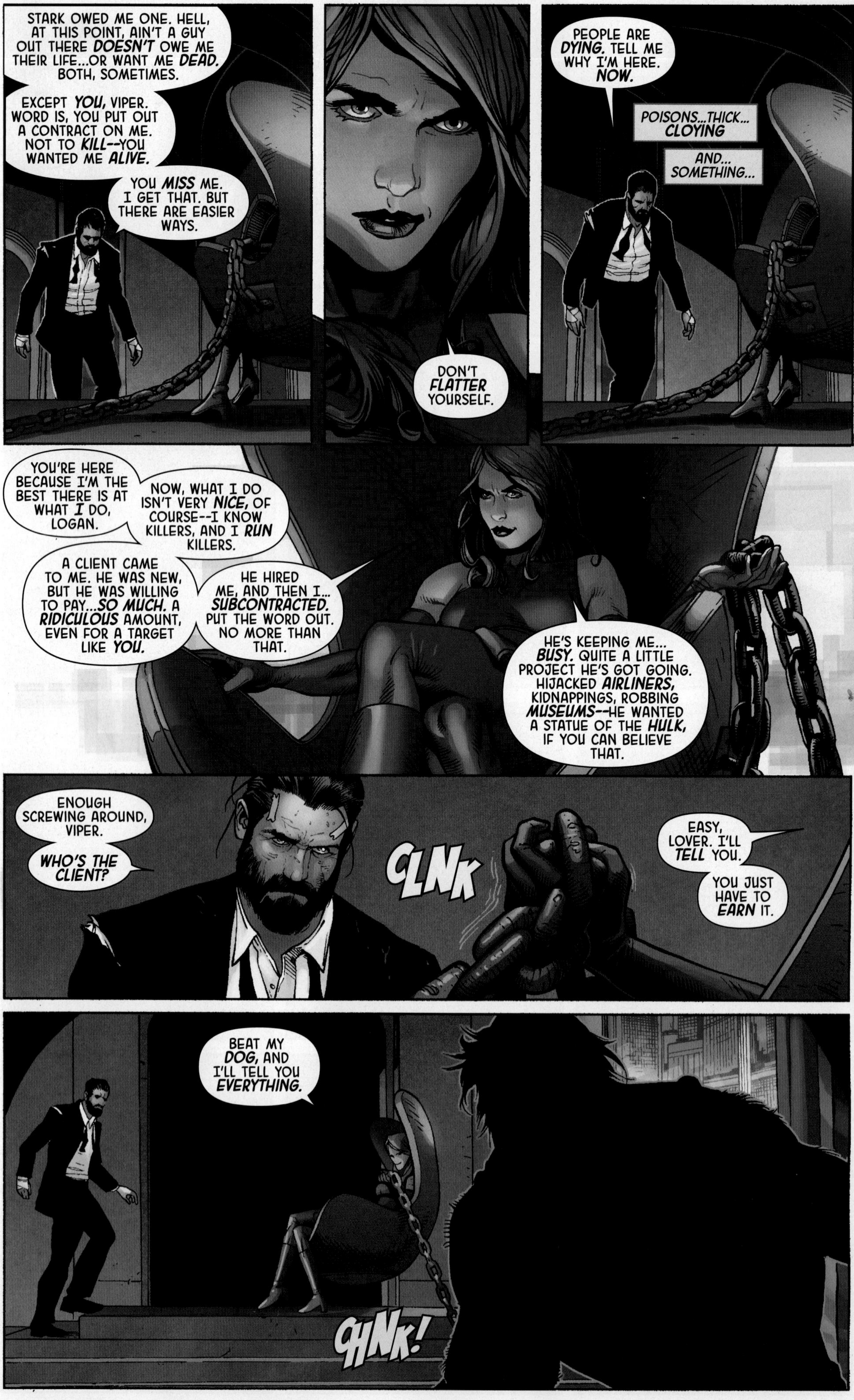
STARK OWED ME ONE. HELL, AT THIS POINT, AIN'T A GUY OUT THERE DOESN'T OWE ME THEIR LIFE...OR WANT ME DEAD. BOTH, SOMETIMES.
EXCEPT YOU, VIPER. WORD IS, YOU PUT OUT A CONTRACT ON ME. NOT TO KILL--YOU WANTED ME ALIVE.
YOU MISS ME. I GET THAT. BUT THERE ARE EASIER WAYS.
DON'T FLATTER YOURSELF.
PEOPLE ARE DYING. TELL ME WHY I'M HERE. NOW.
POISONS...THICK... CLOYING
AND... SOMETHING...
YOU'RE HERE BECAUSE I'M THE BEST THERE IS AT WHAT I DO, LOGAN.
NOW, WHAT I DO ISN'T VERY NICE, OF COURSE--I KNOW KILLERS, AND I RUN KILLERS.
A CLIENT CAME TO ME. HE WAS NEW, BUT HE WAS WILLING TO PAY...SO MUCH. A RIDICULOUS AMOUNT, EVEN FOR A TARGET LIKE YOU.
HE HIRED ME, AND THEN I... SUBCONTRACTED. PUT THE WORD OUT. NO MORE THAN THAT.
HE'S KEEPING ME... BUSY. QUITE A LITTLE PROJECT HE'S GOT GOING. HIJACKED AIRLINERS, KIDNAPPINGS, ROBBING MUSEUMS--HE WANTED A STATUE OF THE HULK, IF YOU CAN BELIEVE THAT.
ENOUGH SCREWING AROUND, VIPER.
WHO'S THE CLIENT?
CLNK
EASY, LOVER. I'LL TELL YOU.
YOU JUST HAVE TO EARN IT.
BEAT MY DOG, AND I'LL TELL YOU EVERYTHING.
CHNK!

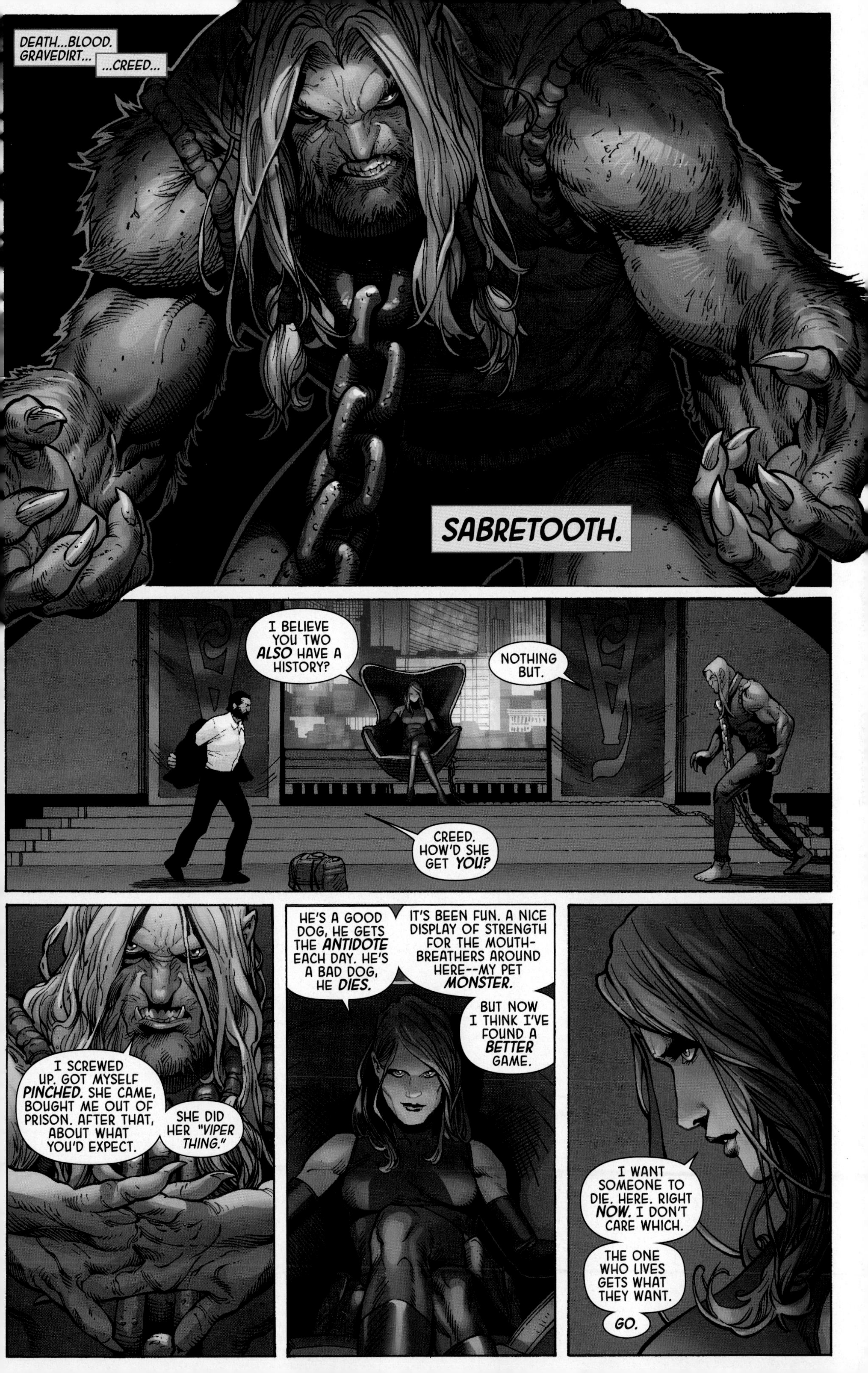
DEATH...BLOOD. GRAVEDIRT...
...CREED...
SABRETOOTH.
I BELIEVE YOU TWO ALSO HAVE A HISTORY?
NOTHING BUT.
CREED. HOW'D SHE GET YOU?
I SCREWED UP. GOT MYSELF PINCHED. SHE CAME, BOUGHT ME OUT OF PRISON. AFTER THAT, ABOUT WHAT YOU'D EXPECT.
SHE DID HER "VIPER THING."
HE'S A GOOD DOG, HE GETS THE ANTIDOTE EACH DAY. HE'S A BAD DOG, HE DIES.
IT'S BEEN FUN. A NICE DISPLAY OF STRENGTH FOR THE MOUTH-BREATHERS AROUND HERE--MY PET MONSTER.
BUT NOW I THINK I'VE FOUND A BETTER GAME.
I WANT SOMEONE TO DIE. HERE. RIGHT NOW. I DON'T CARE WHICH.
THE ONE WHO LIVES GETS WHAT THEY WANT.
GO.

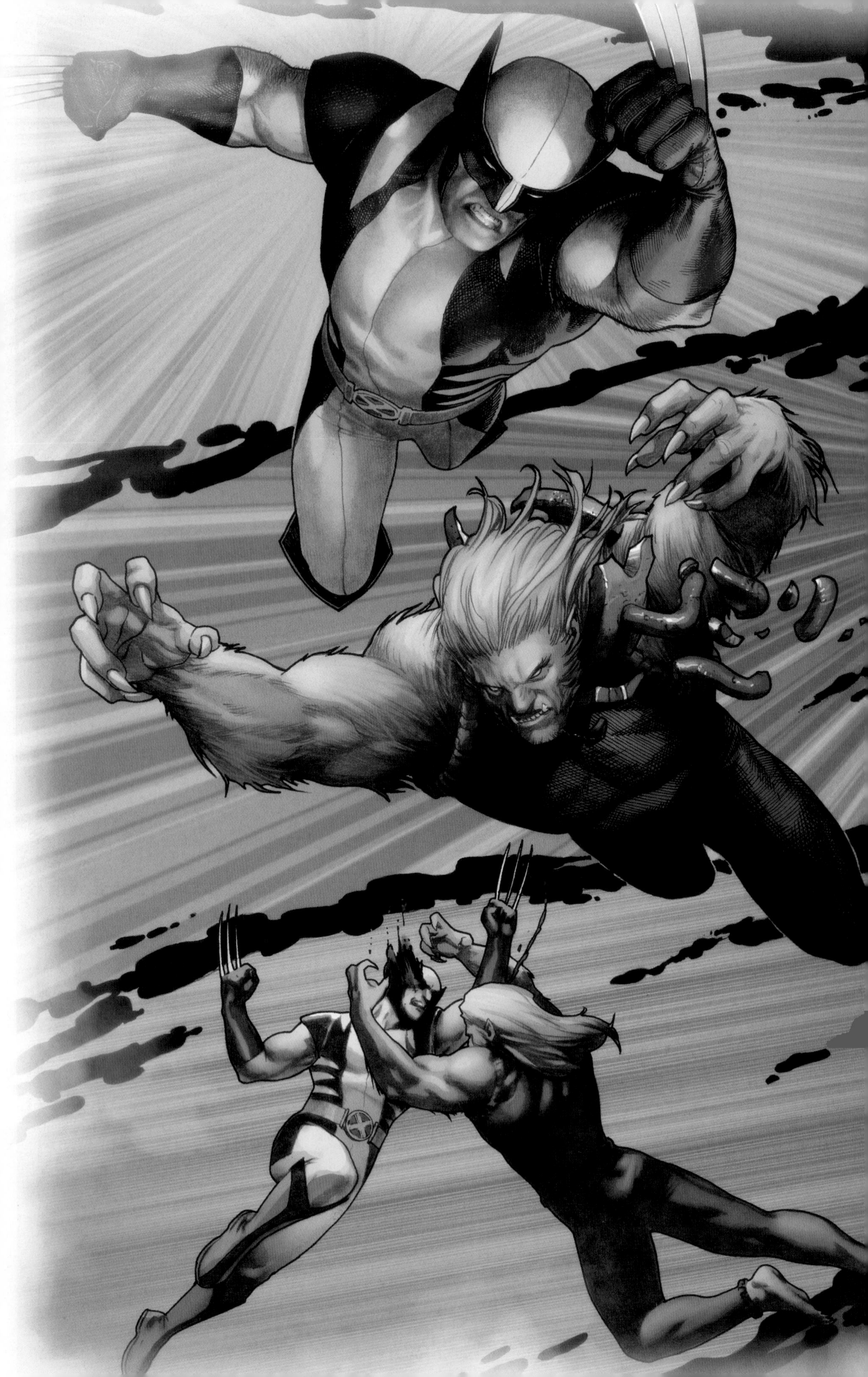

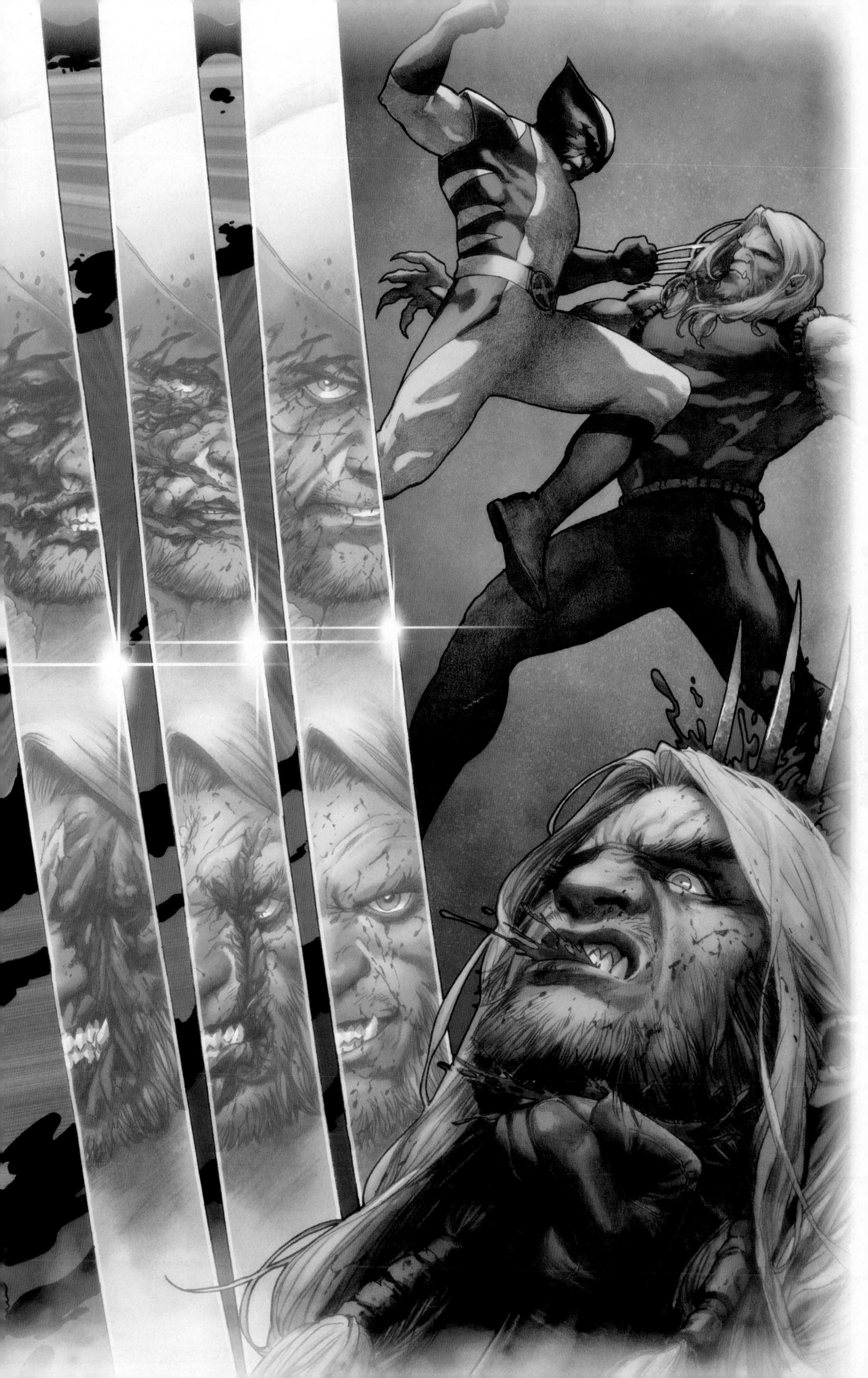

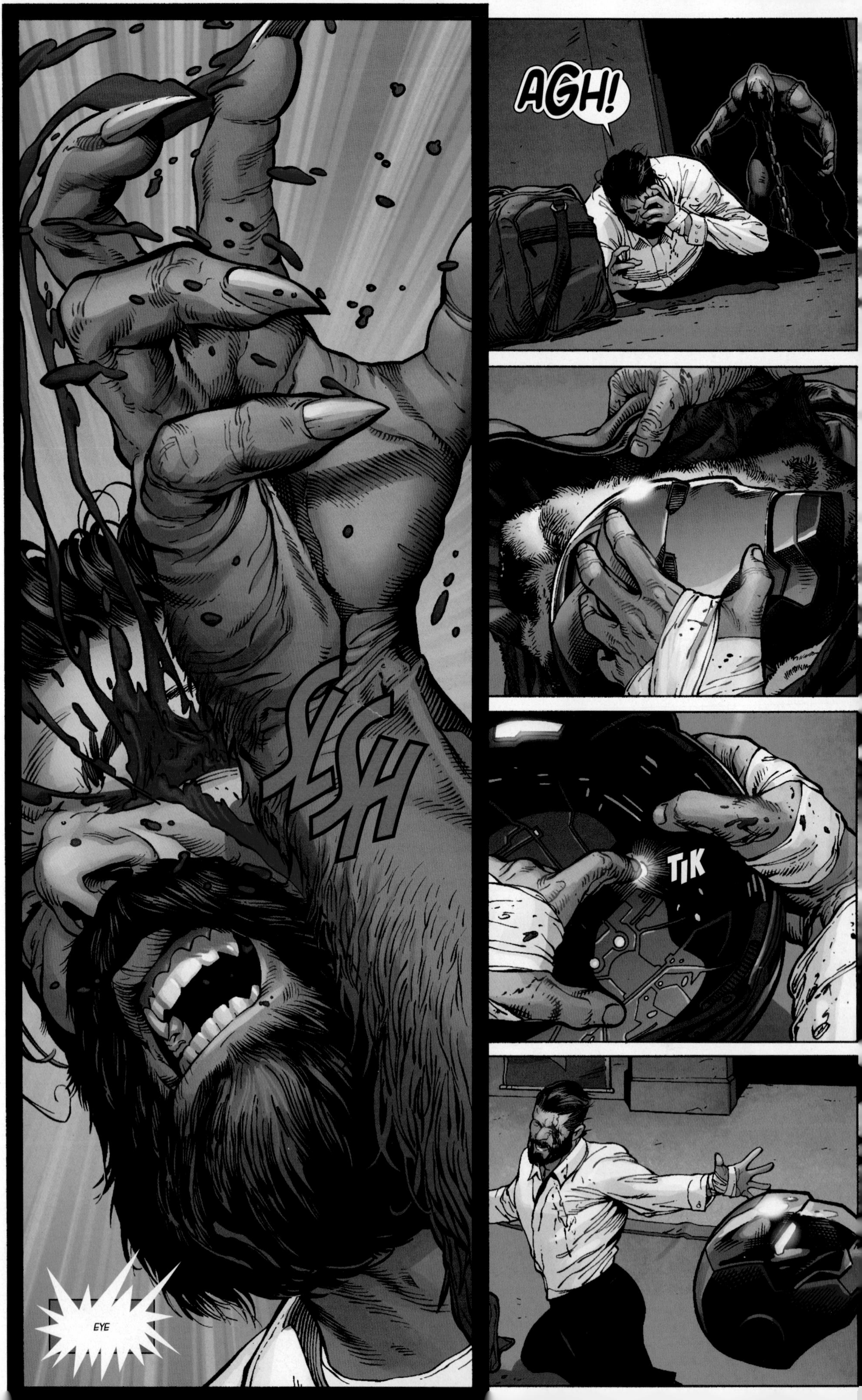
SSHH
EYE
AGH!
TIK

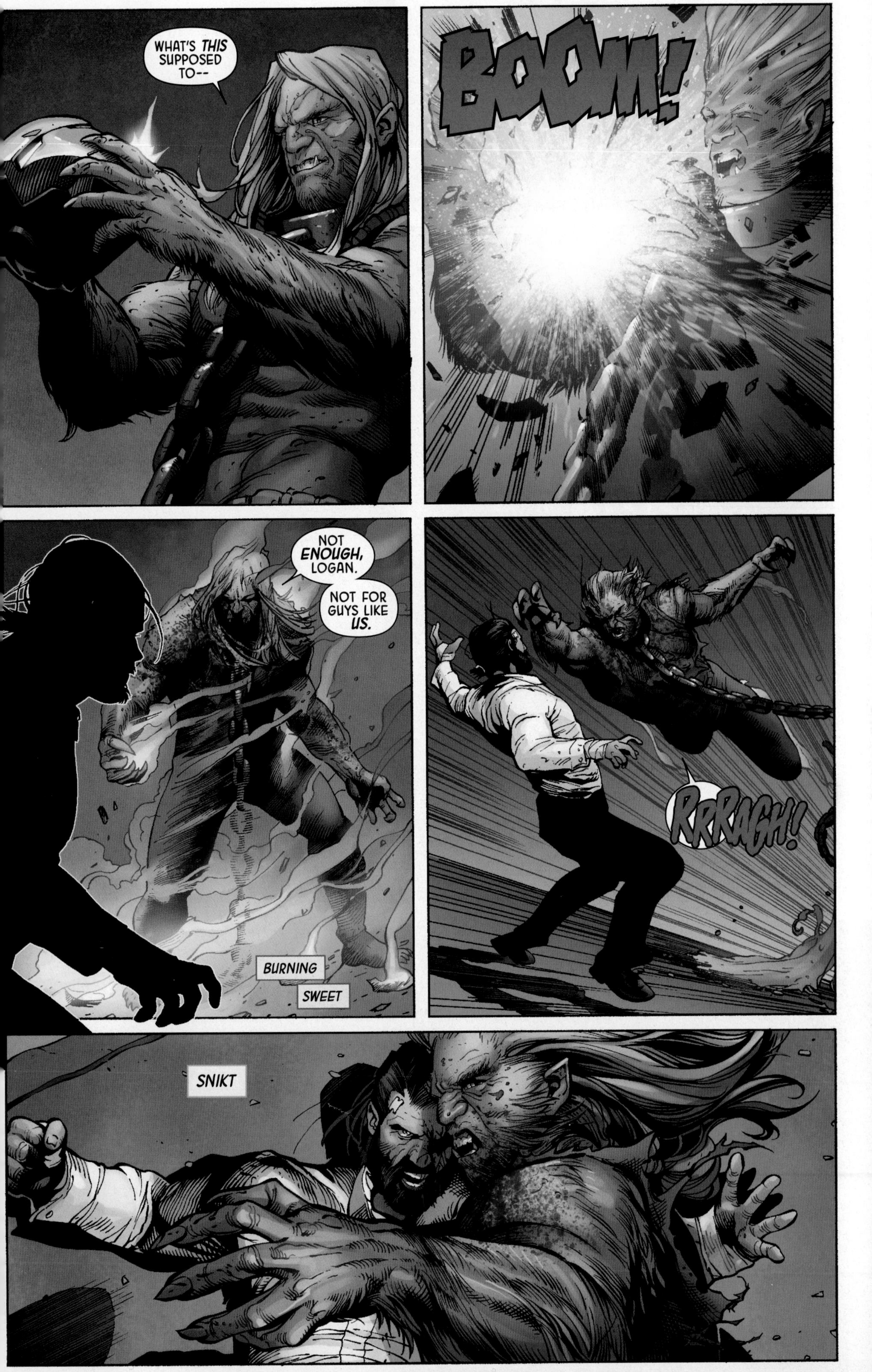

WHAT'S *THIS* SUPPOSED TO--
BOOM!
NOT *ENOUGH*, LOGAN.
NOT FOR GUYS LIKE *US*.
BURNING
SWEET
RRRAGH!
SNIKT

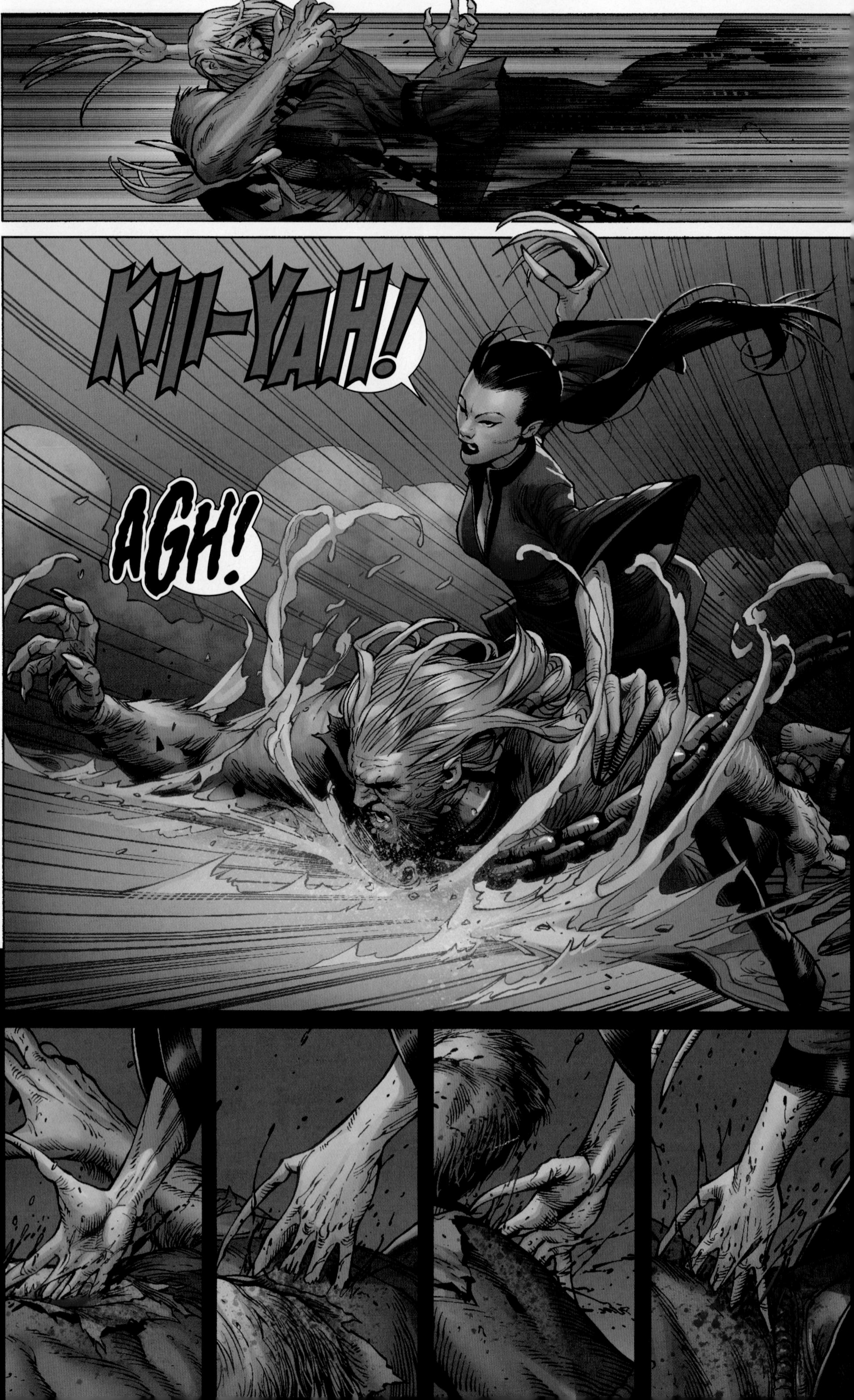
KII-YAH!
AGH!

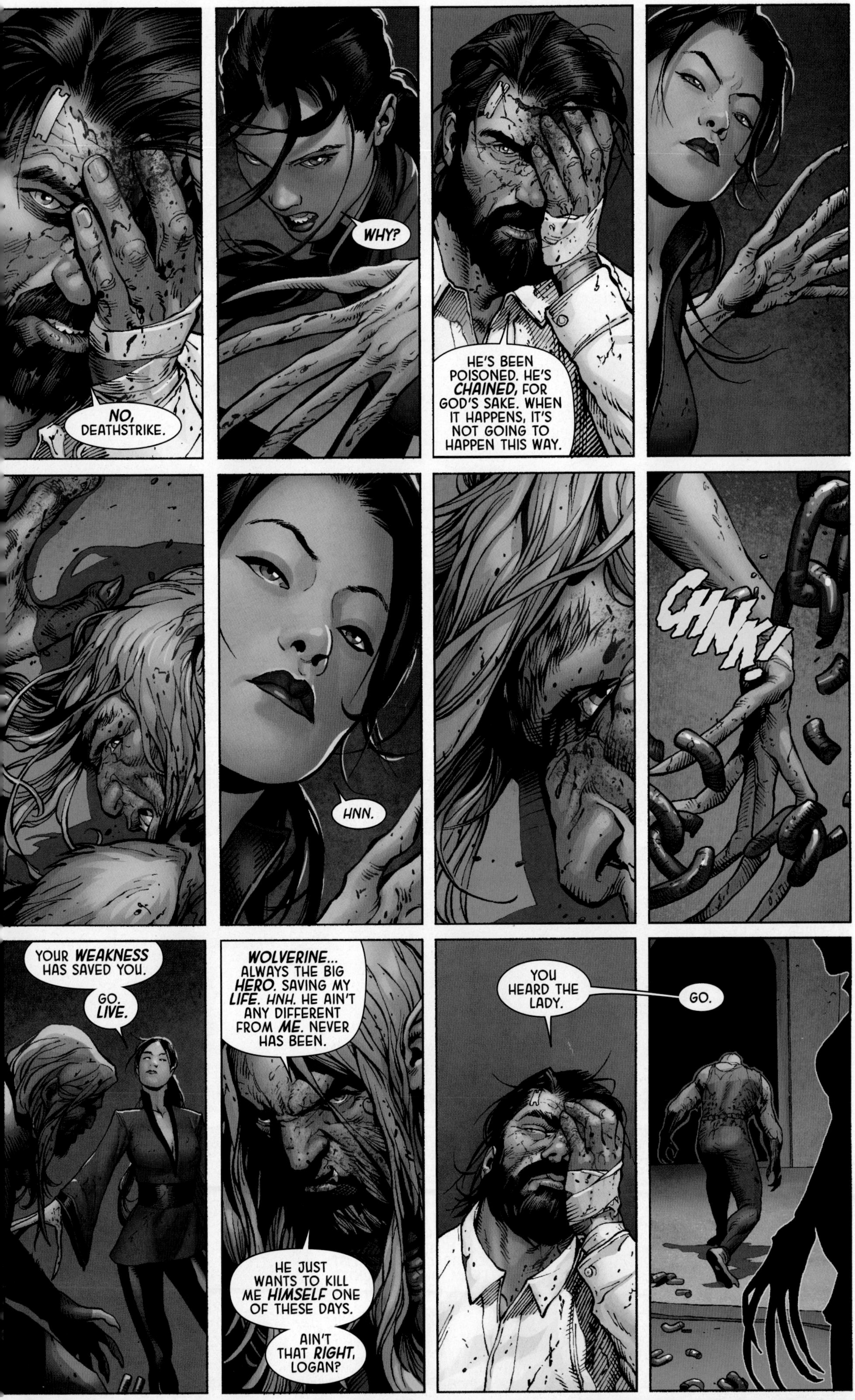
NO, DEATHSTRIKE.
WHY?
HE'S BEEN POISONED. HE'S CHAINED, FOR GOD'S SAKE. WHEN IT HAPPENS, IT'S NOT GOING TO HAPPEN THIS WAY.
HNN.
CHNK!
YOUR WEAKNESS HAS SAVED YOU.
GO. LIVE.
WOLVERINE... ALWAYS THE BIG HERO. SAVING MY LIFE. HNH. HE AIN'T ANY DIFFERENT FROM ME. NEVER HAS BEEN.
HE JUST WANTS TO KILL ME HIMSELF ONE OF THESE DAYS.
AIN'T THAT RIGHT, LOGAN?
YOU HEARD THE LADY.
GO.

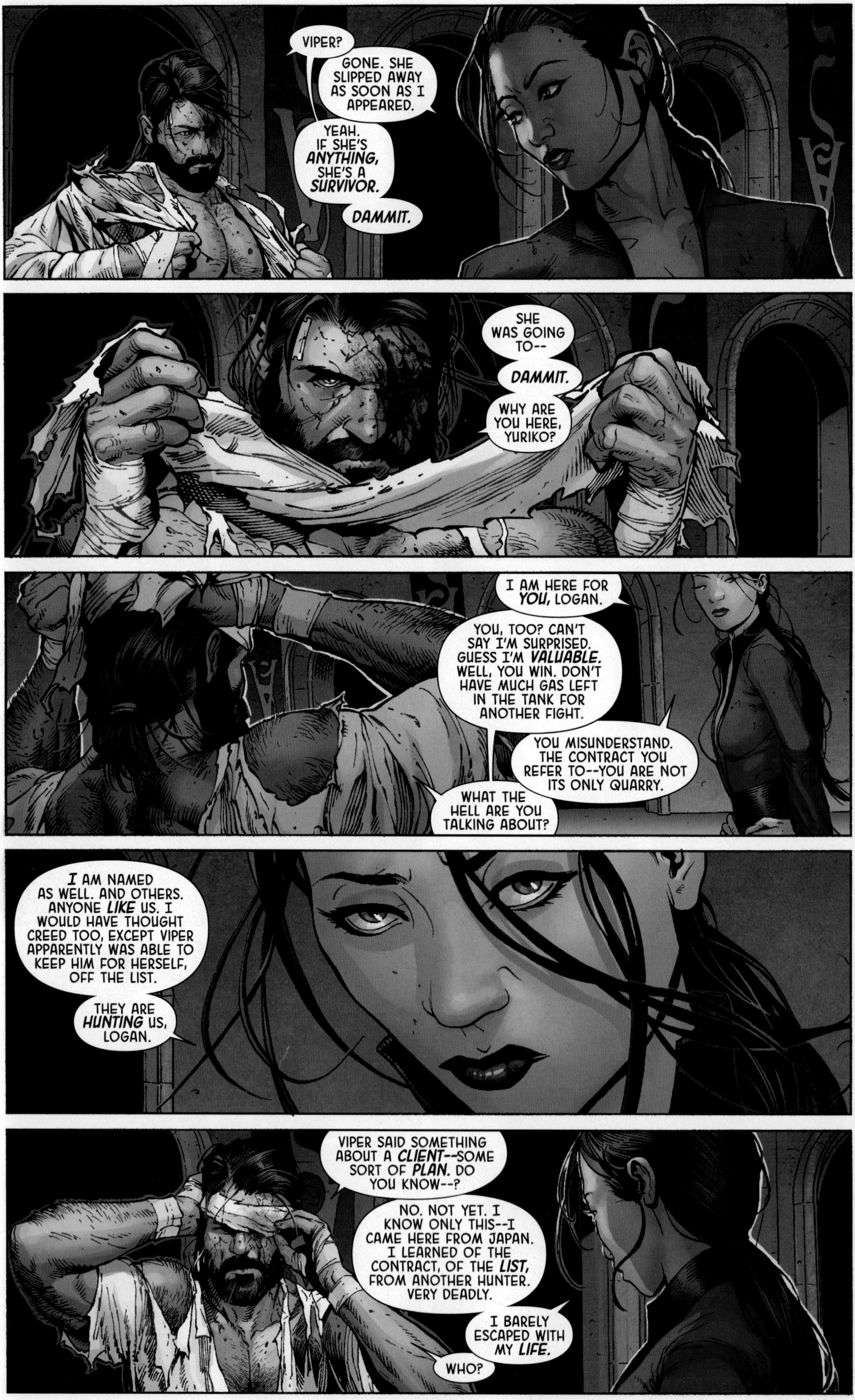
VIPER?
GONE. SHE SLIPPED AWAY AS SOON AS I APPEARED.
YEAH. IF SHE'S ANYTHING, SHE'S A SURVIVOR.
DAMMIT.
SHE WAS GOING TO--
DAMMIT.
WHY ARE YOU HERE, YURIKO?
I AM HERE FOR YOU, LOGAN.
YOU, TOO? CAN'T SAY I'M SURPRISED. GUESS I'M VALUABLE. WELL, YOU WIN. DON'T HAVE MUCH GAS LEFT IN THE TANK FOR ANOTHER FIGHT.
YOU MISUNDERSTAND. THE CONTRACT YOU REFER TO--YOU ARE NOT ITS ONLY QUARRY.
WHAT THE HELL ARE YOU TALKING ABOUT?
I AM NAMED AS WELL. AND OTHERS. ANYONE LIKE US. I WOULD HAVE THOUGHT CREED TOO, EXCEPT VIPER APPARENTLY WAS ABLE TO KEEP HIM FOR HERSELF, OFF THE LIST.
THEY ARE HUNTING US, LOGAN.
VIPER SAID SOMETHING ABOUT A CLIENT--SOME SORT OF PLAN. DO YOU KNOW--?
NO. NOT YET. I KNOW ONLY THIS--I CAME HERE FROM JAPAN. I LEARNED OF THE CONTRACT, OF THE LIST, FROM ANOTHER HUNTER. VERY DEADLY.
I BARELY ESCAPED WITH MY LIFE.
WHO?

OGUN.

LORD. OGUN.

YES. THAT IS WHY I TRACKED YOU HERE, TO MADRIPOOR. I THOUGHT WE MIGHT PUT ASIDE OUR DIFFERENCES, WORK *TOGETHER* TO DISCOVER THE TRUTH AND DEFEAT OUR ENEMY.

THIS IS VERY BAD. I HESITATE TO SAY THIS, BUT I NEED YOUR STRENGTH, LOGAN. I--

...HNN.

WHY DOES YOUR *EYE* NOT HEAL?

AND WHY DID YOU NOT USE YOUR *CLAWS* IN THE FIGHT WITH CREED? WHAT IS THE *MATTER* WITH YOU, LOGAN?

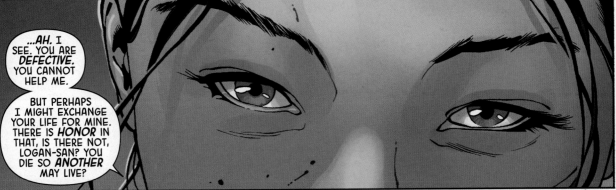

...AH. I SEE. YOU ARE *DEFECTIVE*. YOU CANNOT HELP ME.

BUT PERHAPS I MIGHT EXCHANGE YOUR LIFE FOR MINE. THERE IS *HONOR* IN THAT, IS THERE NOT, LOGAN-SAN? YOU DIE SO *ANOTHER* MAY LIVE?

AHH, COME ON.

SHKK!

YOU KNOW...

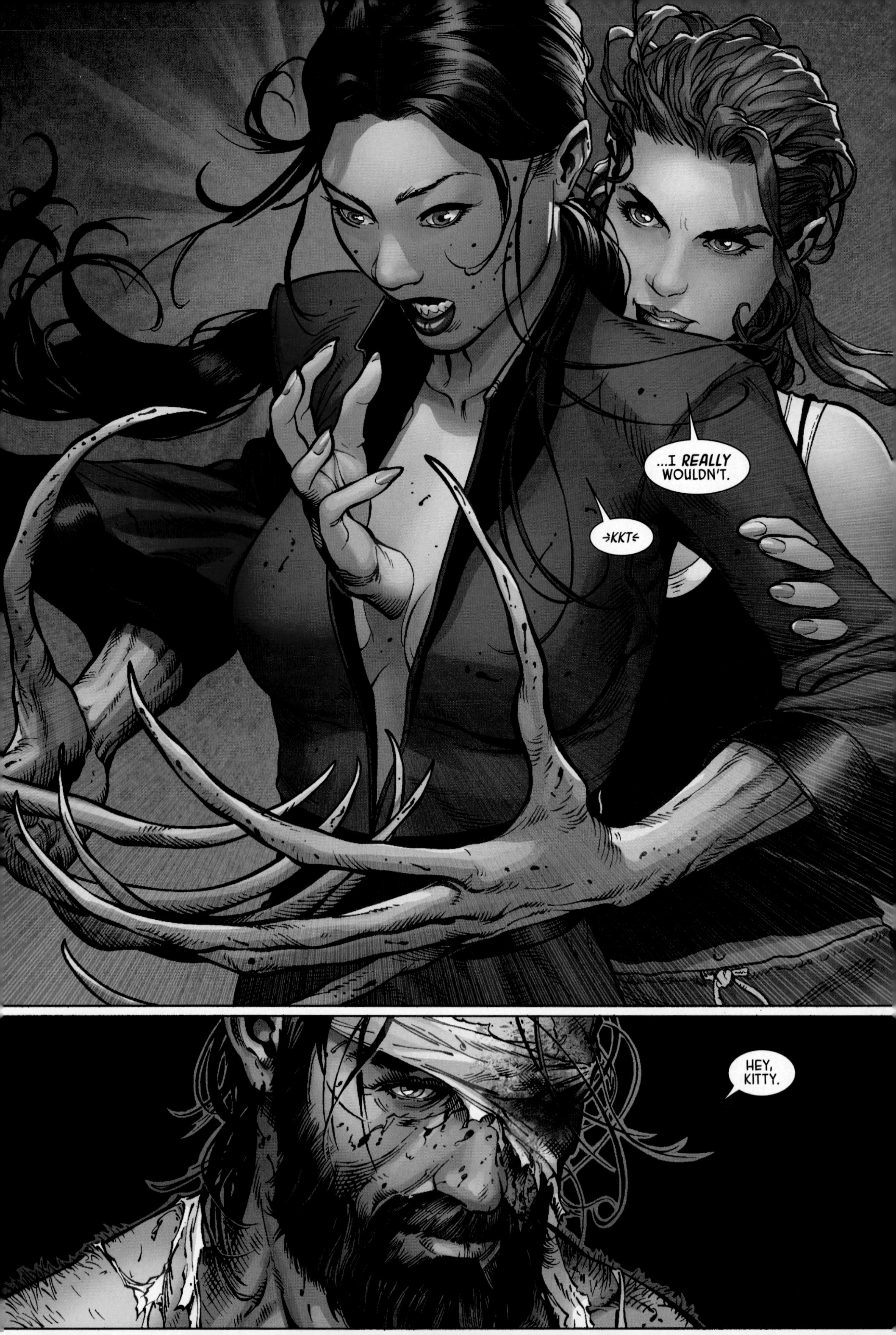
...I *REALLY* WOULDN'T.
KKT
HEY, KITTY.

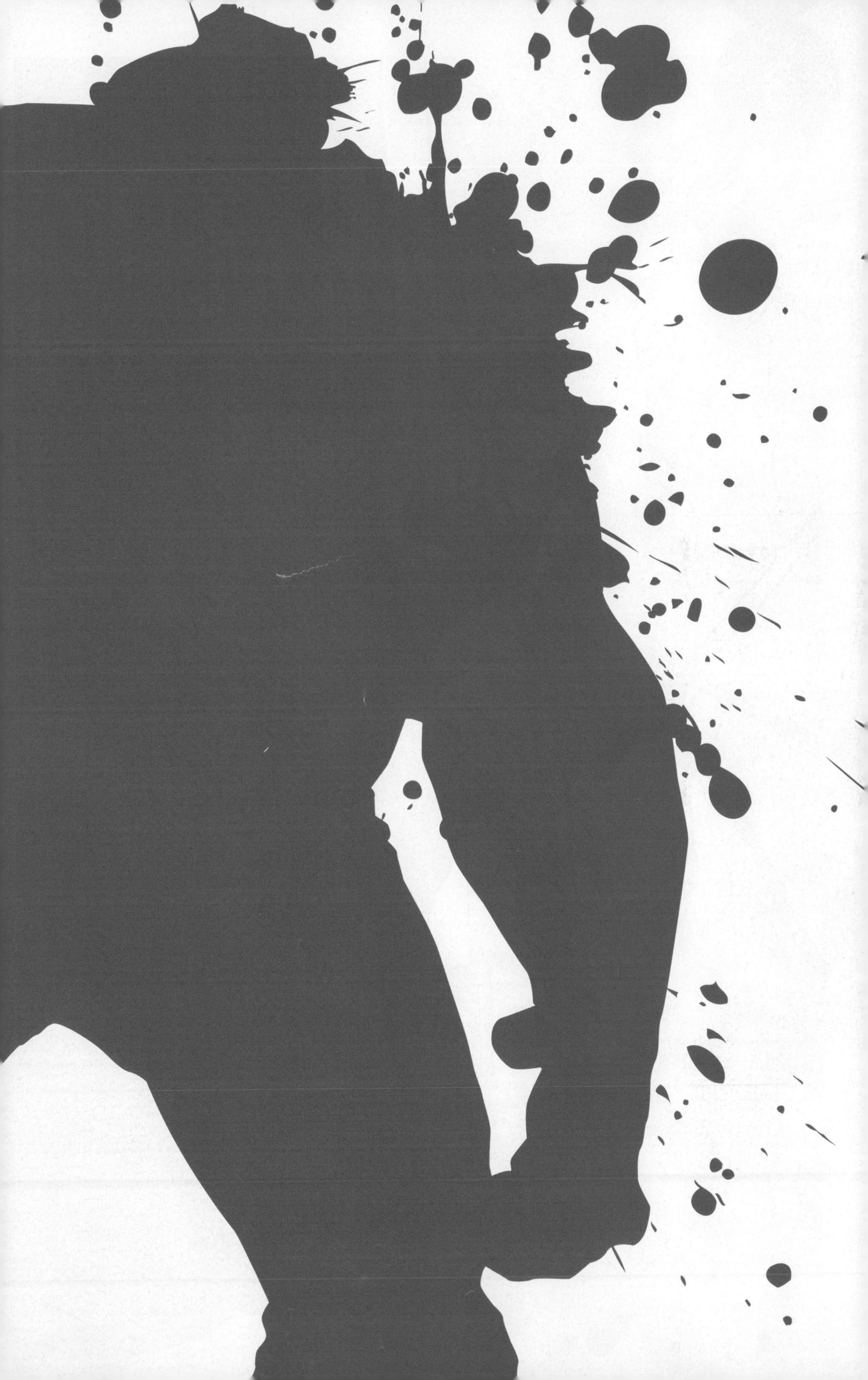

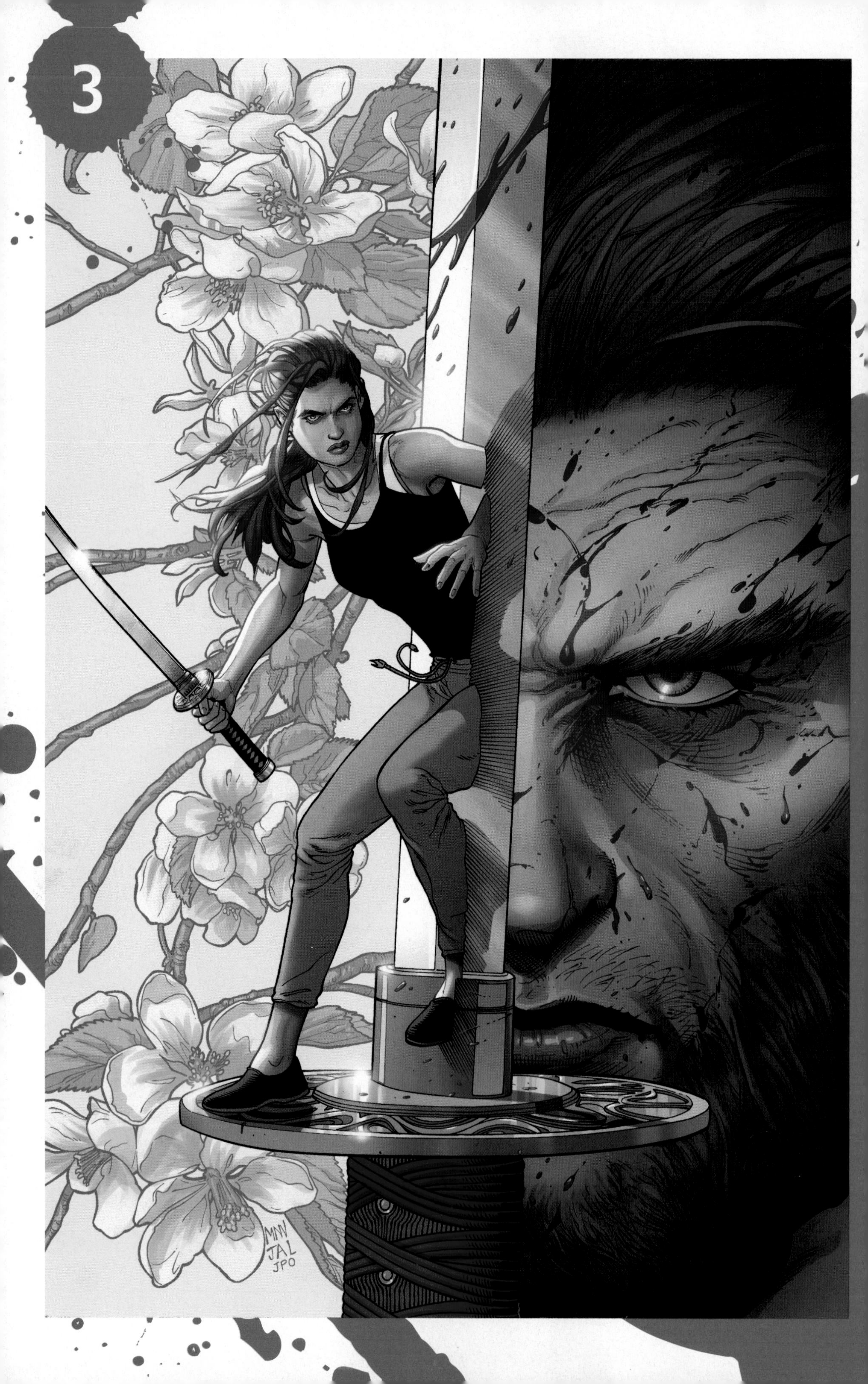
3
MW
JAL
JPO

SEPPUKU

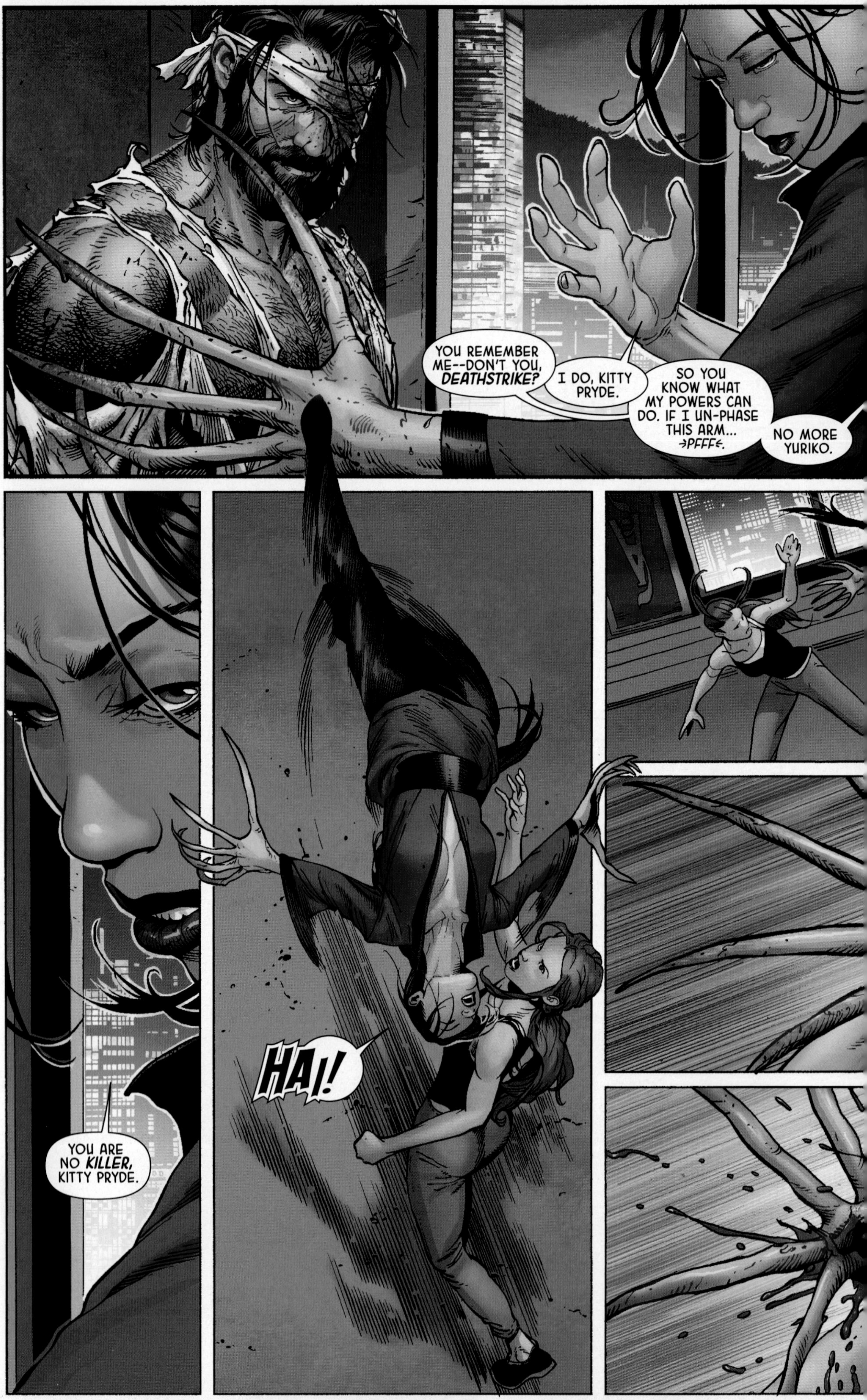

YOU REMEMBER ME--DON'T YOU, DEATHSTRIKE?
I DO, KITTY PRYDE.
SO YOU KNOW WHAT MY POWERS CAN DO. IF I UN-PHASE THIS ARM... →PFFF←.
NO MORE YURIKO.
YOU ARE NO KILLER, KITTY PRYDE.
HAI!

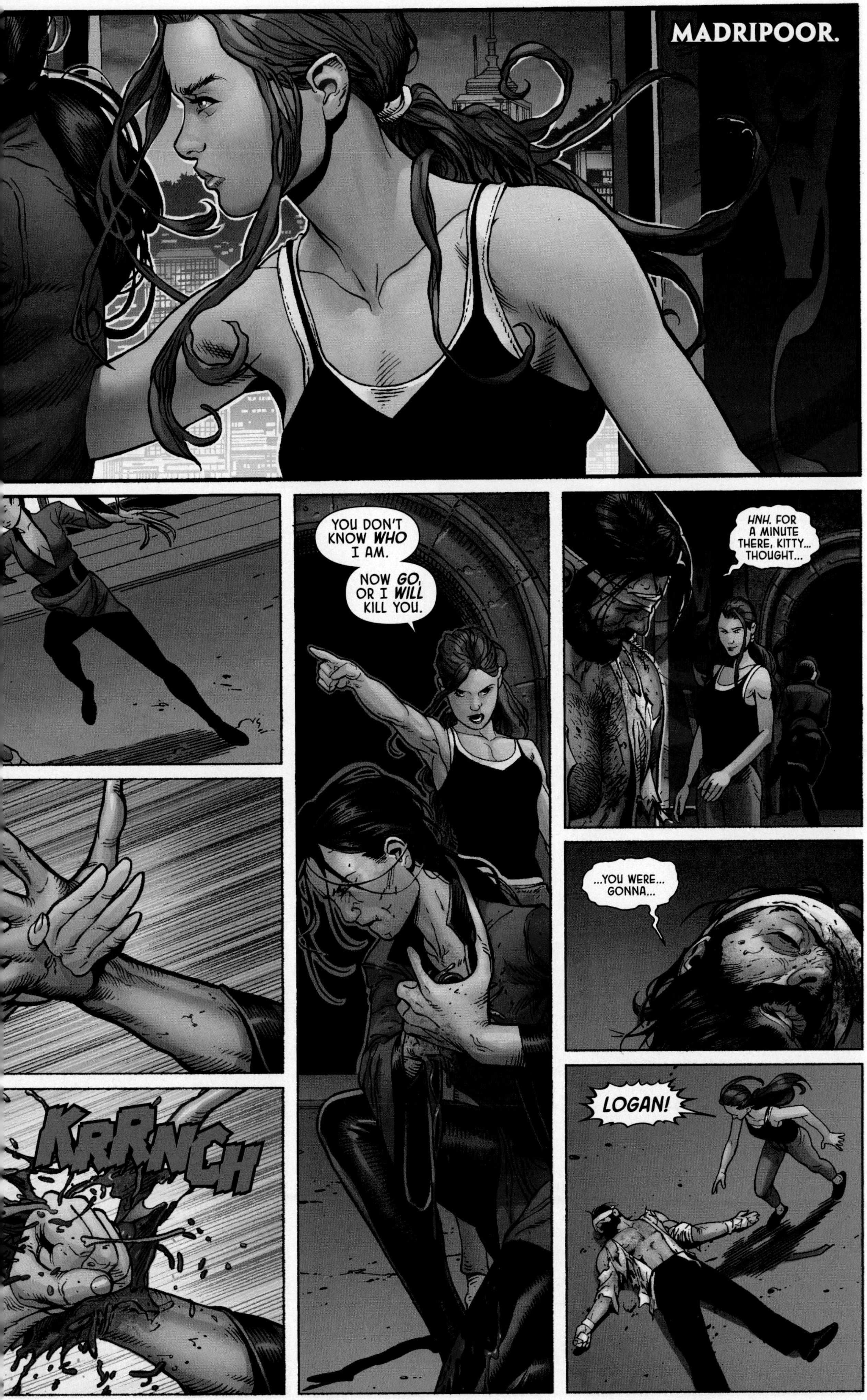
MADRIPOOR.
KRRNCH
YOU DON'T KNOW WHO I AM.
NOW GO, OR I WILL KILL YOU.
HNH. FOR A MINUTE THERE, KITTY... THOUGHT...
...YOU WERE... GONNA...
LOGAN!

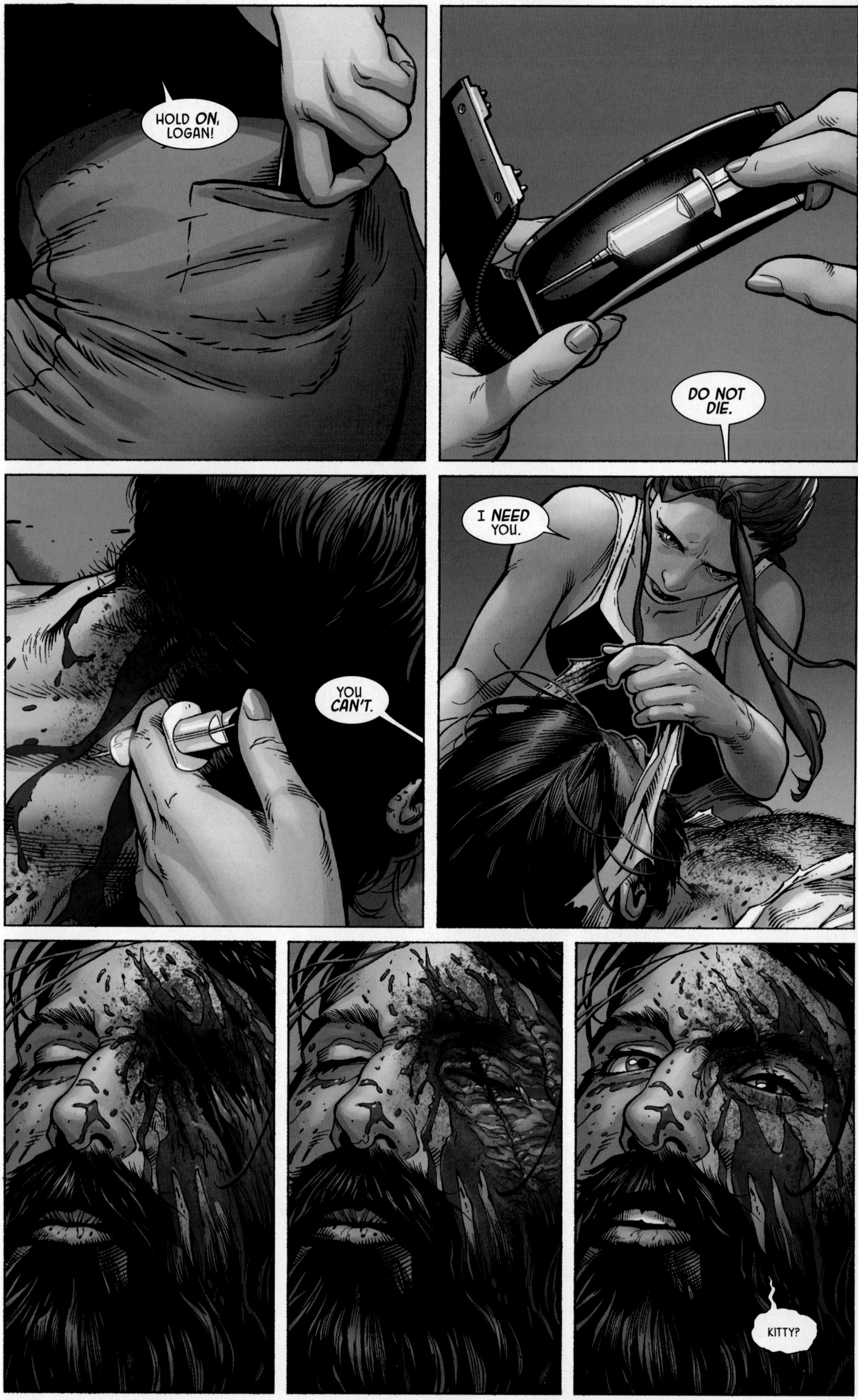
HOLD ON, LOGAN!
DO NOT DIE.
YOU CAN'T.
I NEED YOU.
KITTY?

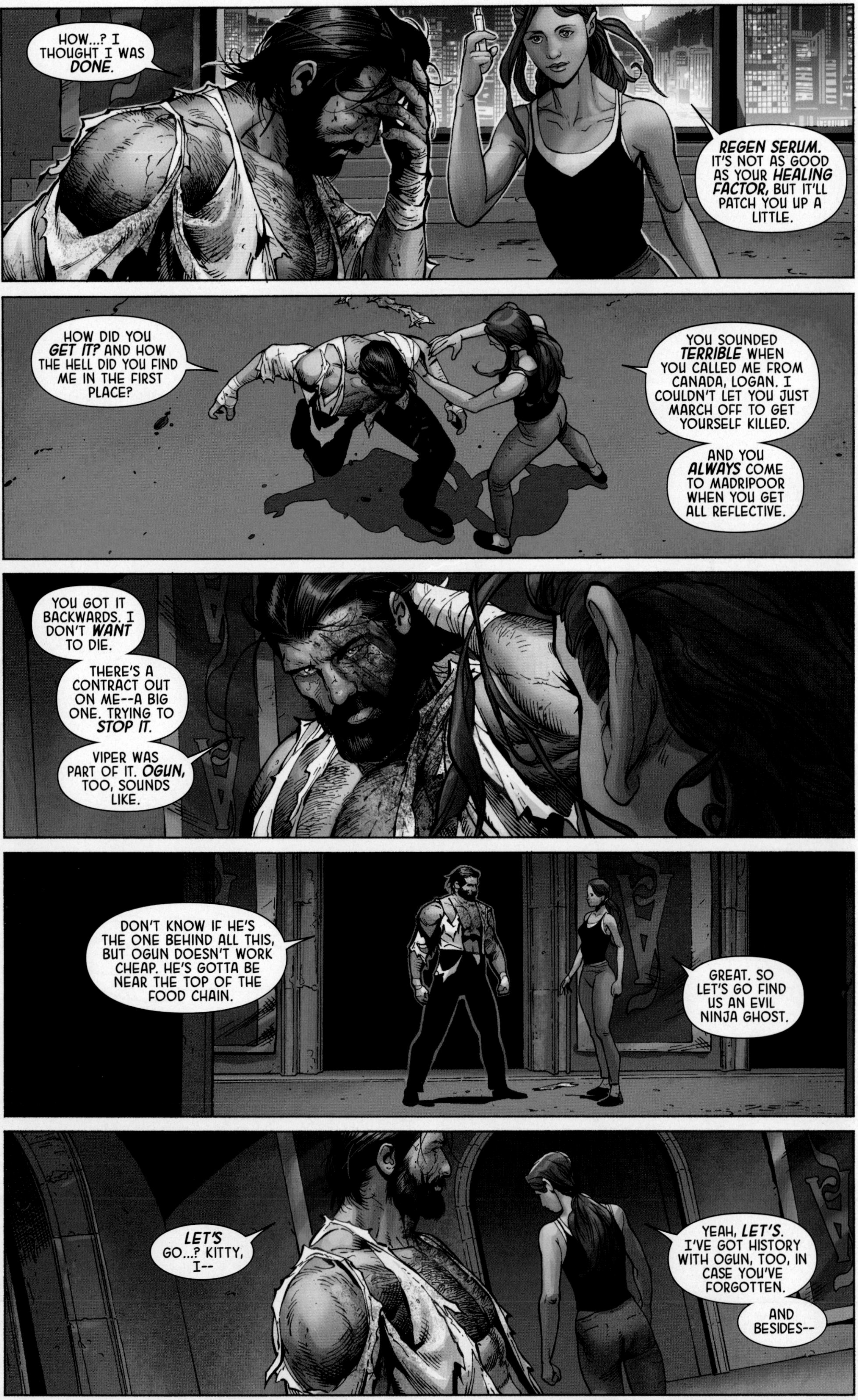
HOW...? I THOUGHT I WAS DONE.
REGEN SERUM. IT'S NOT AS GOOD AS YOUR HEALING FACTOR, BUT IT'LL PATCH YOU UP A LITTLE.
HOW DID YOU GET IT? AND HOW THE HELL DID YOU FIND ME IN THE FIRST PLACE?
YOU SOUNDED TERRIBLE WHEN YOU CALLED ME FROM CANADA, LOGAN. I COULDN'T LET YOU JUST MARCH OFF TO GET YOURSELF KILLED.
AND YOU ALWAYS COME TO MADRIPOOR WHEN YOU GET ALL REFLECTIVE.
YOU GOT IT BACKWARDS. I DON'T WANT TO DIE.
THERE'S A CONTRACT OUT ON ME--A BIG ONE. TRYING TO STOP IT.
VIPER WAS PART OF IT. OGUN, TOO, SOUNDS LIKE.
DON'T KNOW IF HE'S THE ONE BEHIND ALL THIS, BUT OGUN DOESN'T WORK CHEAP. HE'S GOTTA BE NEAR THE TOP OF THE FOOD CHAIN.
GREAT. SO LET'S GO FIND US AN EVIL NINJA GHOST.
LET'S GO...? KITTY, I--
YEAH, LET'S. I'VE GOT HISTORY WITH OGUN, TOO, IN CASE YOU'VE FORGOTTEN.
AND BESIDES--

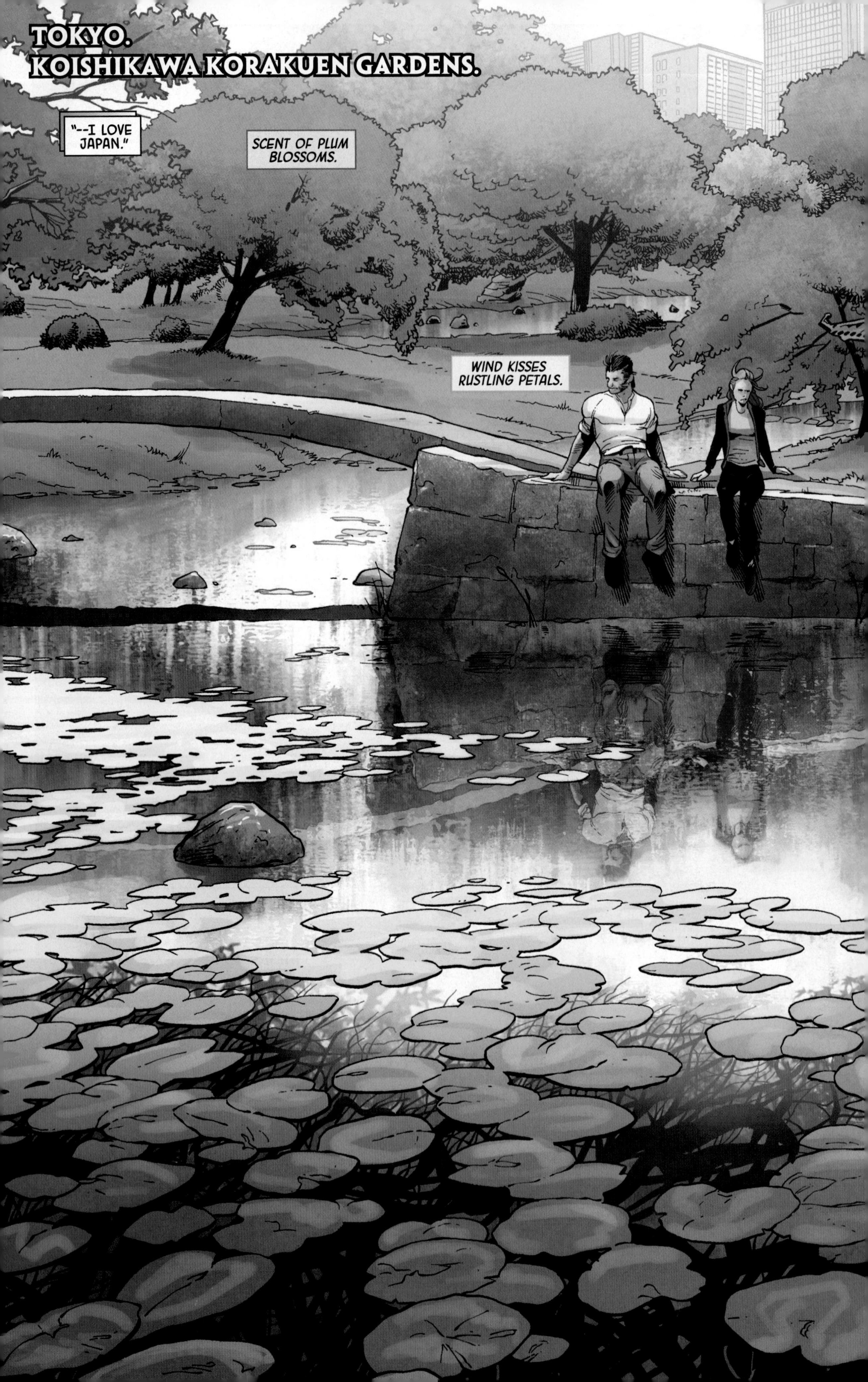
TOKYO.
KOISHIKAWA KORAKUEN GARDENS.
"--I LOVE JAPAN."
SCENT OF PLUM BLOSSOMS.
WIND KISSES RUSTLING PETALS.

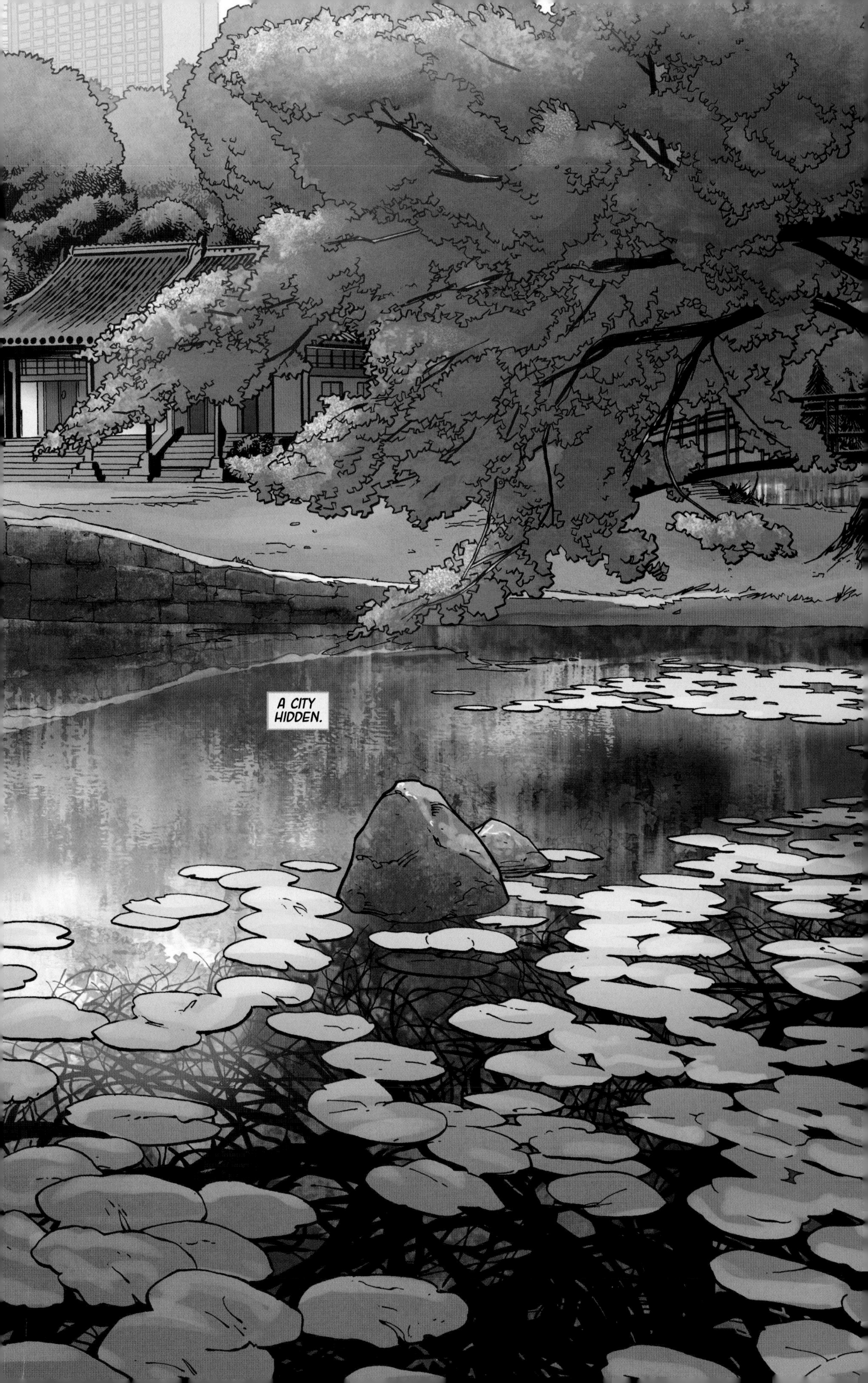
A CITY HIDDEN.

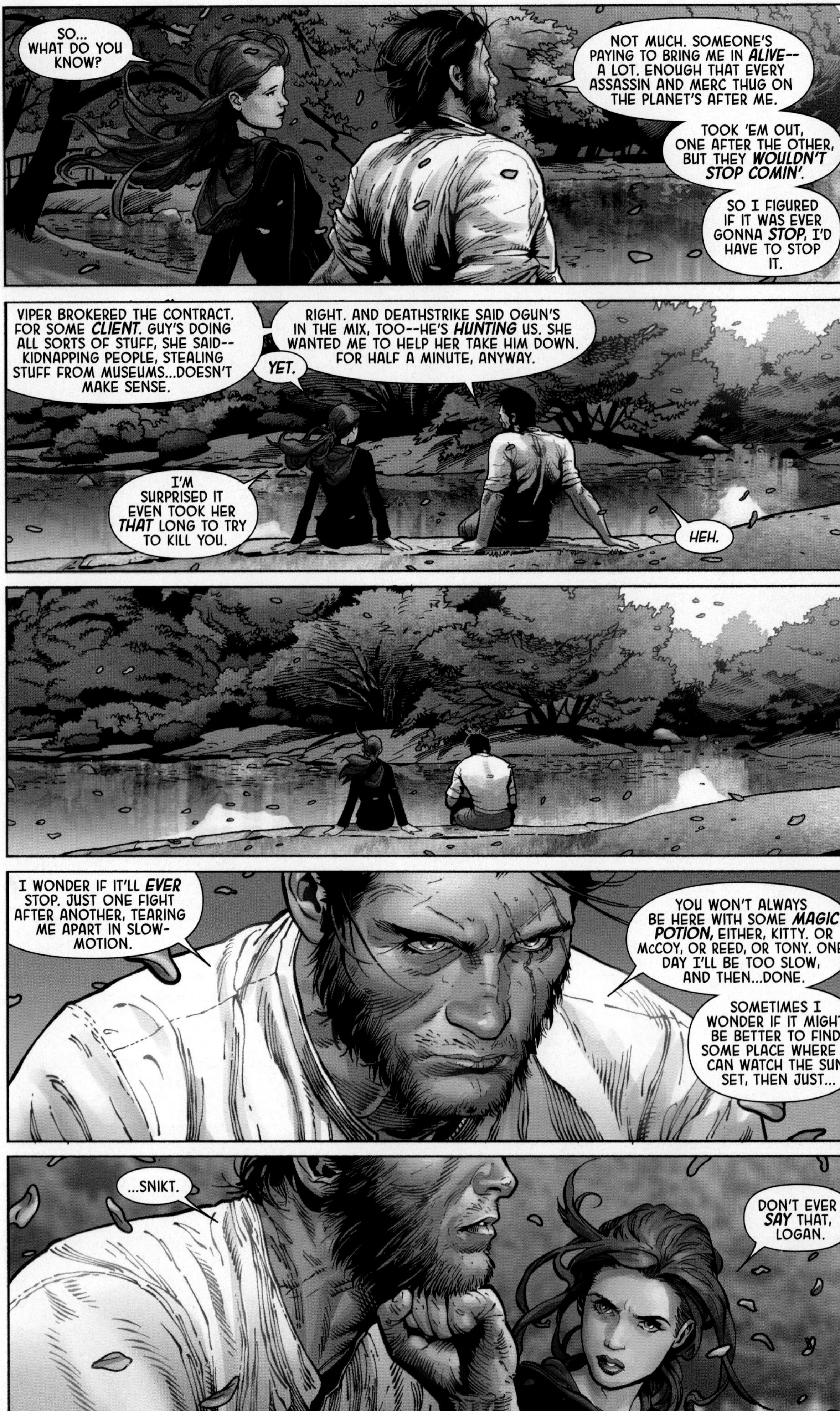
SO... WHAT DO YOU KNOW?
NOT MUCH. SOMEONE'S PAYING TO BRING ME IN ALIVE-- A LOT. ENOUGH THAT EVERY ASSASSIN AND MERC THUG ON THE PLANET'S AFTER ME.
TOOK 'EM OUT, ONE AFTER THE OTHER, BUT THEY WOULDN'T STOP COMIN'.
SO I FIGURED IF IT WAS EVER GONNA STOP, I'D HAVE TO STOP IT.
VIPER BROKERED THE CONTRACT. FOR SOME CLIENT. GUY'S DOING ALL SORTS OF STUFF, SHE SAID-- KIDNAPPING PEOPLE, STEALING STUFF FROM MUSEUMS...DOESN'T MAKE SENSE.
RIGHT. AND DEATHSTRIKE SAID OGUN'S IN THE MIX, TOO--HE'S HUNTING US. SHE WANTED ME TO HELP HER TAKE HIM DOWN. FOR HALF A MINUTE, ANYWAY.
YET.
I'M SURPRISED IT EVEN TOOK HER THAT LONG TO TRY TO KILL YOU.
HEH.
I WONDER IF IT'LL EVER STOP. JUST ONE FIGHT AFTER ANOTHER, TEARING ME APART IN SLOW-MOTION.
YOU WON'T ALWAYS BE HERE WITH SOME MAGIC POTION, EITHER, KITTY. OR McCOY, OR REED, OR TONY. ONE DAY I'LL BE TOO SLOW, AND THEN...DONE.
SOMETIMES I WONDER IF IT MIGHT BE BETTER TO FIND SOME PLACE WHERE I CAN WATCH THE SUN SET, THEN JUST...
...SNIKT.
DON'T EVER SAY THAT, LOGAN.

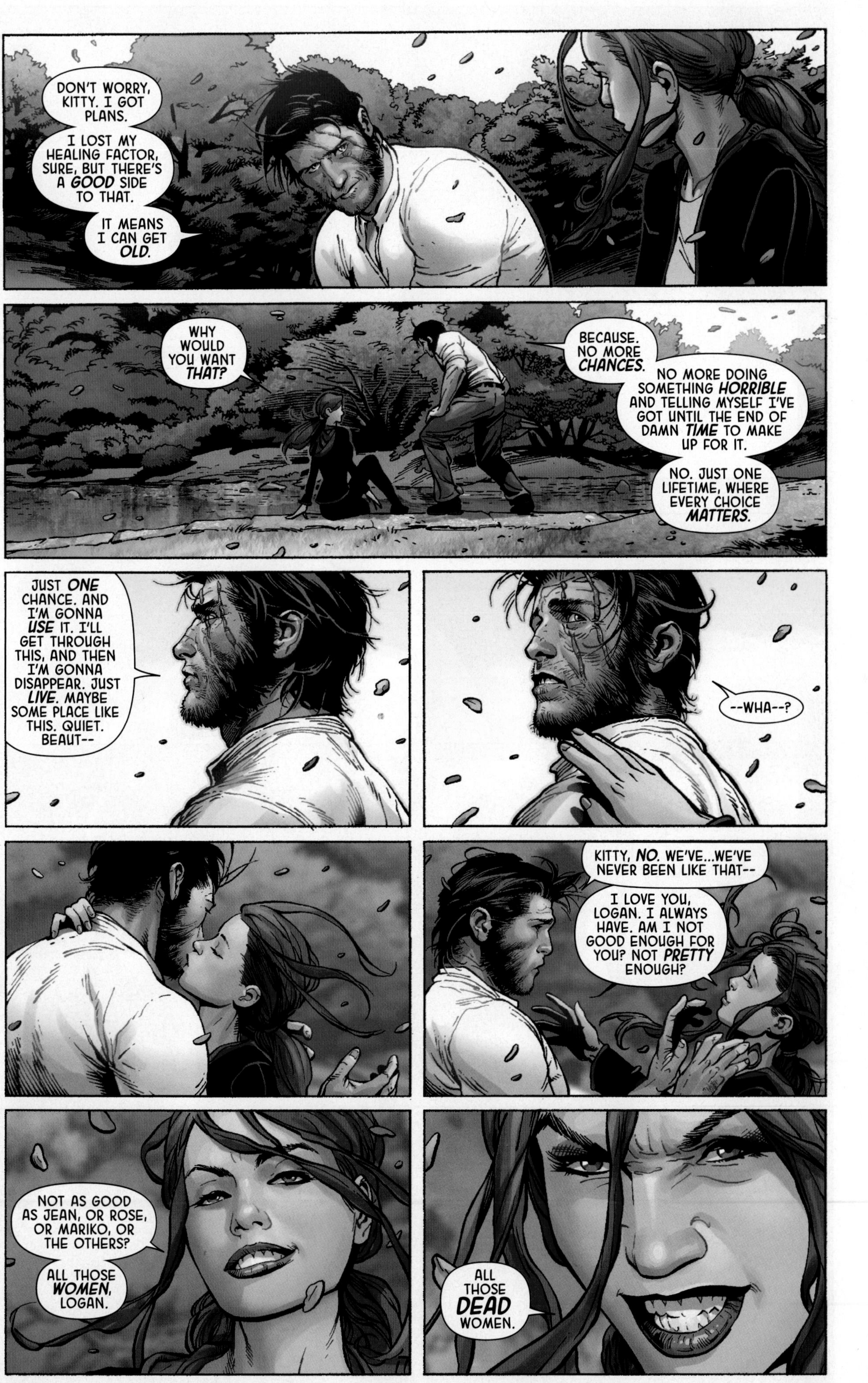
DON'T WORRY, KITTY. I GOT PLANS.
I LOST MY HEALING FACTOR, SURE, BUT THERE'S A GOOD SIDE TO THAT.
IT MEANS I CAN GET OLD.
WHY WOULD YOU WANT THAT?
BECAUSE. NO MORE CHANCES.
NO MORE DOING SOMETHING HORRIBLE AND TELLING MYSELF I'VE GOT UNTIL THE END OF DAMN TIME TO MAKE UP FOR IT.
NO. JUST ONE LIFETIME, WHERE EVERY CHOICE MATTERS.
JUST ONE CHANCE. AND I'M GONNA USE IT. I'LL GET THROUGH THIS, AND THEN I'M GONNA DISAPPEAR. JUST LIVE. MAYBE SOME PLACE LIKE THIS. QUIET. BEAUT--
--WHA--?
KITTY, NO. WE'VE...WE'VE NEVER BEEN LIKE THAT--
I LOVE YOU, LOGAN. I ALWAYS HAVE. AM I NOT GOOD ENOUGH FOR YOU? NOT PRETTY ENOUGH?
NOT AS GOOD AS JEAN, OR ROSE, OR MARIKO, OR THE OTHERS?
ALL THOSE WOMEN, LOGAN.
ALL THOSE DEAD WOMEN.

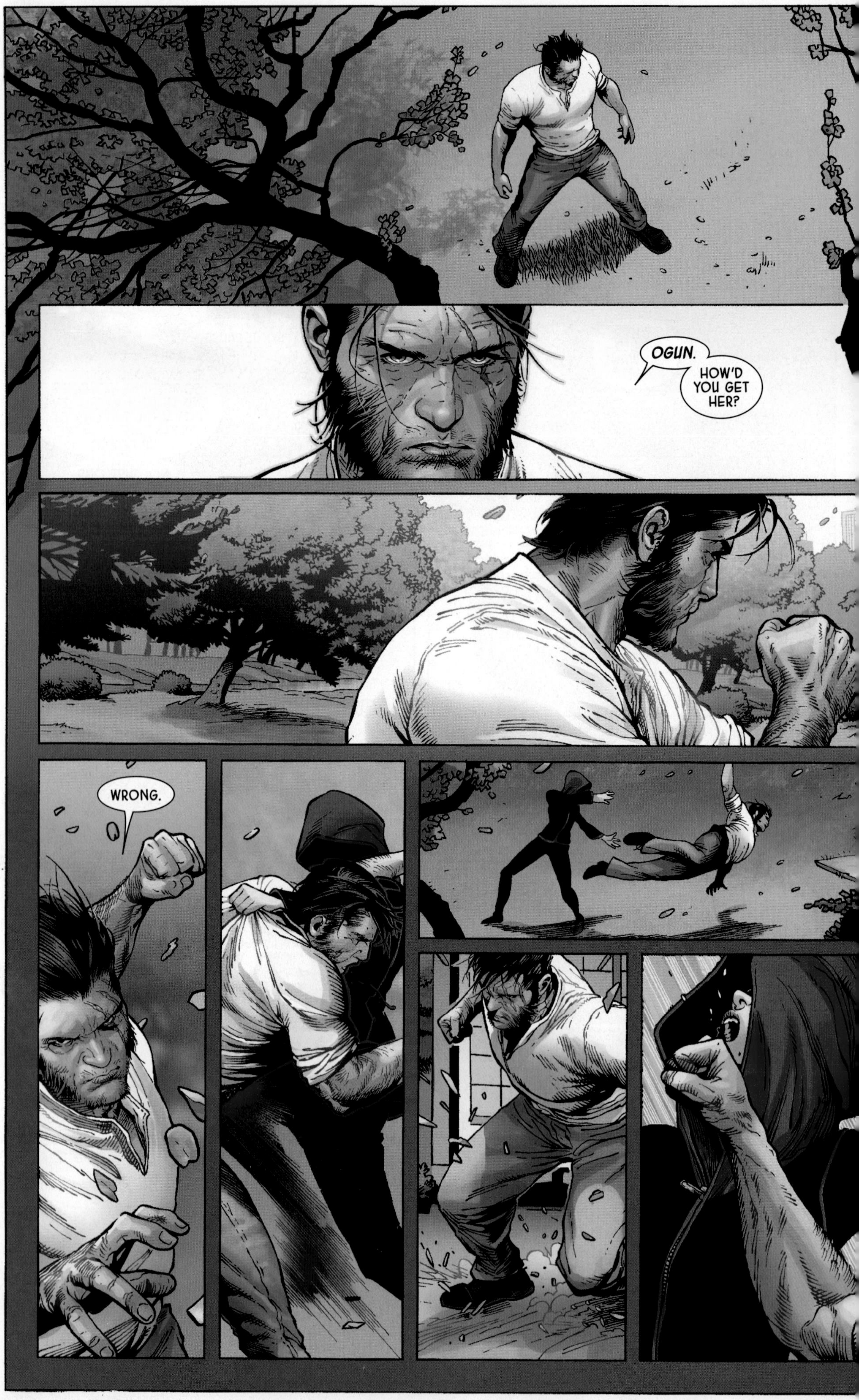

OGUN.
HOW'D YOU GET HER?
WRONG.

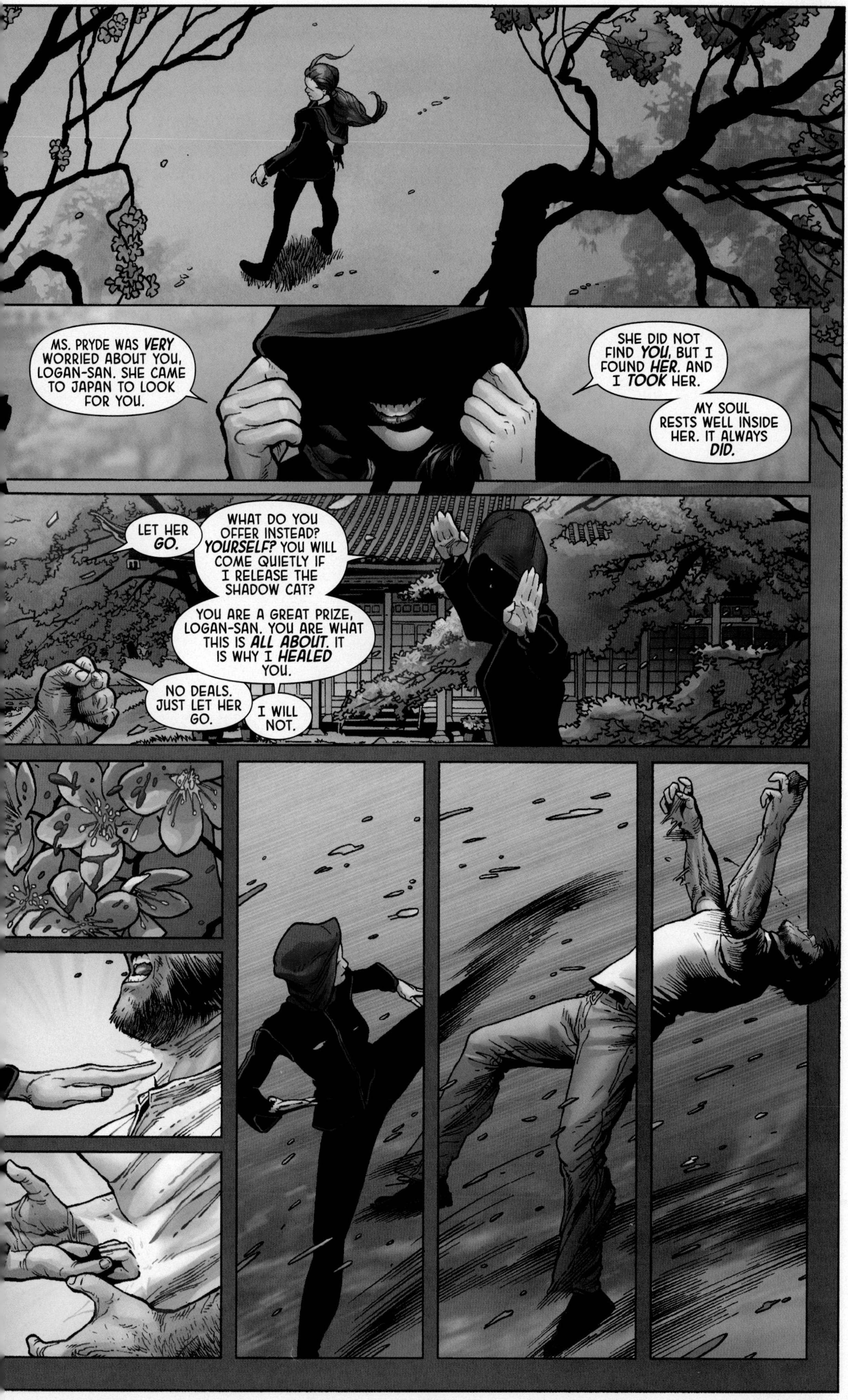
MS. PRYDE WAS VERY WORRIED ABOUT YOU, LOGAN-SAN. SHE CAME TO JAPAN TO LOOK FOR YOU.
SHE DID NOT FIND YOU, BUT I FOUND HER. AND I TOOK HER.
MY SOUL RESTS WELL INSIDE HER. IT ALWAYS DID.
LET HER GO.
WHAT DO YOU OFFER INSTEAD? YOURSELF? YOU WILL COME QUIETLY IF I RELEASE THE SHADOW CAT?
YOU ARE A GREAT PRIZE, LOGAN-SAN. YOU ARE WHAT THIS IS ALL ABOUT. IT IS WHY I HEALED YOU.
NO DEALS. JUST LET HER GO.
I WILL NOT.

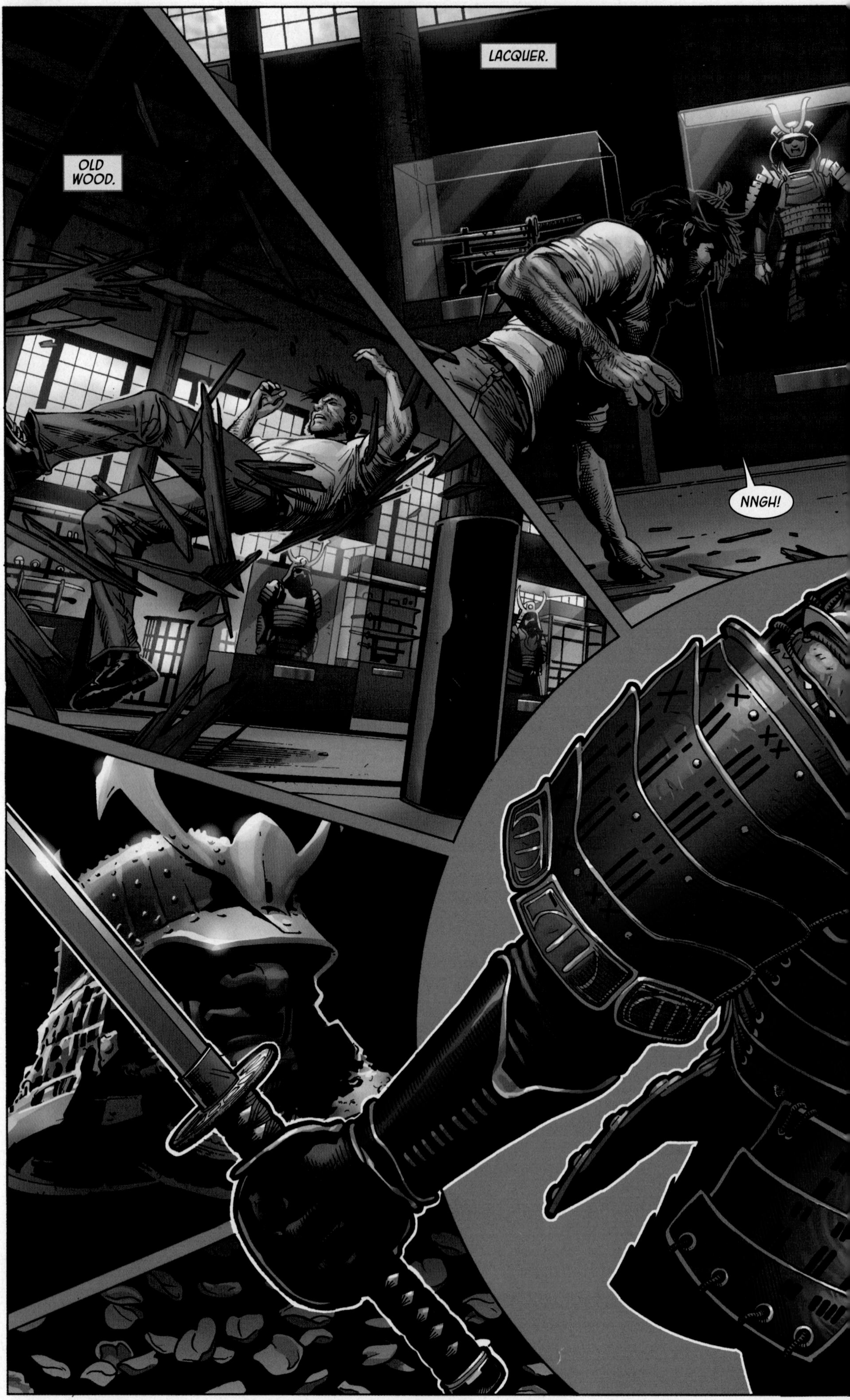
OLD WOOD.
LACQUER.
NNGH!

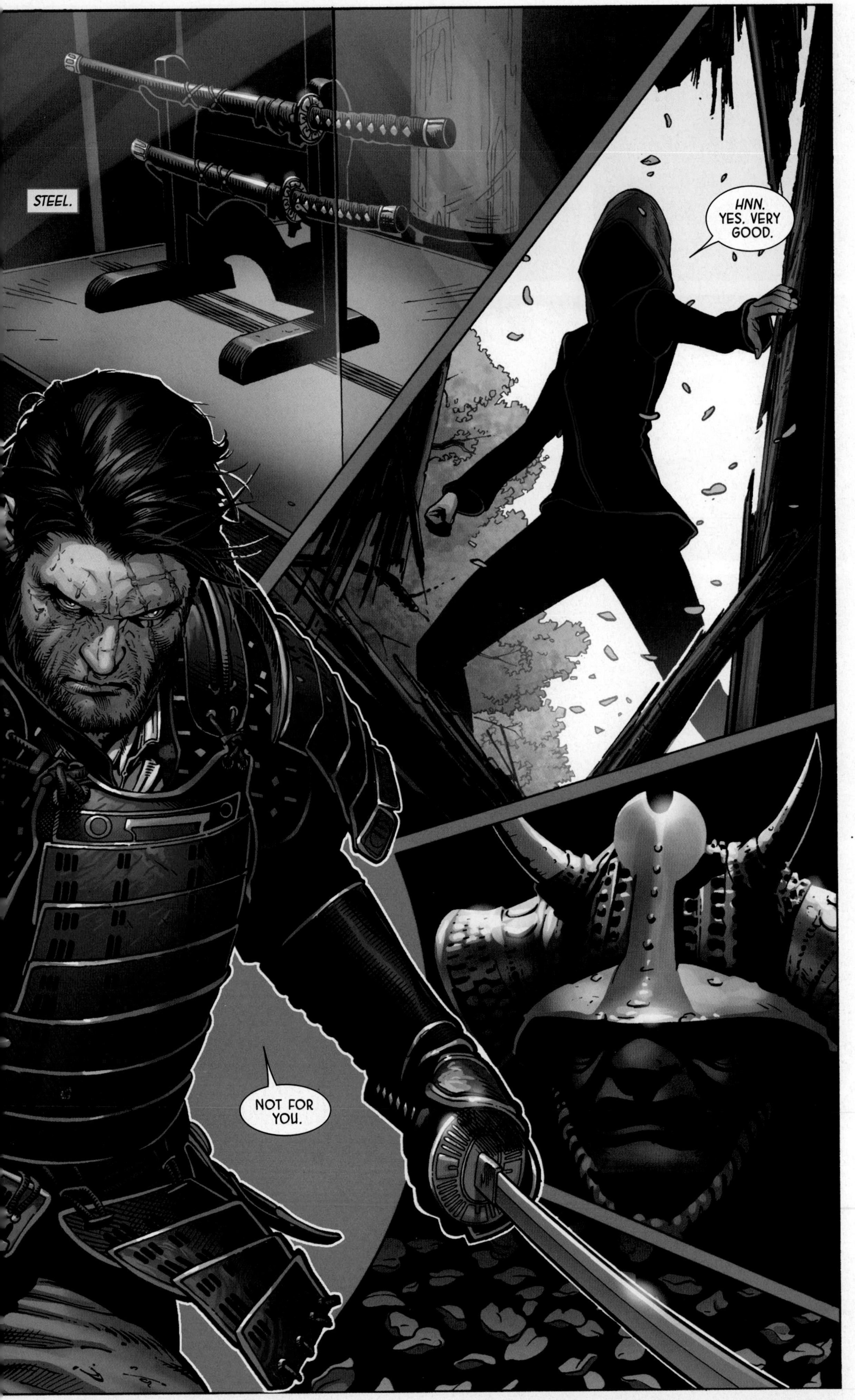
STEEL.
HNN. YES. VERY GOOD.
NOT FOR YOU.

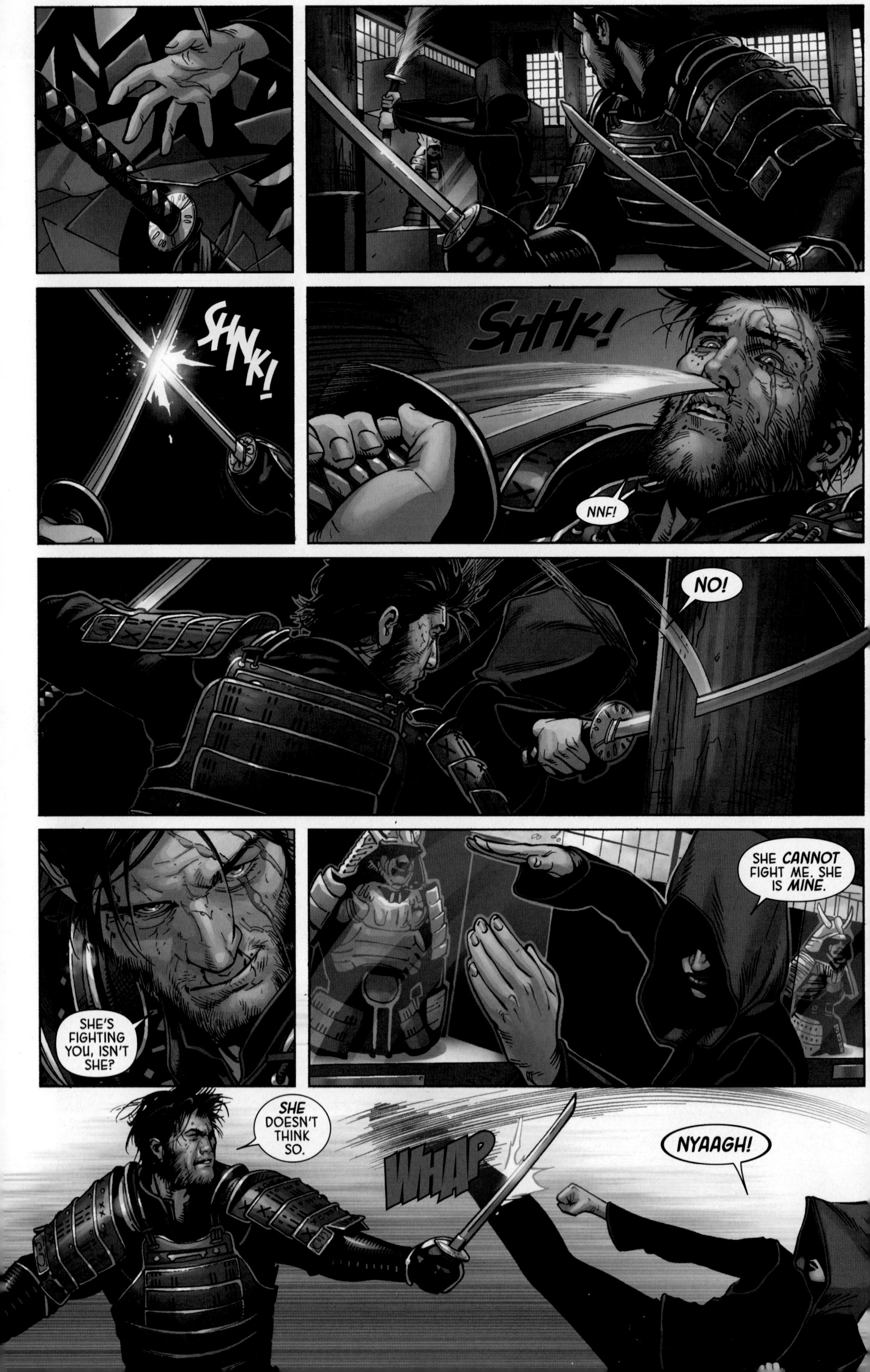
SHNK!
SHHK!
NNF!
NO!
SHE'S FIGHTING YOU, ISN'T SHE?
SHE CANNOT FIGHT ME. SHE IS MINE.
SHE DOESN'T THINK SO.
WHAP
NYAAGH!

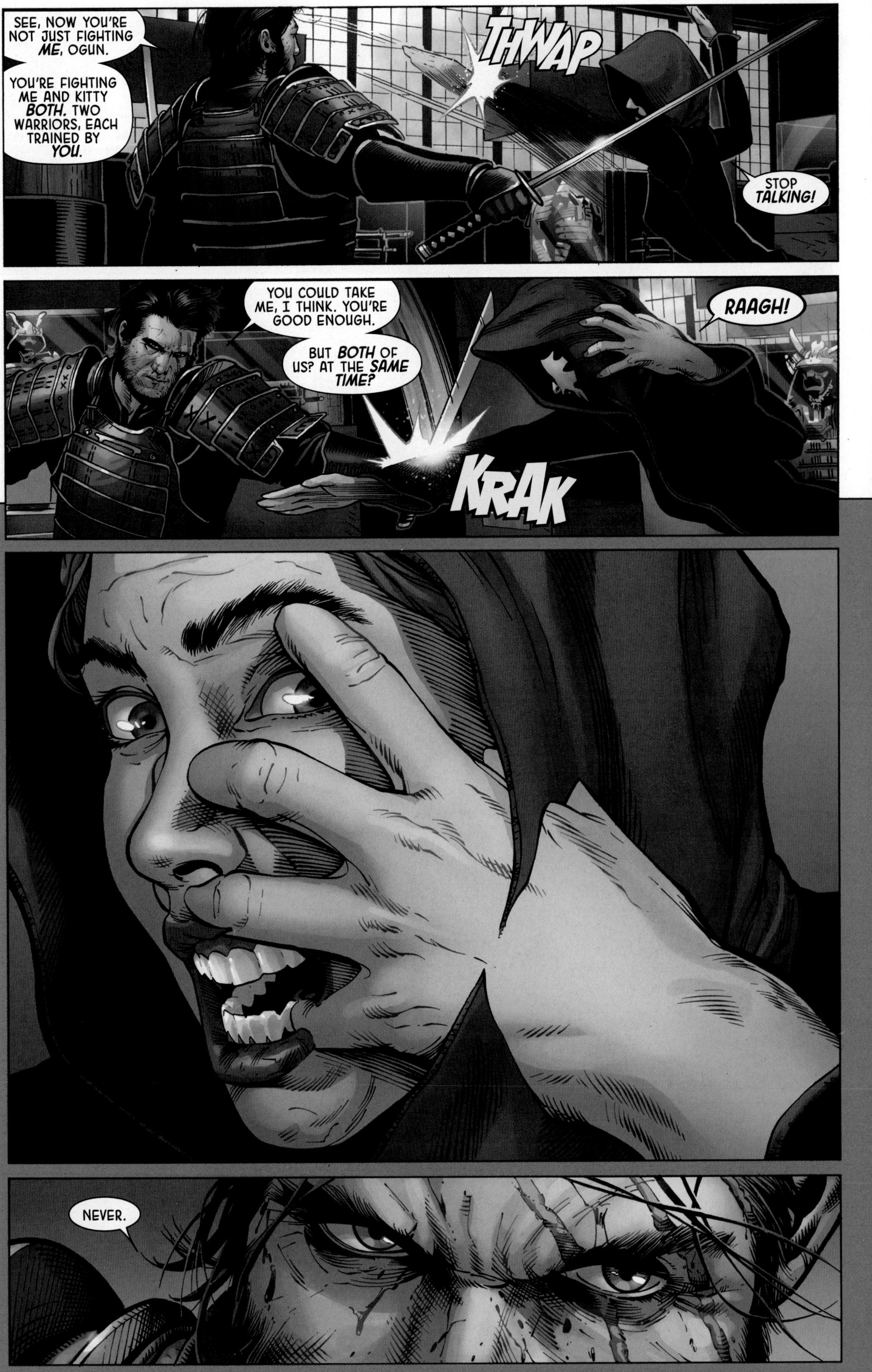
SEE, NOW YOU'RE NOT JUST FIGHTING *ME*, OGUN.
YOU'RE FIGHTING ME AND KITTY *BOTH*. TWO WARRIORS, EACH TRAINED BY *YOU*.
THWAP
STOP *TALKING!*
YOU COULD TAKE ME, I THINK. YOU'RE GOOD ENOUGH.
BUT *BOTH* OF US? AT THE *SAME TIME?*
RAAGH!
KRAK
NEVER.

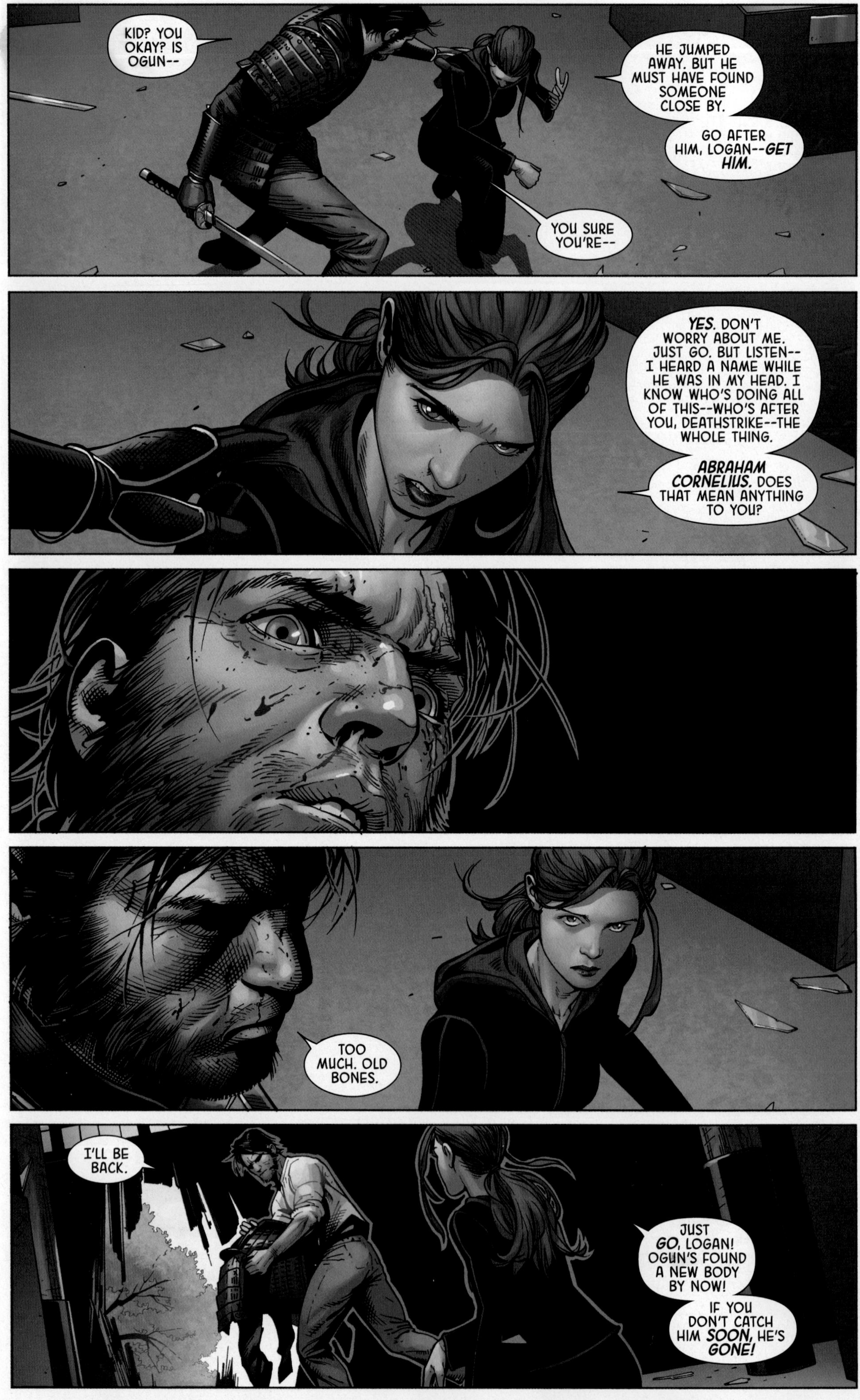

KID? YOU OKAY? IS OGUN--
HE JUMPED AWAY. BUT HE MUST HAVE FOUND SOMEONE CLOSE BY.
GO AFTER HIM, LOGAN--GET HIM.
YOU SURE YOU'RE--
YES. DON'T WORRY ABOUT ME. JUST GO. BUT LISTEN-- I HEARD A NAME WHILE HE WAS IN MY HEAD. I KNOW WHO'S DOING ALL OF THIS--WHO'S AFTER YOU, DEATHSTRIKE--THE WHOLE THING.
ABRAHAM CORNELIUS. DOES THAT MEAN ANYTHING TO YOU?
TOO MUCH. OLD BONES.
I'LL BE BACK.
JUST GO, LOGAN! OGUN'S FOUND A NEW BODY BY NOW!
IF YOU DON'T CATCH HIM SOON, HE'S GONE!

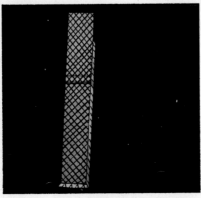

ROT.

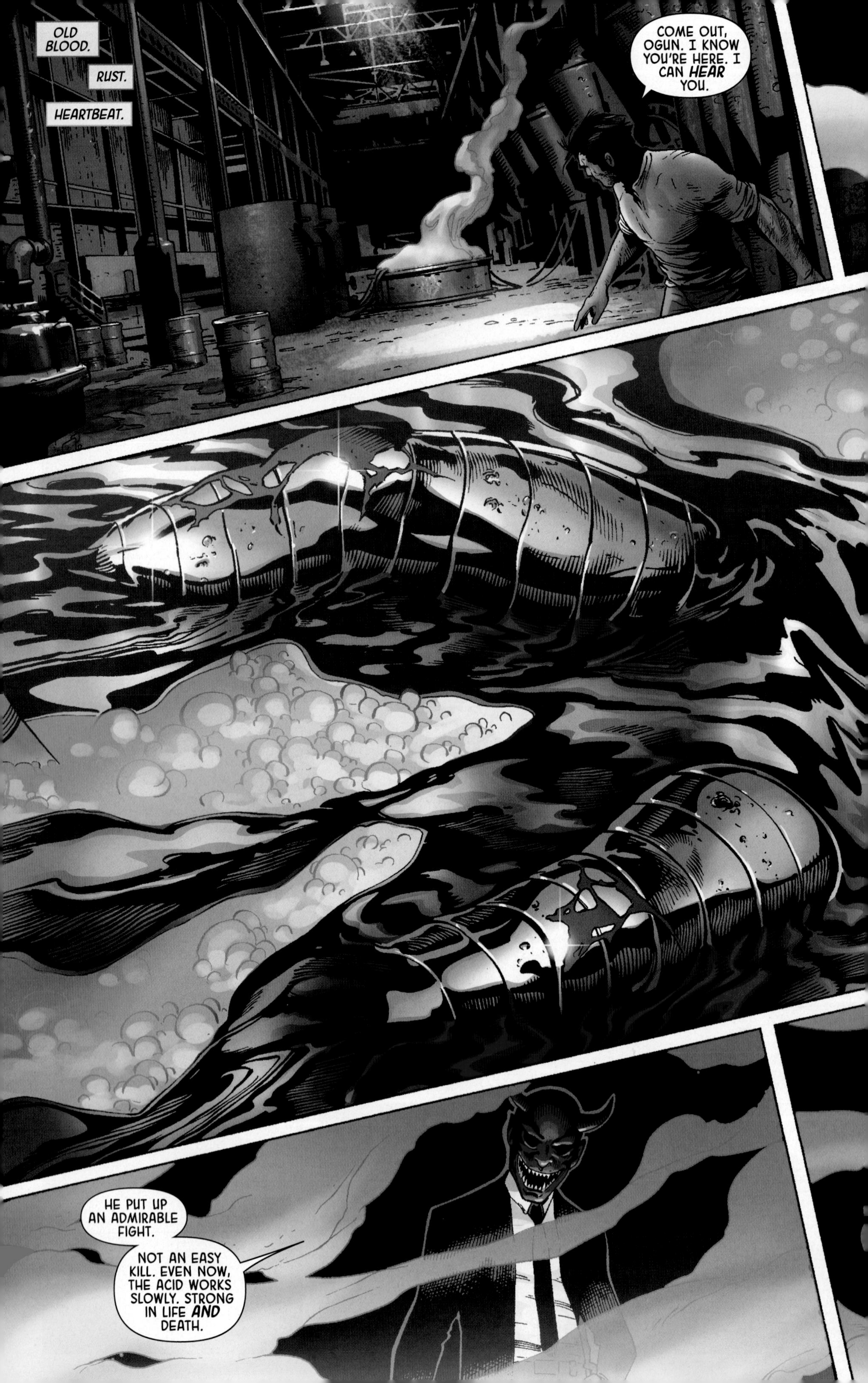
OLD BLOOD.
RUST.
HEARTBEAT.
COME OUT, OGUN. I KNOW YOU'RE HERE. I CAN HEAR YOU.
HE PUT UP AN ADMIRABLE FIGHT.
NOT AN EASY KILL. EVEN NOW, THE ACID WORKS SLOWLY. STRONG IN LIFE AND DEATH.

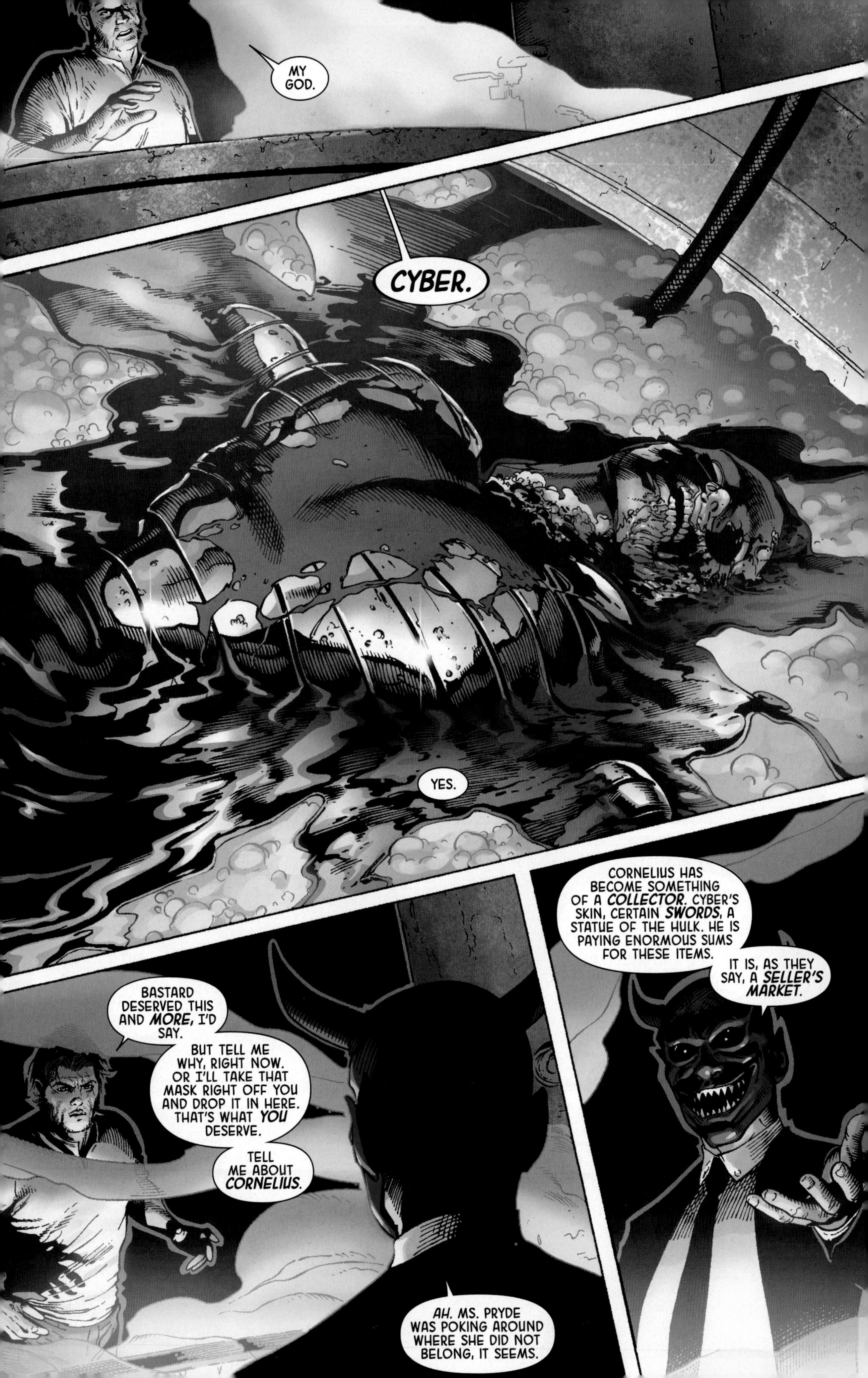
MY GOD.
CYBER.
YES.
BASTARD DESERVED THIS AND MORE, I'D SAY.
BUT TELL ME WHY, RIGHT NOW. OR I'LL TAKE THAT MASK RIGHT OFF YOU AND DROP IT IN HERE. THAT'S WHAT YOU DESERVE.
TELL ME ABOUT CORNELIUS.
AH. MS. PRYDE WAS POKING AROUND WHERE SHE DID NOT BELONG, IT SEEMS.
CORNELIUS HAS BECOME SOMETHING OF A COLLECTOR. CYBER'S SKIN, CERTAIN SWORDS, A STATUE OF THE HULK. HE IS PAYING ENORMOUS SUMS FOR THESE ITEMS.
IT IS, AS THEY SAY, A SELLER'S MARKET.

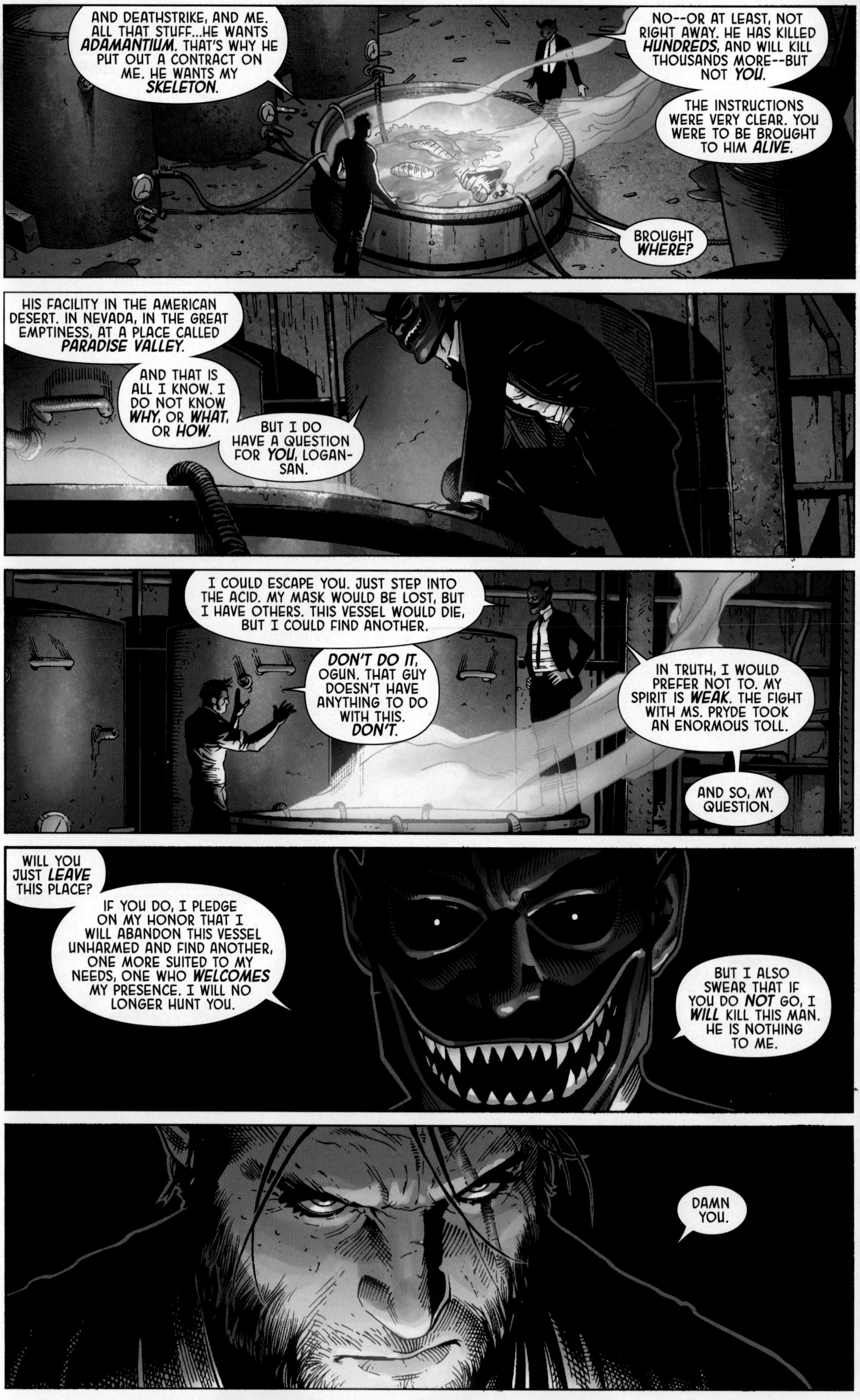
AND DEATHSTRIKE, AND ME. ALL THAT STUFF...HE WANTS ADAMANTIUM. THAT'S WHY HE PUT OUT A CONTRACT ON ME. HE WANTS MY SKELETON.
NO--OR AT LEAST, NOT RIGHT AWAY. HE HAS KILLED HUNDREDS, AND WILL KILL THOUSANDS MORE--BUT NOT YOU.
THE INSTRUCTIONS WERE VERY CLEAR. YOU WERE TO BE BROUGHT TO HIM ALIVE.
BROUGHT WHERE?
HIS FACILITY IN THE AMERICAN DESERT. IN NEVADA, IN THE GREAT EMPTINESS, AT A PLACE CALLED PARADISE VALLEY.
AND THAT IS ALL I KNOW. I DO NOT KNOW WHY, OR WHAT, OR HOW.
BUT I DO HAVE A QUESTION FOR YOU, LOGAN-SAN.
I COULD ESCAPE YOU. JUST STEP INTO THE ACID. MY MASK WOULD BE LOST, BUT I HAVE OTHERS. THIS VESSEL WOULD DIE, BUT I COULD FIND ANOTHER.
DON'T DO IT, OGUN. THAT GUY DOESN'T HAVE ANYTHING TO DO WITH THIS. DON'T.
IN TRUTH, I WOULD PREFER NOT TO. MY SPIRIT IS WEAK. THE FIGHT WITH MS. PRYDE TOOK AN ENORMOUS TOLL.
AND SO, MY QUESTION.
WILL YOU JUST LEAVE THIS PLACE?
IF YOU DO, I PLEDGE ON MY HONOR THAT I WILL ABANDON THIS VESSEL UNHARMED AND FIND ANOTHER, ONE MORE SUITED TO MY NEEDS, ONE WHO WELCOMES MY PRESENCE. I WILL NO LONGER HUNT YOU.
BUT I ALSO SWEAR THAT IF YOU DO NOT GO, I WILL KILL THIS MAN. HE IS NOTHING TO ME.
DAMN YOU.

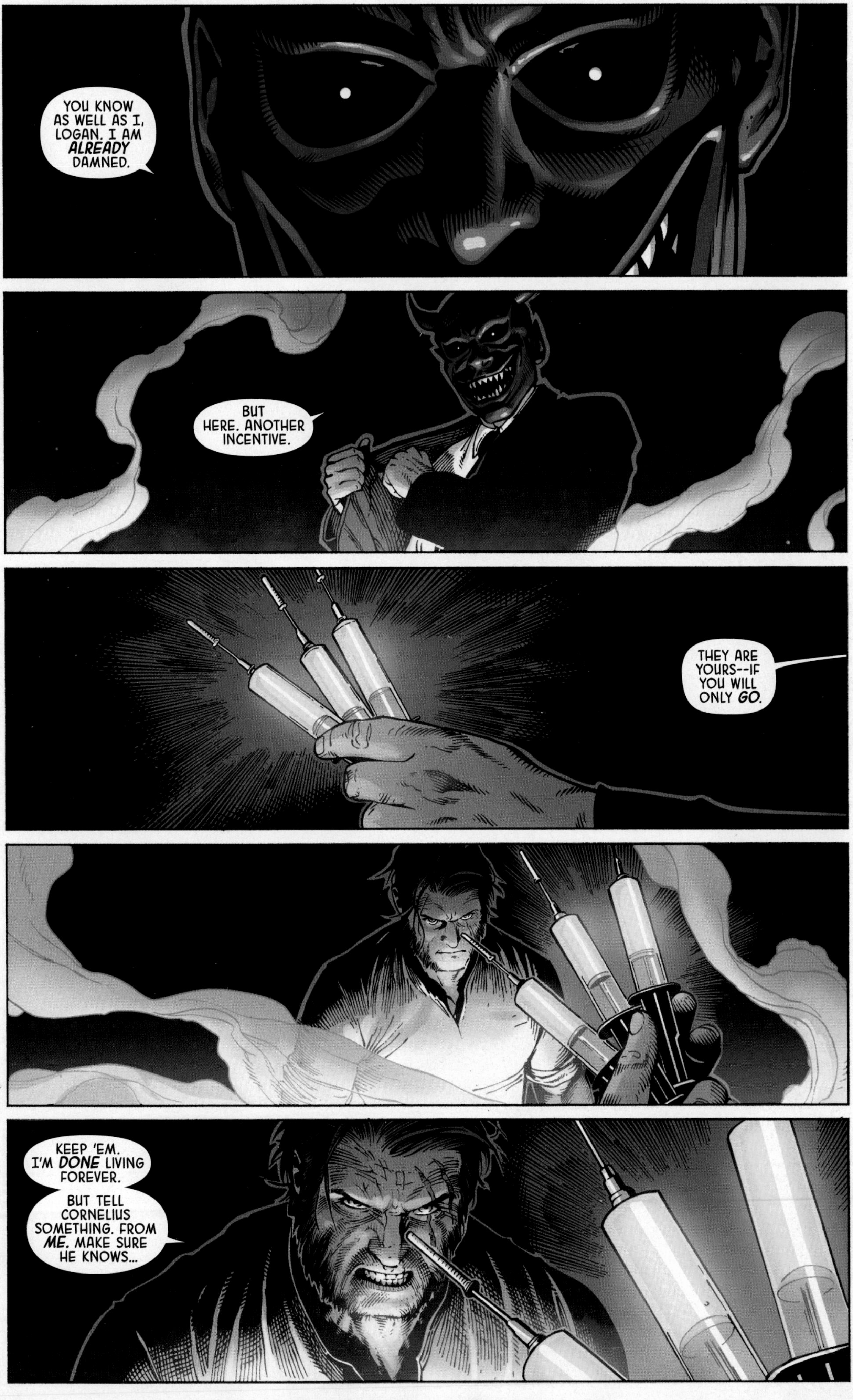
YOU KNOW AS WELL AS I, LOGAN. I AM ALREADY DAMNED.
BUT HERE. ANOTHER INCENTIVE.
THEY ARE YOURS--IF YOU WILL ONLY GO.
KEEP 'EM. I'M DONE LIVING FOREVER.
BUT TELL CORNELIUS SOMETHING. FROM ME. MAKE SURE HE KNOWS...

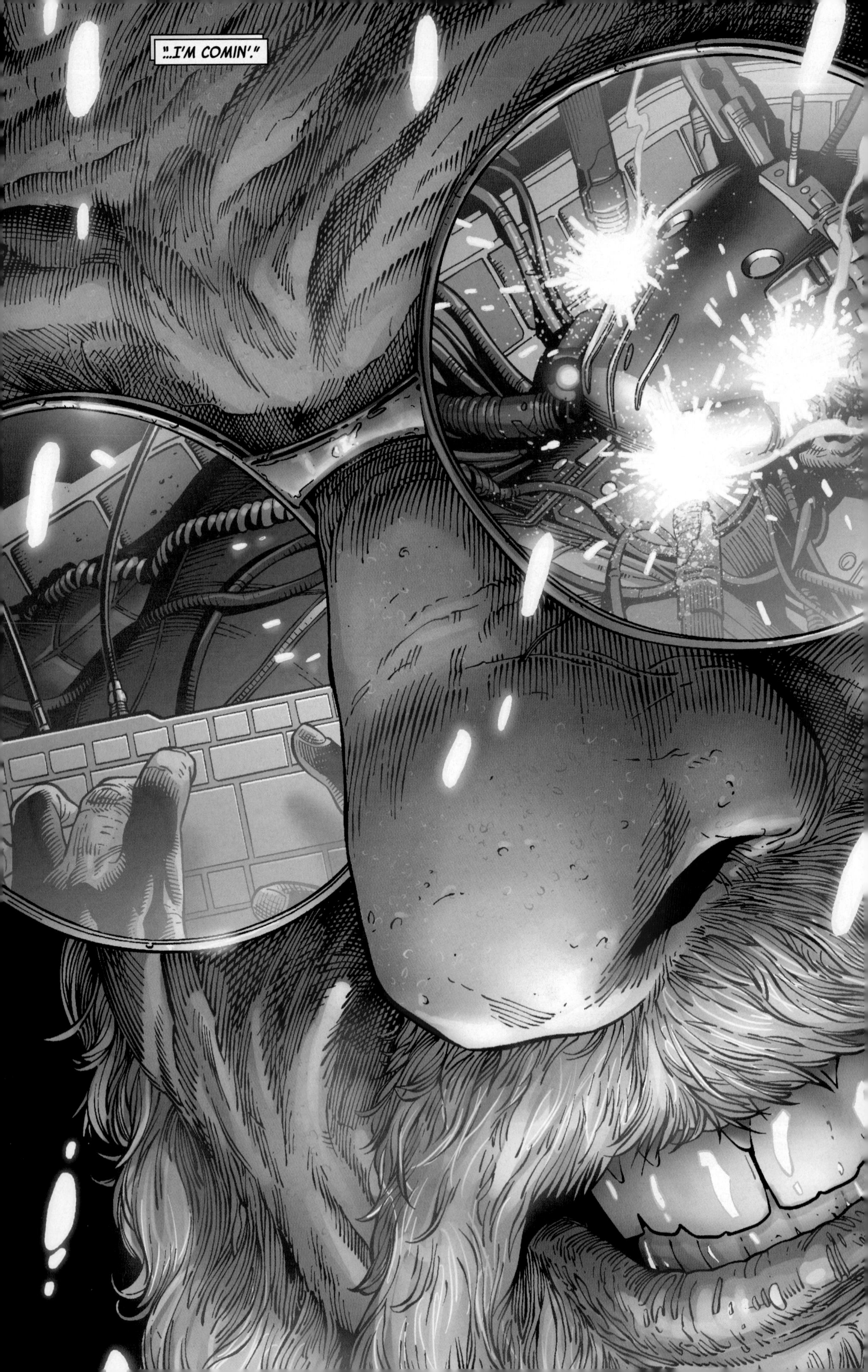
"...I'M COMIN'."

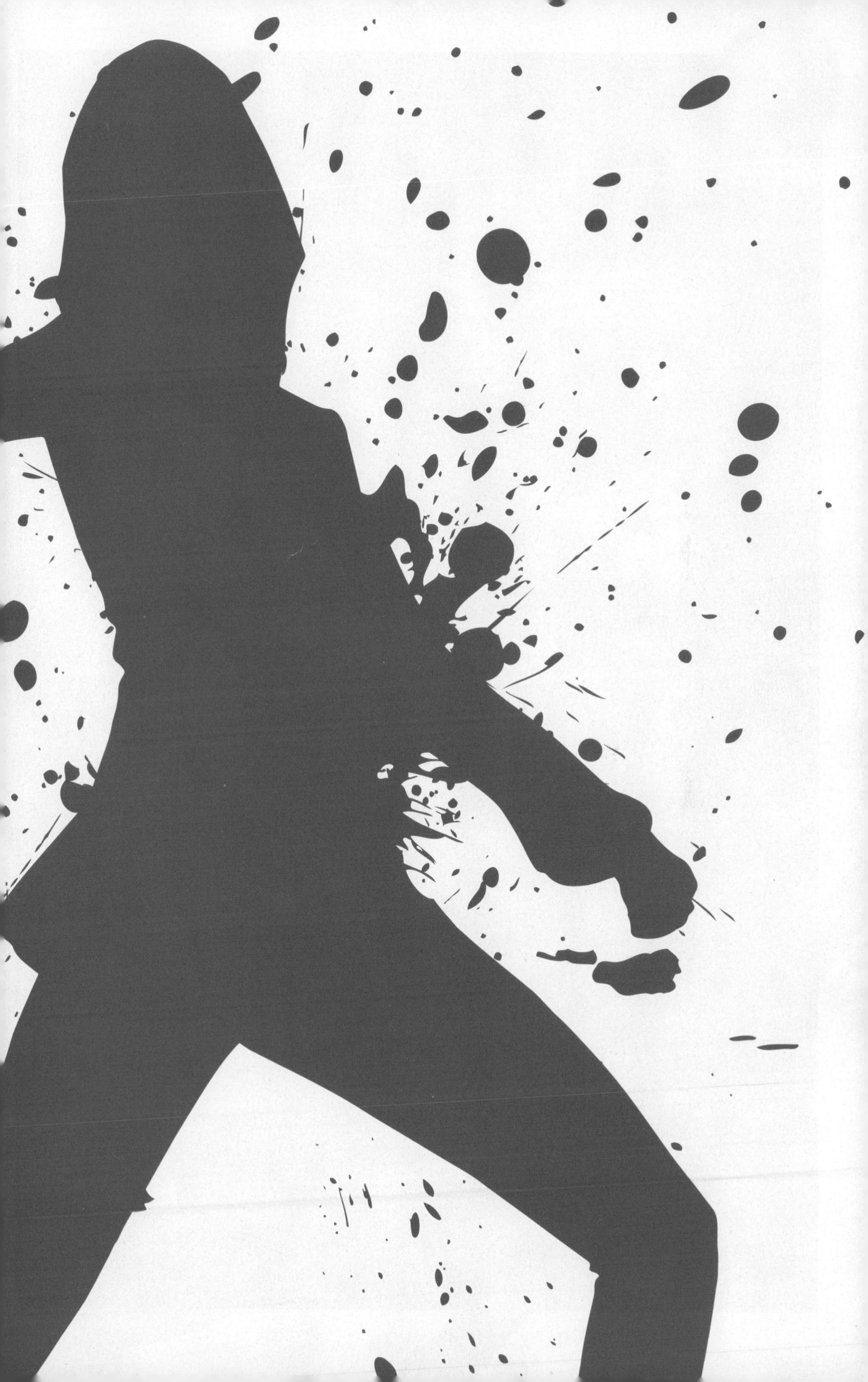

4

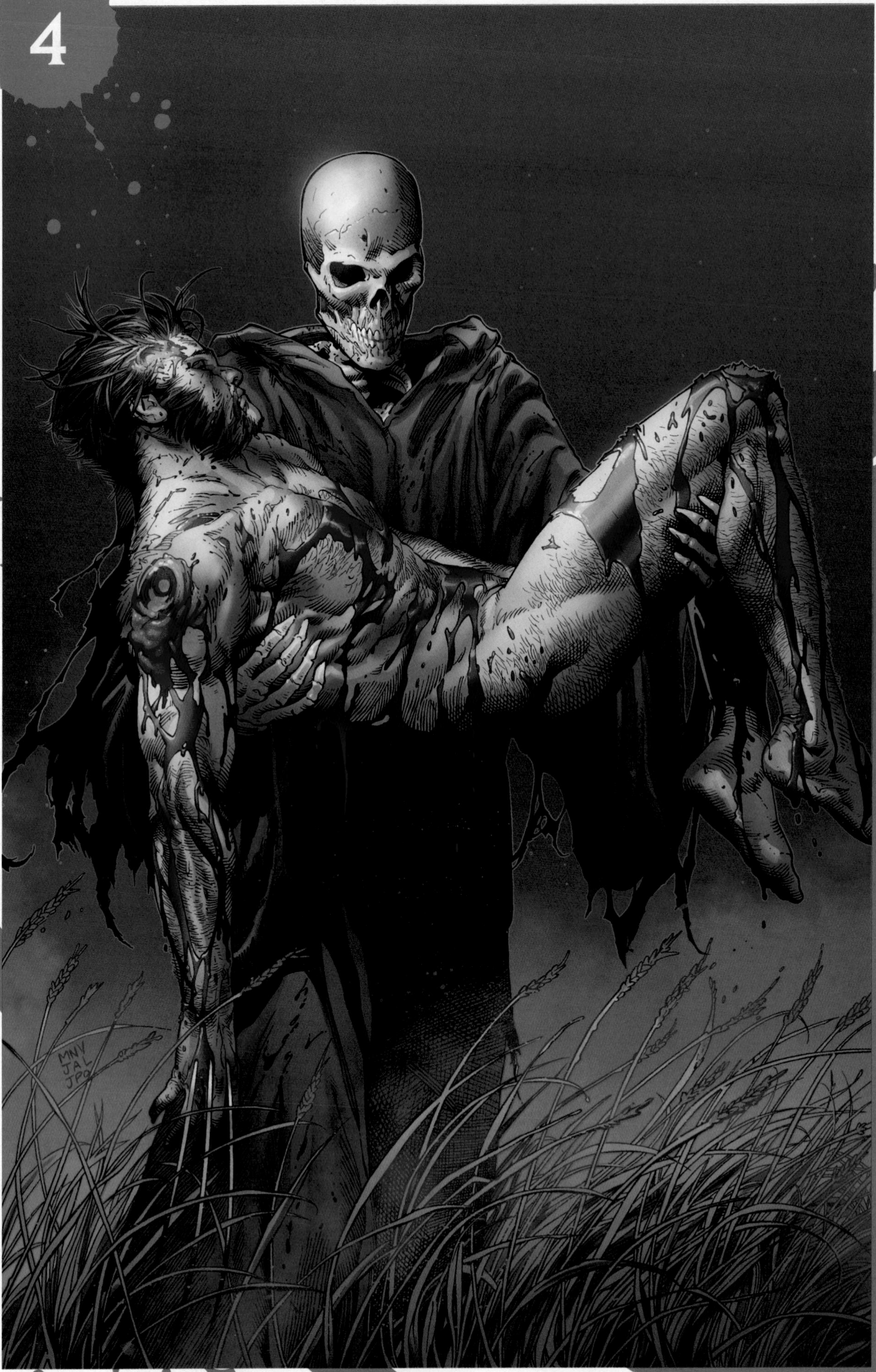

HISTORY

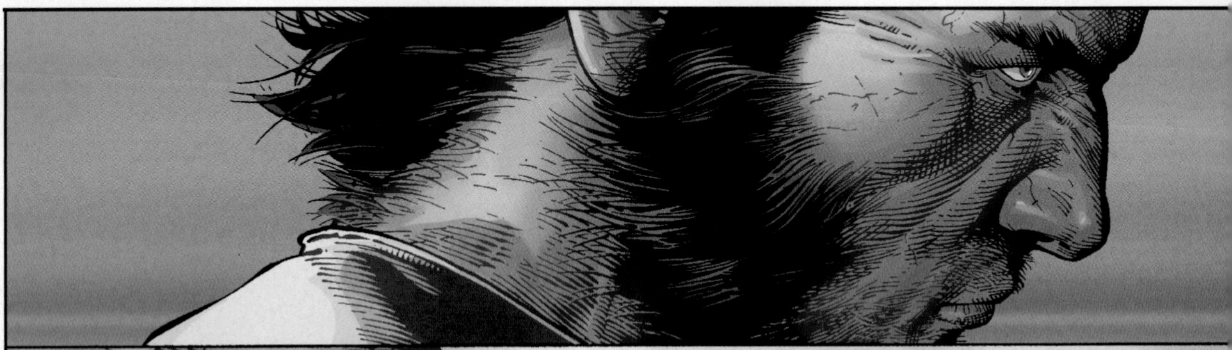
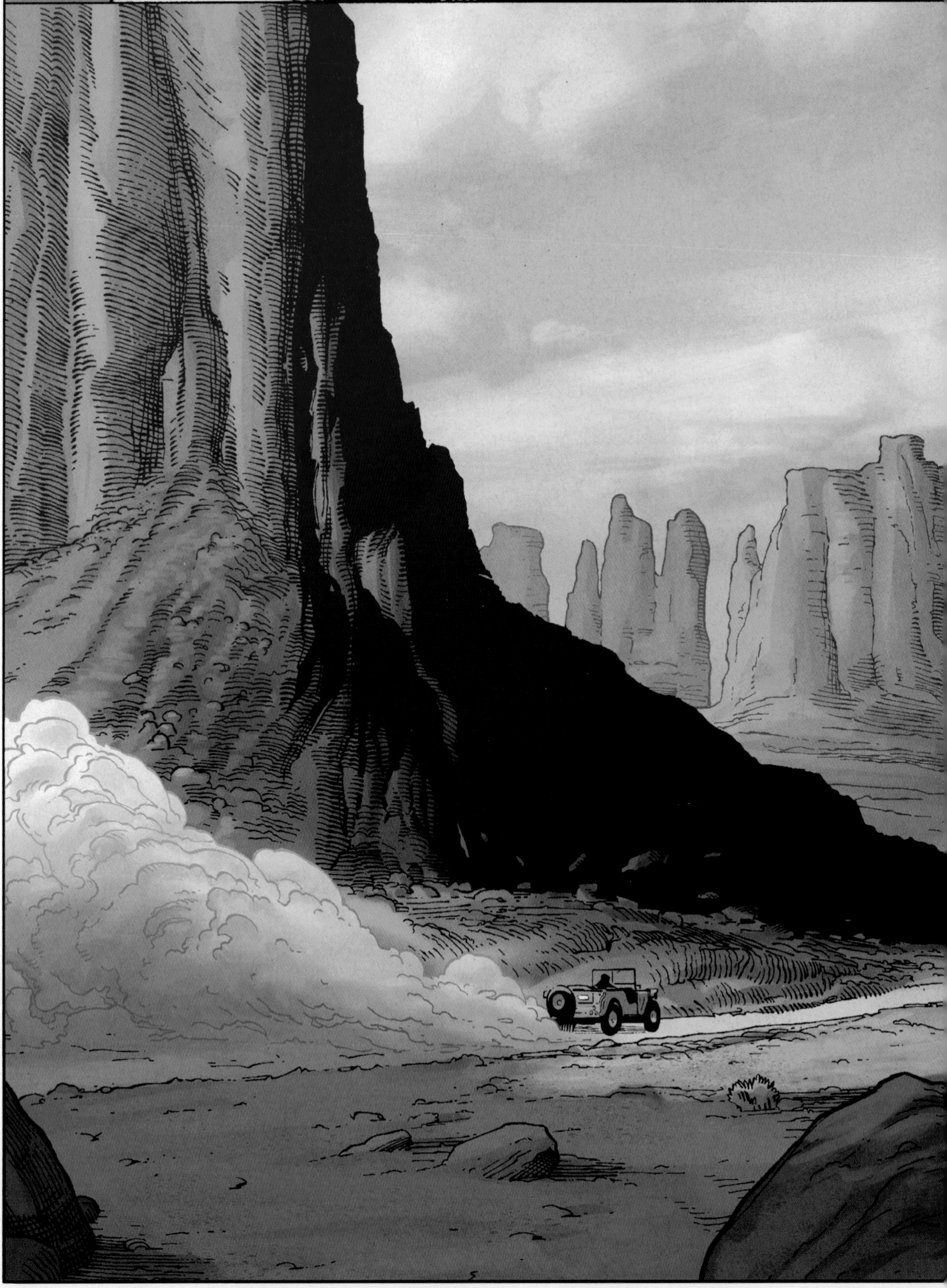

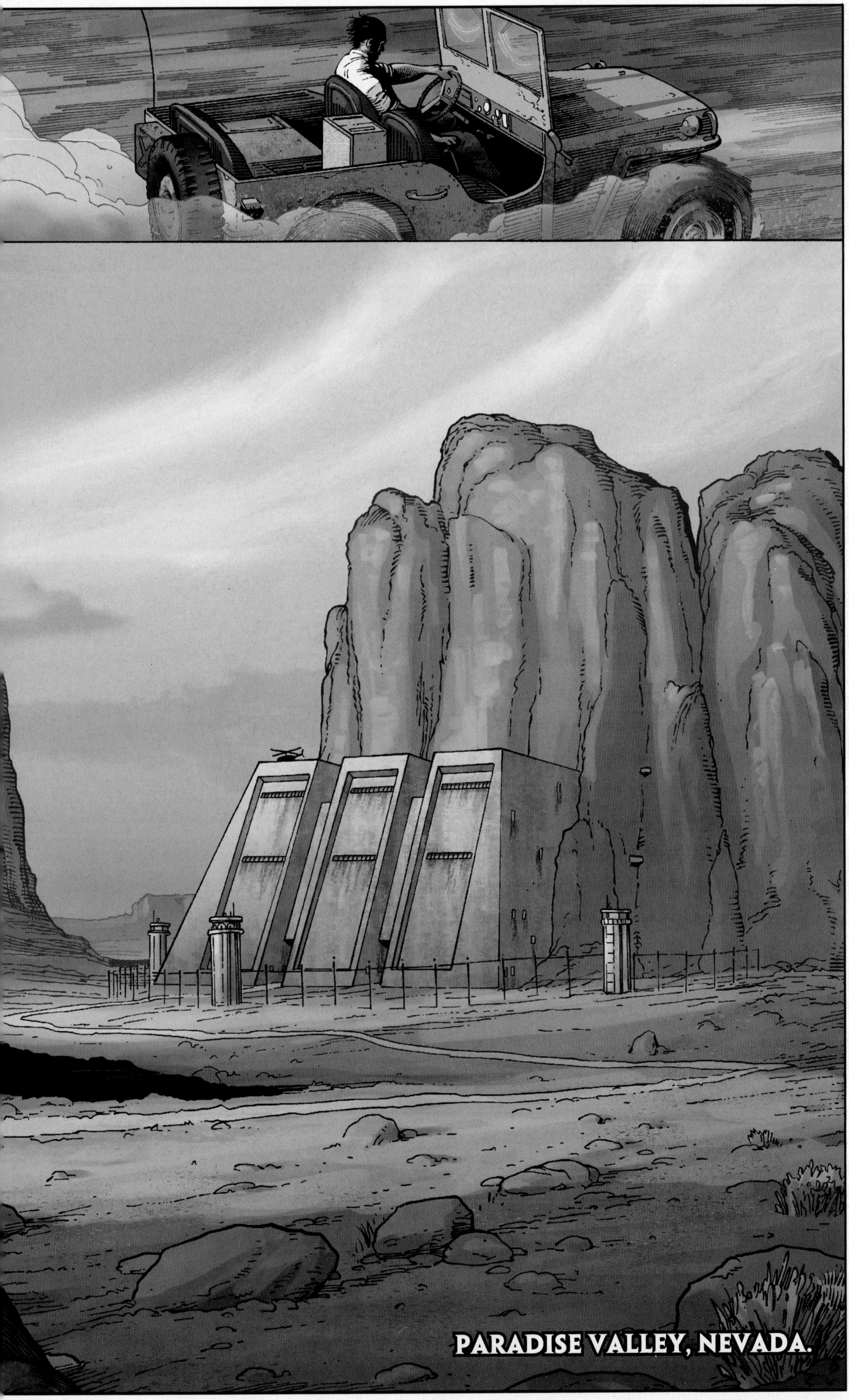
PARADISE VALLEY, NEVADA.

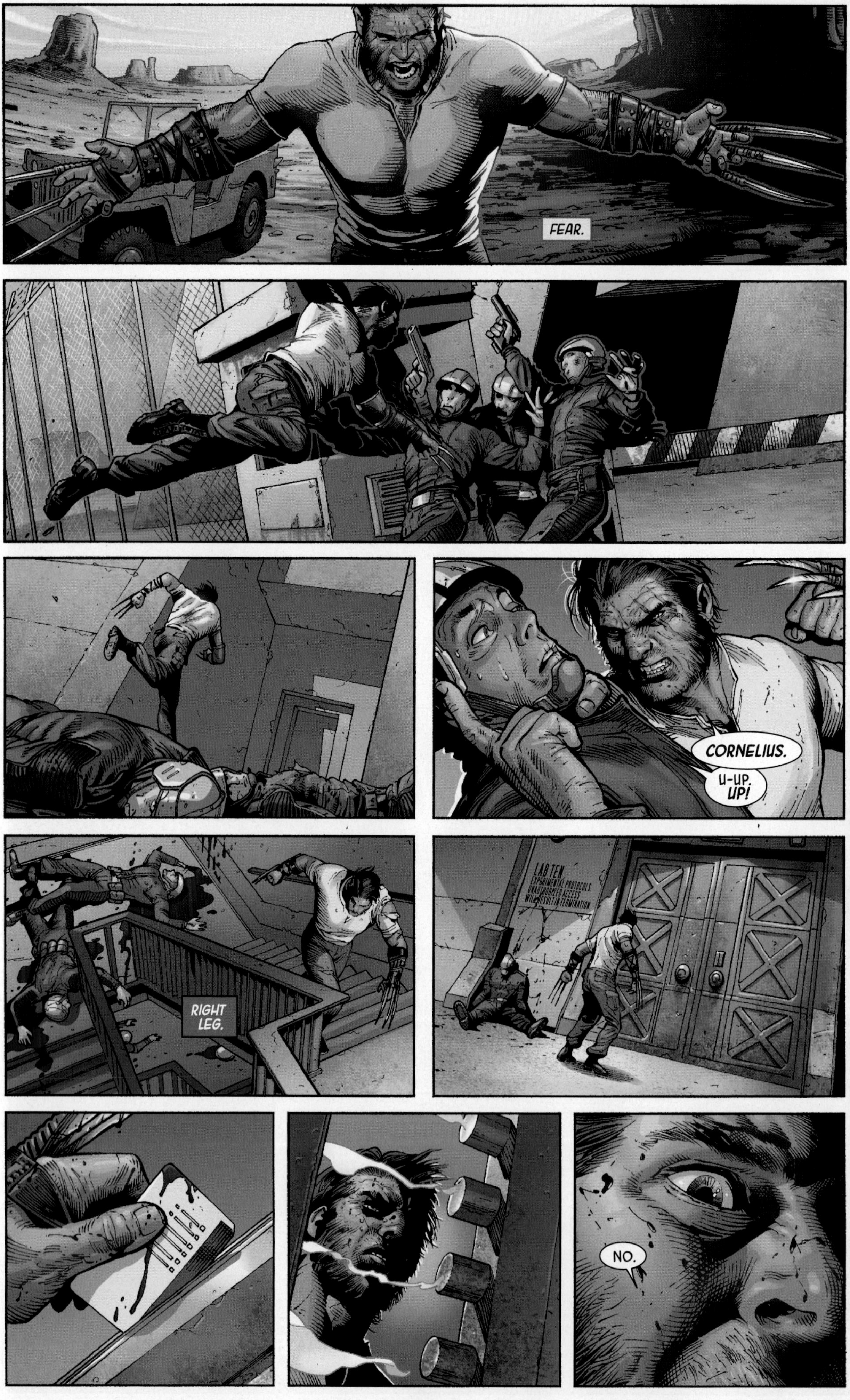
FEAR.
CORNELIUS.
U-UP. UP!
RIGHT LEG.
LAB TEN
EXPERIMENTAL PROTOCOLS.
UNAUTHORIZED ACCESS
WILL RESULT IN TERMINATION
NO.

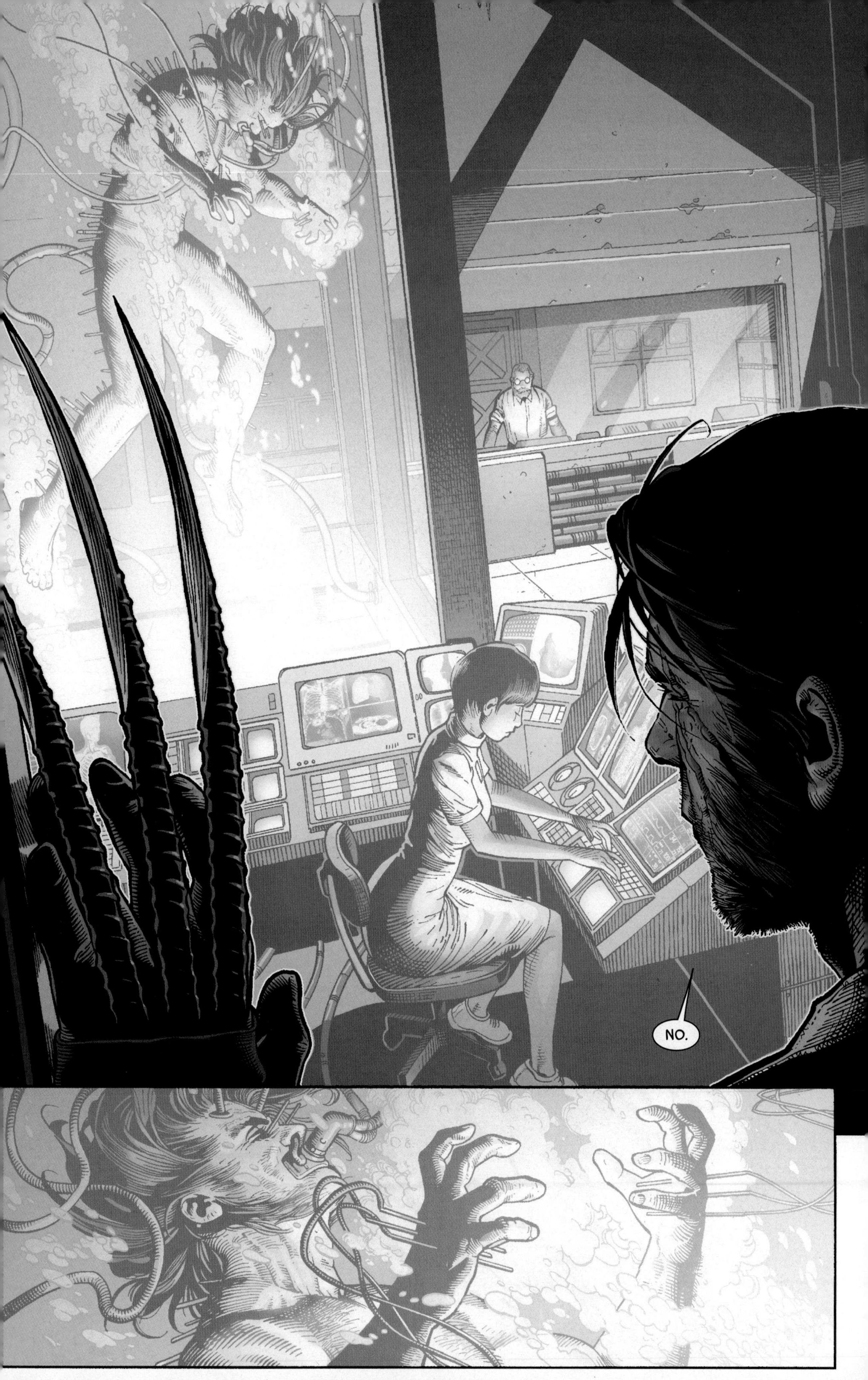
NO.

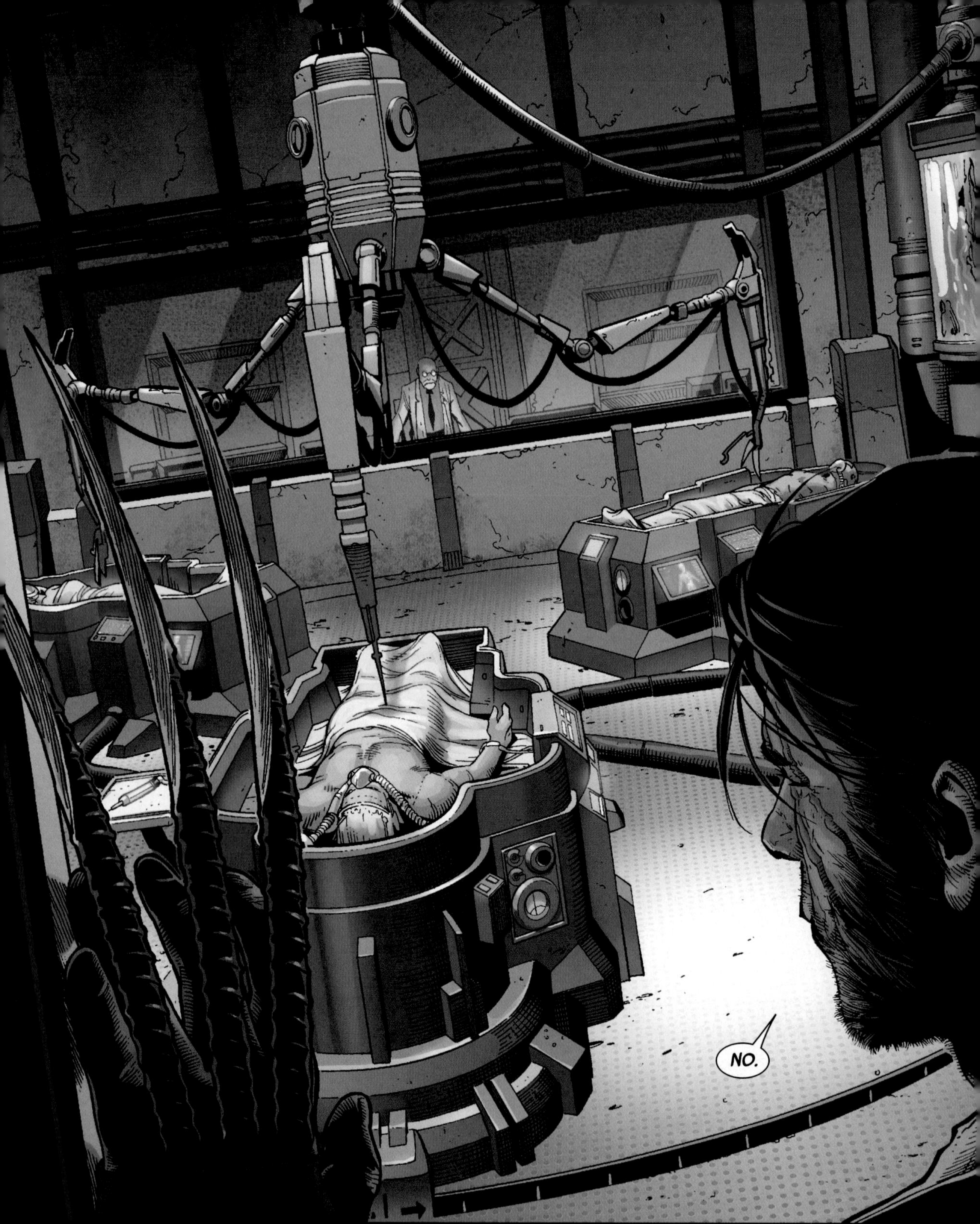
NO.

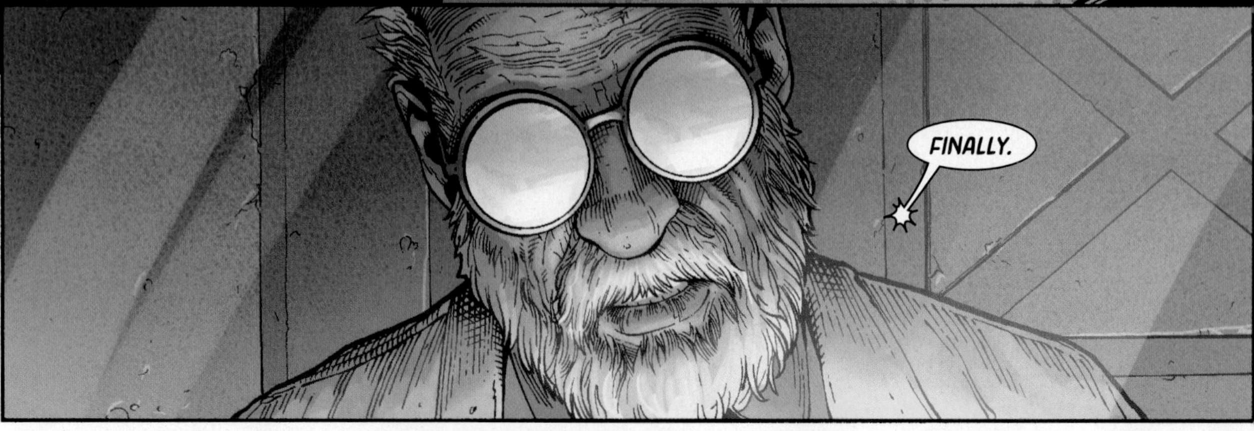
FINALLY.

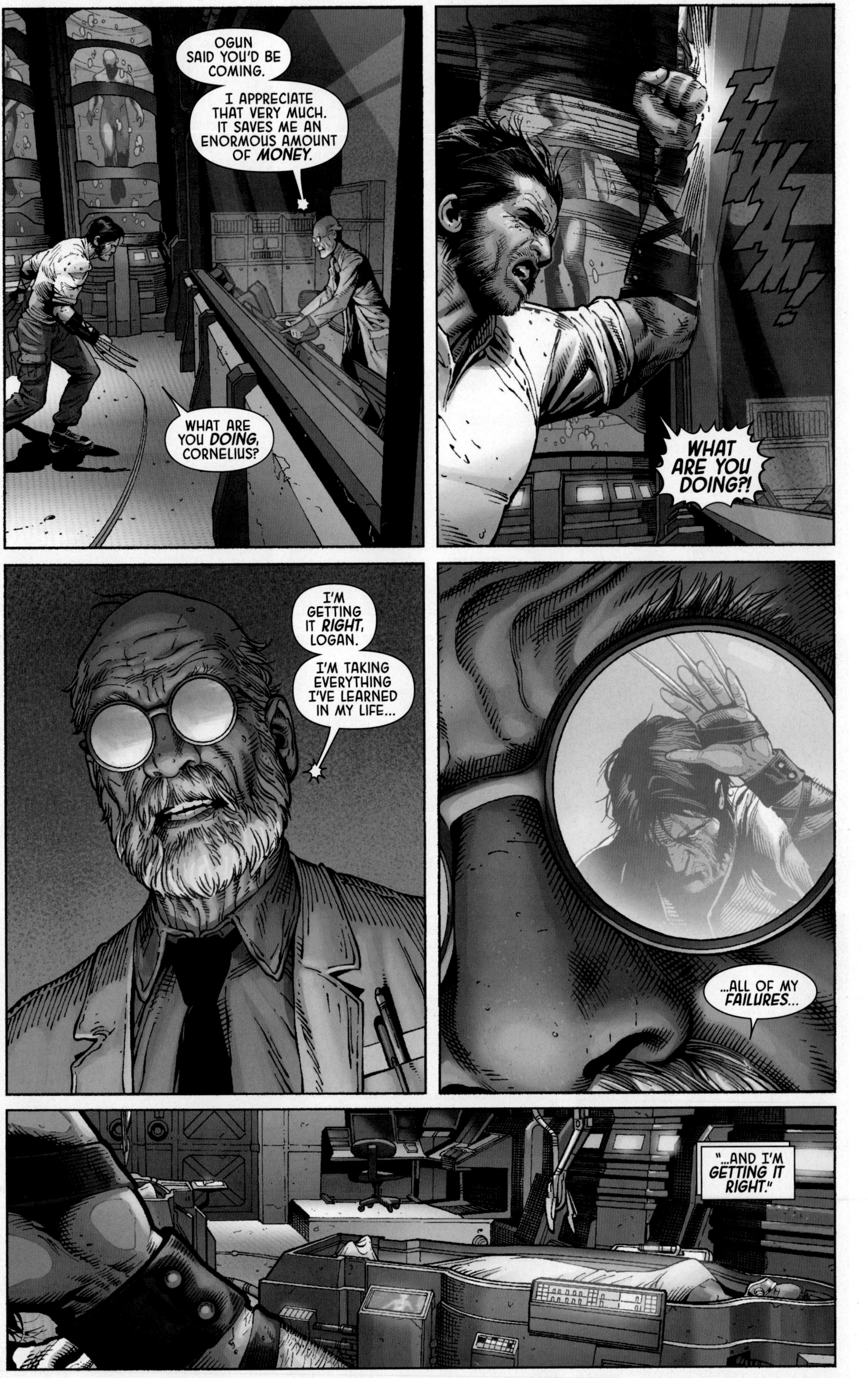
OGUN SAID YOU'D BE COMING.
I APPRECIATE THAT VERY MUCH. IT SAVES ME AN ENORMOUS AMOUNT OF MONEY.
WHAT ARE YOU DOING, CORNELIUS?
THWAM!
WHAT ARE YOU DOING?!
I'M GETTING IT RIGHT, LOGAN.
I'M TAKING EVERYTHING I'VE LEARNED IN MY LIFE...
...ALL OF MY FAILURES...
"...AND I'M GETTING IT RIGHT."

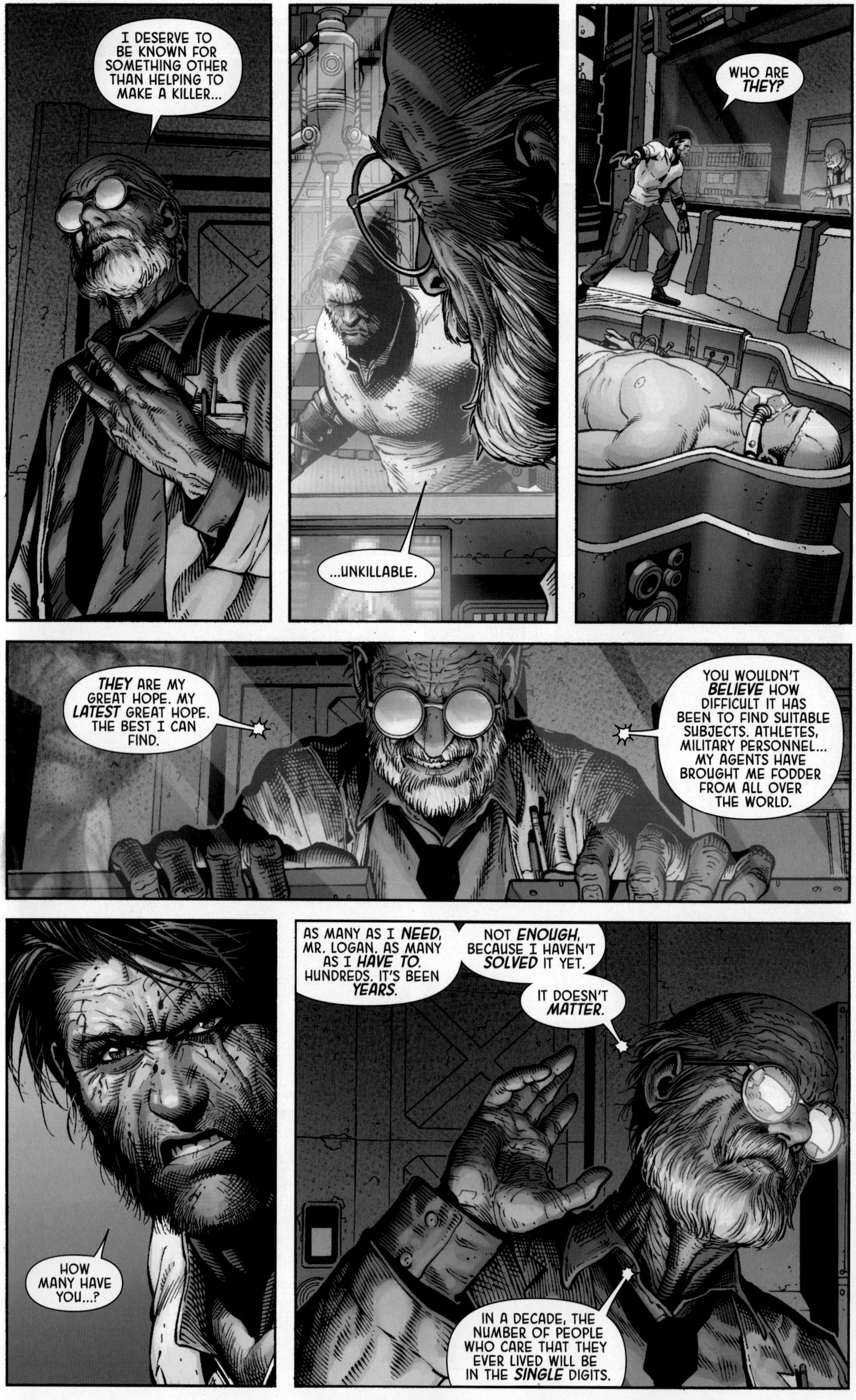
I DESERVE TO BE KNOWN FOR SOMETHING OTHER THAN HELPING TO MAKE A KILLER...
...UNKILLABLE.
WHO ARE THEY?
THEY ARE MY GREAT HOPE. MY LATEST GREAT HOPE. THE BEST I CAN FIND.
YOU WOULDN'T BELIEVE HOW DIFFICULT IT HAS BEEN TO FIND SUITABLE SUBJECTS. ATHLETES, MILITARY PERSONNEL... MY AGENTS HAVE BROUGHT ME FODDER FROM ALL OVER THE WORLD.
HOW MANY HAVE YOU...?
AS MANY AS I NEED, MR. LOGAN. AS MANY AS I HAVE TO. HUNDREDS. IT'S BEEN YEARS.
NOT ENOUGH, BECAUSE I HAVEN'T SOLVED IT YET.
IT DOESN'T MATTER.
IN A DECADE, THE NUMBER OF PEOPLE WHO CARE THAT THEY EVER LIVED WILL BE IN THE SINGLE DIGITS.

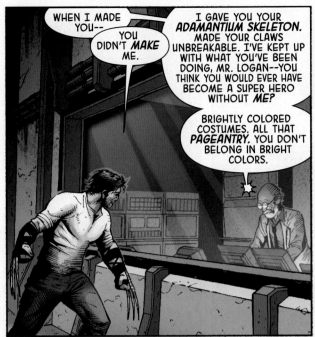

WHEN I MADE YOU--

YOU DIDN'T *MAKE* ME.

I GAVE YOU YOUR *ADAMANTIUM SKELETON.* MADE YOUR CLAWS UNBREAKABLE. I'VE KEPT UP WITH WHAT YOU'VE BEEN DOING, MR. LOGAN--YOU THINK YOU WOULD EVER HAVE BECOME A SUPER HERO WITHOUT *ME*?

BRIGHTLY COLORED COSTUMES. ALL THAT *PAGEANTRY.* YOU DON'T BELONG IN BRIGHT COLORS.

"THEY DO.

"MY CHILDREN. MY PRETTY, *DEADLY* CHILDREN."

THEY'RE *CONDITIONED.* THEY'LL *DO WHAT THEY'RE TOLD.* NOT LIKE YOU.

I'VE ENHANCED EVERY SYSTEM...NEUROLOGICAL, ENDOCRINE, MUSCULAR... THEY'RE *PERFECT.*

ALL THEY NEED...

"...IS THE *ADAMANTIUM.*"

THAT'S WHY... YOU WANT MY *SKELETON.*

NO. I HAVE ENOUGH OF THE ALLOY. NOT EASY TO FIND. CRUSHINGLY *EXPENSIVE.* BUT I'VE GATHERED AN ADEQUATE AMOUNT. EVEN CRACKED THE METHOD TO *SMELT* IT.

BUT AS YOU KNOW, THE PROCESS TO BOND THE METAL TO A PERSON IS...*INVASIVE.*

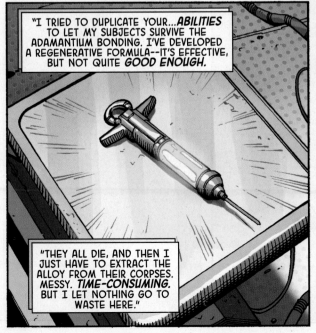

"I TRIED TO DUPLICATE YOUR...*ABILITIES* TO LET MY SUBJECTS SURVIVE THE ADAMANTIUM BONDING. I'VE DEVELOPED A REGENERATIVE FORMULA--IT'S EFFECTIVE, BUT NOT QUITE *GOOD ENOUGH.*

"THEY ALL DIE, AND THEN I JUST HAVE TO EXTRACT THE ALLOY FROM THEIR CORPSES. MESSY. *TIME-CONSUMING.* BUT I LET NOTHING GO TO WASTE HERE."

WHICH IS WHY I'M SO GLAD YOU'VE COME TO ME. YOU CAN TURN ALL OF THIS AROUND. YOU'RE THE REASON I'VE SPENT SO MUCH MONEY. EXPENDED SO MUCH *EFFORT.*

DON'T YOU WANT TO BE PART OF SOMETHING *BETTER,* MR. LOGAN? YOU CAN PLAY THE HERO AGAIN. YOU CAN *SAVE LIVES.*

JUST STOP FIGHTING. HELP ME SAVE THEM. ALL I NEED...IS THAT MARVELOUS *HEALING FACTOR* OF YOURS.

HEH.

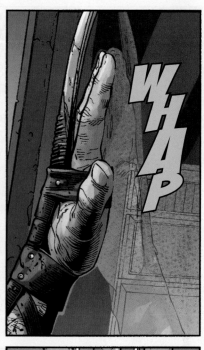

WHAP

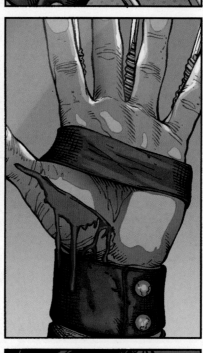

WHY ISN'T IT--?

SORRY, BUB.

I ALWAYS DID HAVE A PROBLEM WITH *TUNNEL VISION.*

KILL HIM, PLEASE.

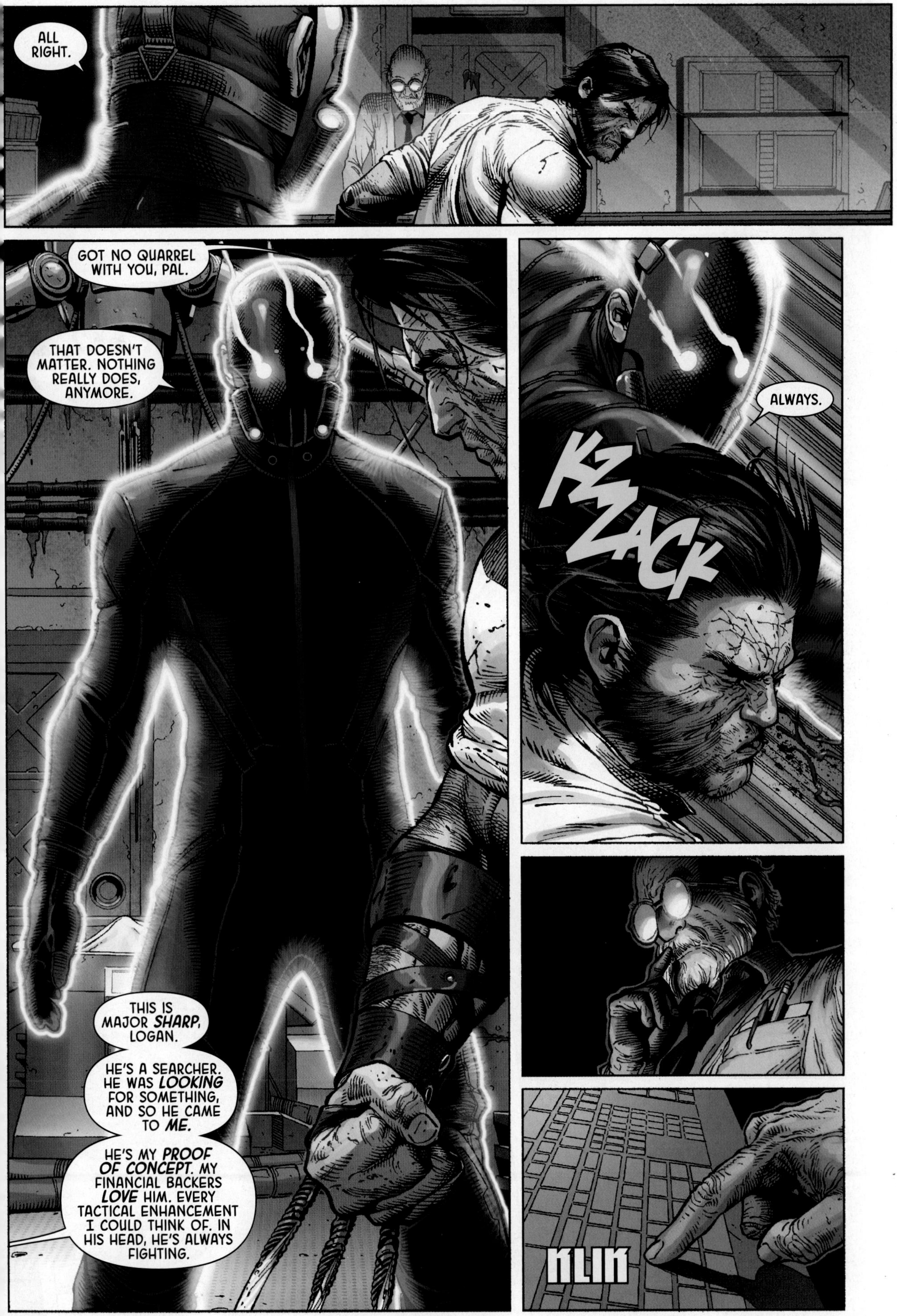
ALL RIGHT.
GOT NO QUARREL WITH YOU, PAL.
THAT DOESN'T MATTER. NOTHING REALLY DOES, ANYMORE.
THIS IS MAJOR SHARP, LOGAN.
HE'S A SEARCHER. HE WAS LOOKING FOR SOMETHING, AND SO HE CAME TO ME.
HE'S MY PROOF OF CONCEPT. MY FINANCIAL BACKERS LOVE HIM. EVERY TACTICAL ENHANCEMENT I COULD THINK OF. IN HIS HEAD, HE'S ALWAYS FIGHTING.
ALWAYS.
KZZACK
KLIK

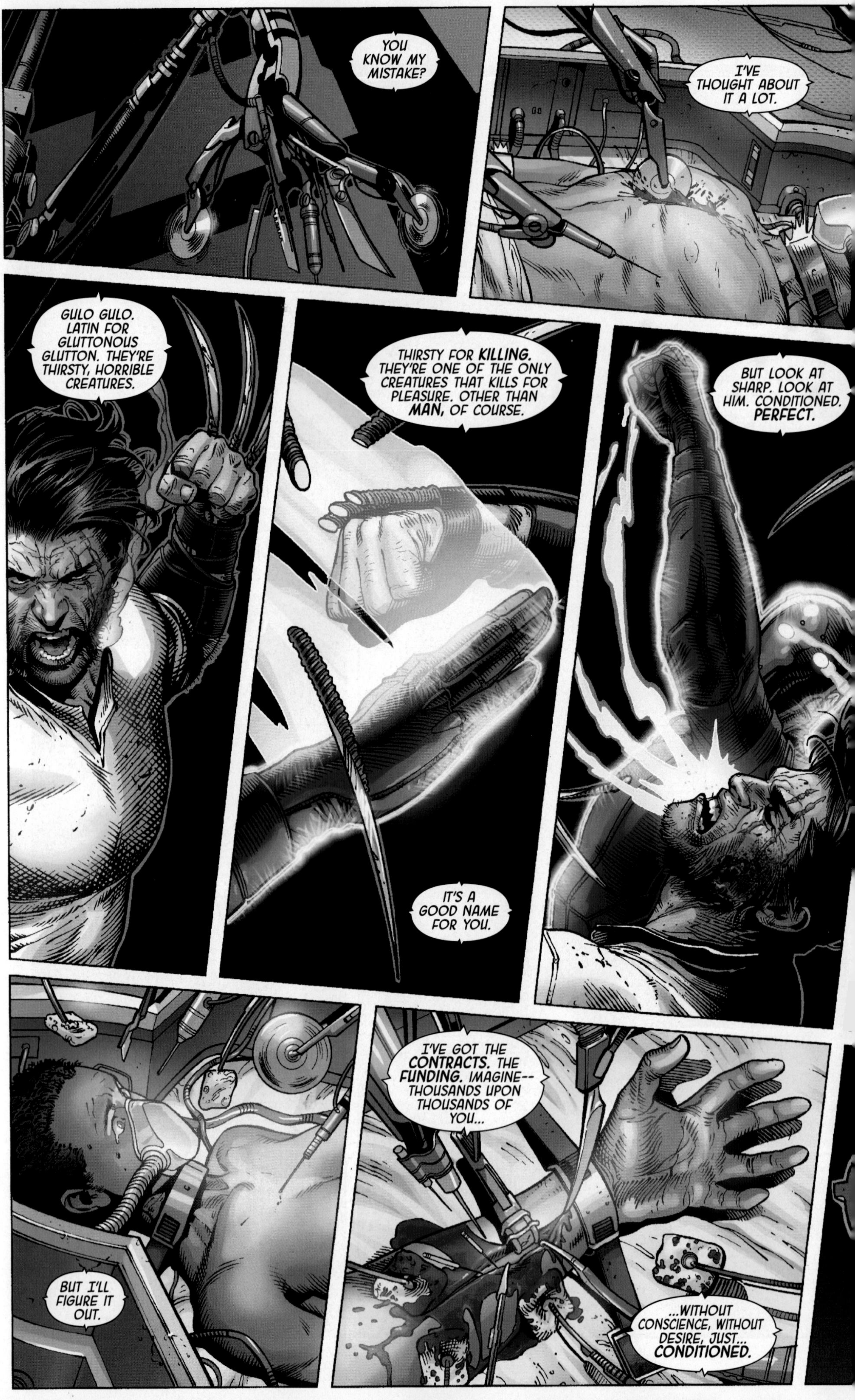
YOU KNOW MY MISTAKE?
I'VE THOUGHT ABOUT IT A LOT.
GULO GULO. LATIN FOR GLUTTONOUS GLUTTON. THEY'RE THIRSTY, HORRIBLE CREATURES.
THIRSTY FOR **KILLING.** THEY'RE ONE OF THE ONLY CREATURES THAT KILLS FOR PLEASURE. OTHER THAN **MAN,** OF COURSE.
IT'S A GOOD NAME FOR YOU.
BUT LOOK AT SHARP. LOOK AT HIM. CONDITIONED. **PERFECT.**
BUT I'LL FIGURE IT OUT.
I'VE GOT THE **CONTRACTS.** THE **FUNDING.** IMAGINE-- THOUSANDS UPON THOUSANDS OF YOU...
...WITHOUT CONSCIENCE, WITHOUT DESIRE, JUST... **CONDITIONED.**

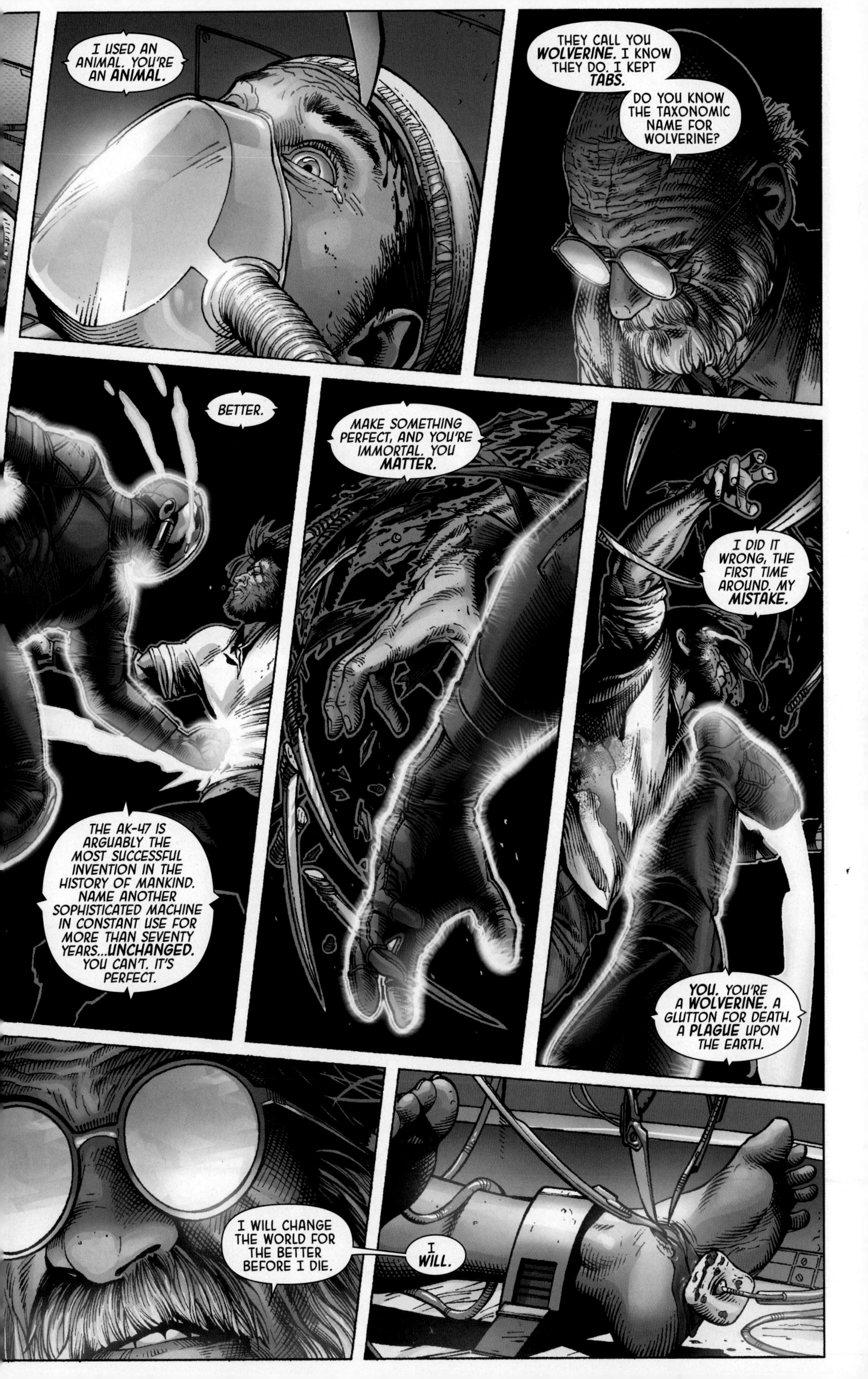

I USED AN ANIMAL. YOU'RE AN ANIMAL.
THEY CALL YOU WOLVERINE. I KNOW THEY DO. I KEPT TABS.
DO YOU KNOW THE TAXONOMIC NAME FOR WOLVERINE?
BETTER.
THE AK-47 IS ARGUABLY THE MOST SUCCESSFUL INVENTION IN THE HISTORY OF MANKIND. NAME ANOTHER SOPHISTICATED MACHINE IN CONSTANT USE FOR MORE THAN SEVENTY YEARS...UNCHANGED. YOU CAN'T. IT'S PERFECT.
MAKE SOMETHING PERFECT, AND YOU'RE IMMORTAL. YOU MATTER.
I DID IT WRONG, THE FIRST TIME AROUND. MY MISTAKE.
YOU. YOU'RE A WOLVERINE. A GLUTTON FOR DEATH. A PLAGUE UPON THE EARTH.
I WILL CHANGE THE WORLD FOR THE BETTER BEFORE I DIE.
I WILL.

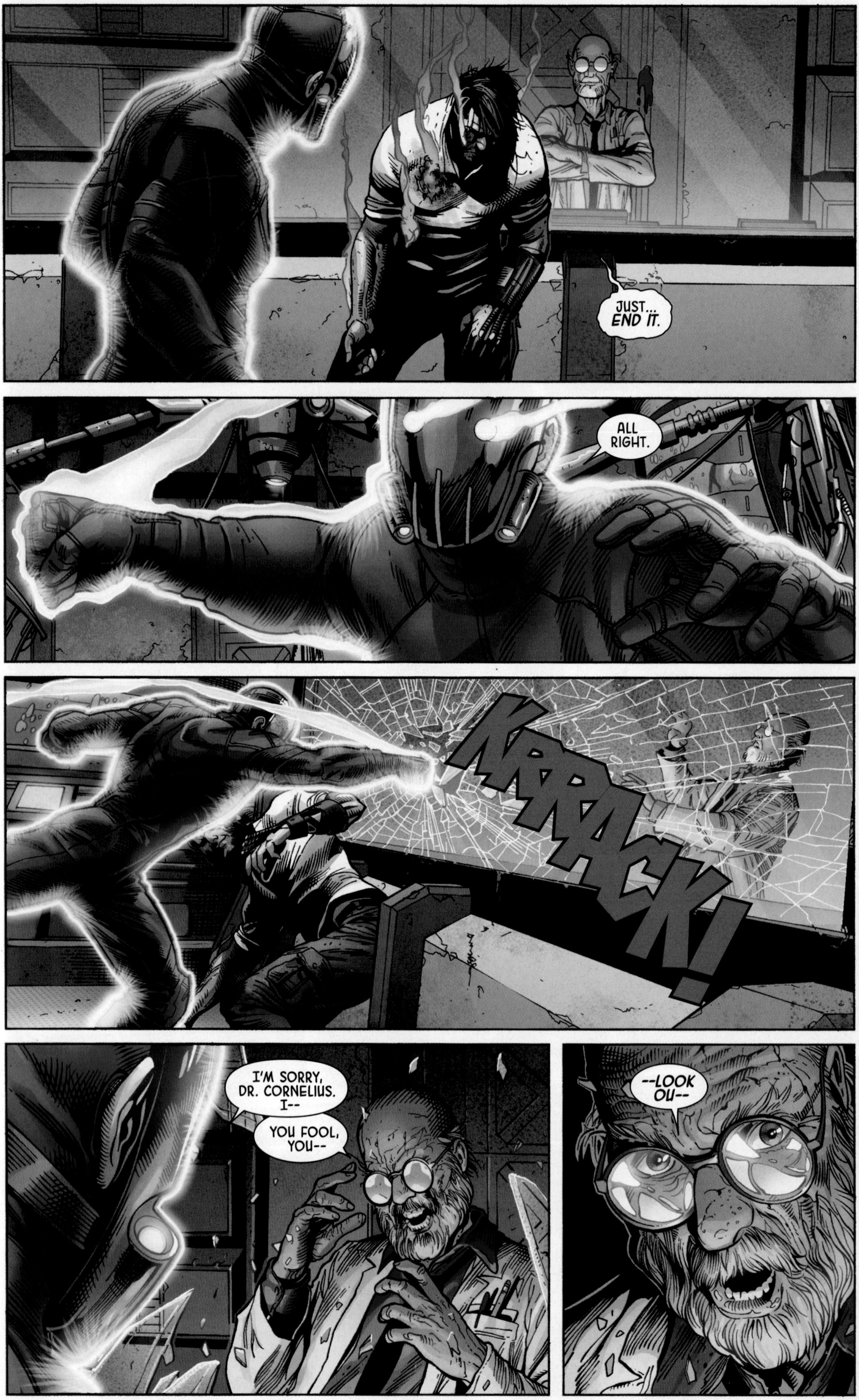
JUST... END IT.
ALL RIGHT.
KRRRACK!
I'M SORRY, DR. CORNELIUS. I--
YOU FOOL, YOU--
--LOOK OU--

THWAM

THE MACHINES.

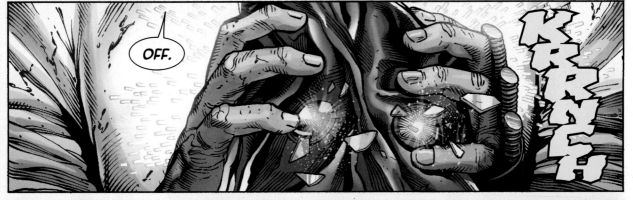

TURN. THEM.

OFF.

KRRNCH

KLIK

NO.

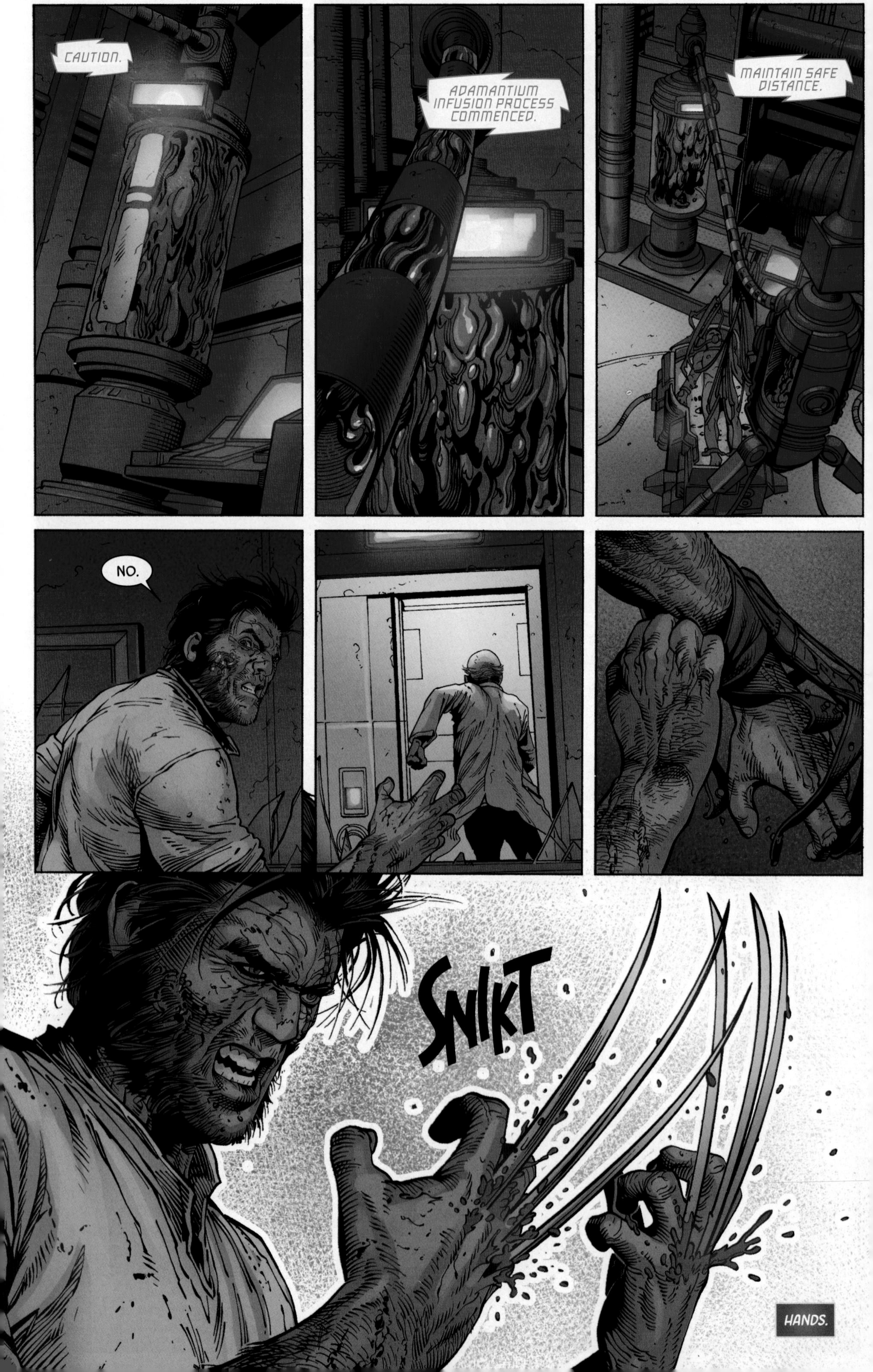
CAUTION.
ADAMANTIUM INFUSION PROCESS COMMENCED.
MAINTAIN SAFE DISTANCE.
NO.
SNIKT
HANDS.

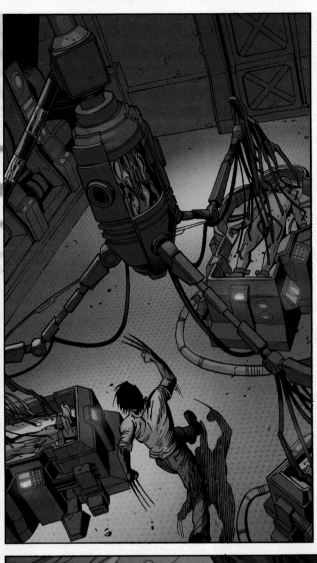

SNSH!

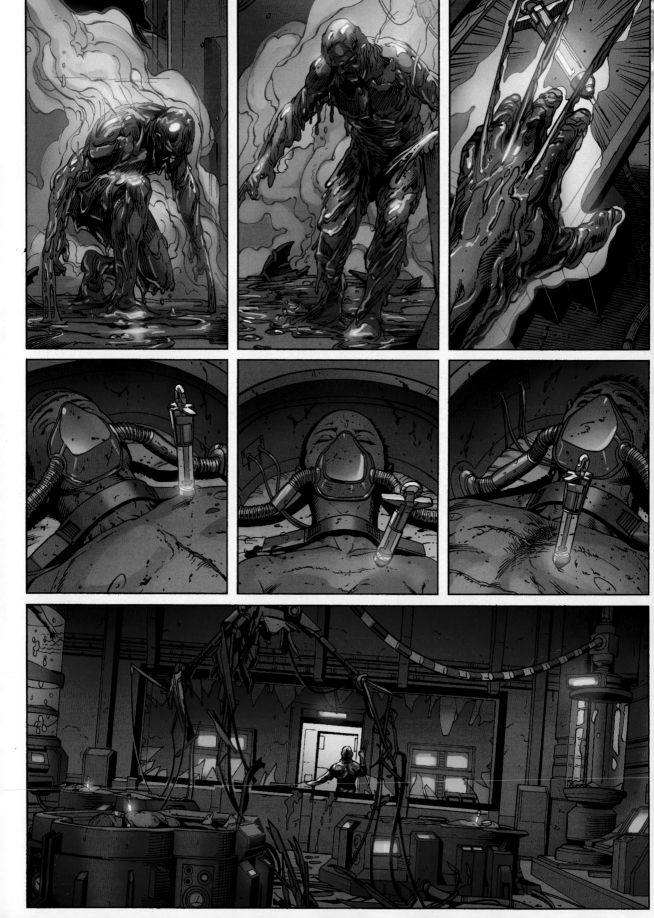

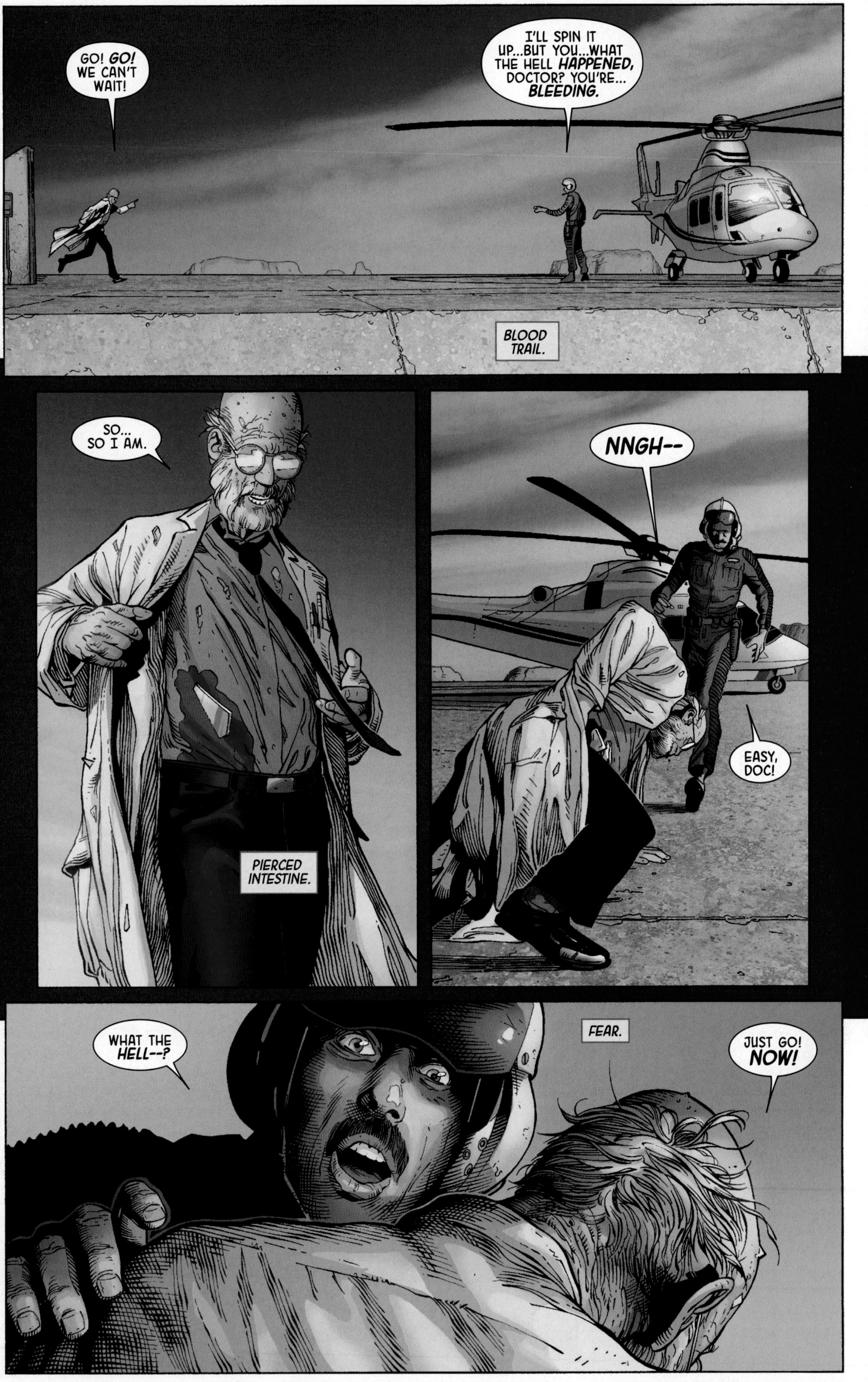
GO! GO! WE CAN'T WAIT!
I'LL SPIN IT UP...BUT YOU...WHAT THE HELL HAPPENED, DOCTOR? YOU'RE... BLEEDING.
BLOOD TRAIL.
SO... SO I AM.
PIERCED INTESTINE.
NNGH--
EASY, DOC!
WHAT THE HELL--?
FEAR.
JUST GO! NOW!

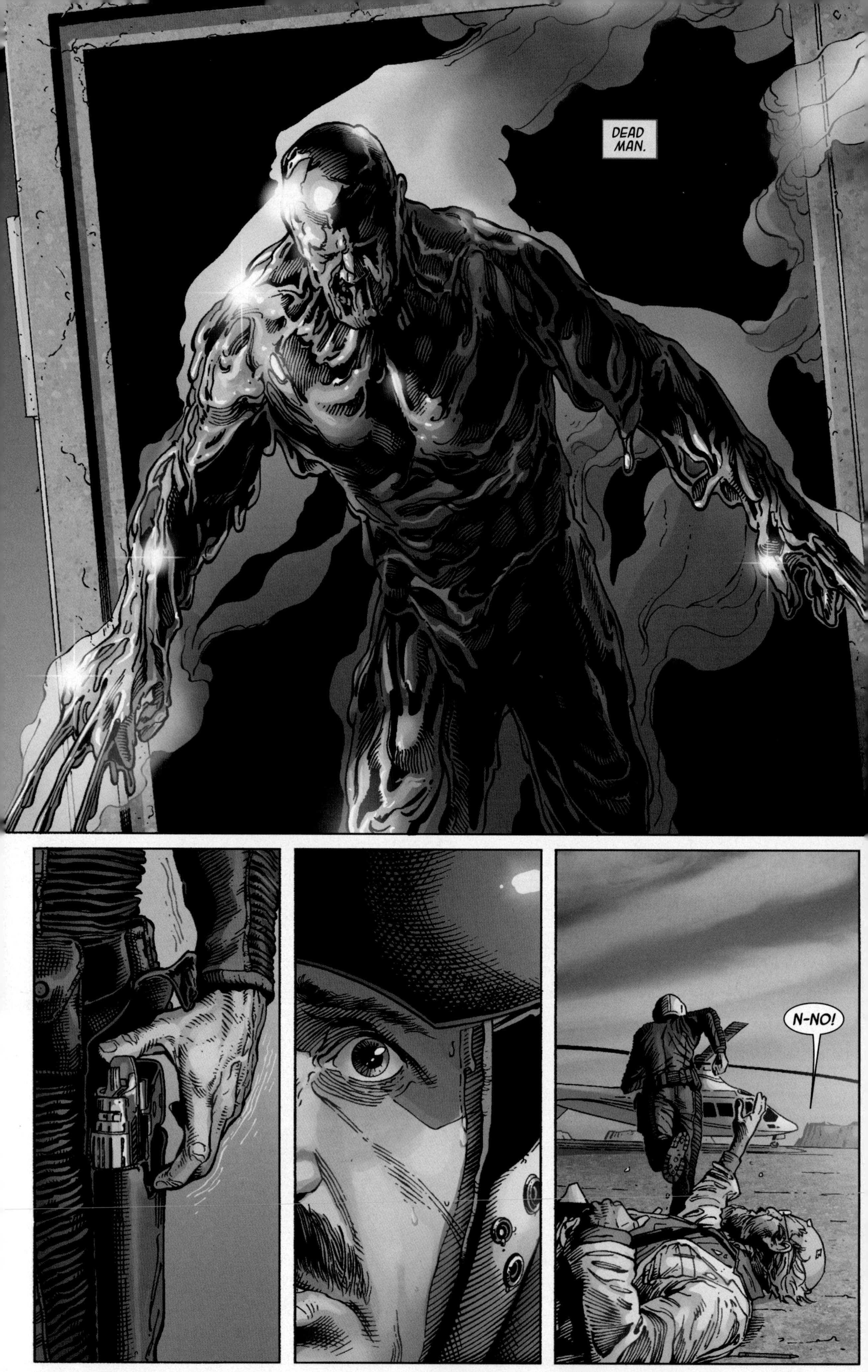
DEAD MAN.
N-NO!

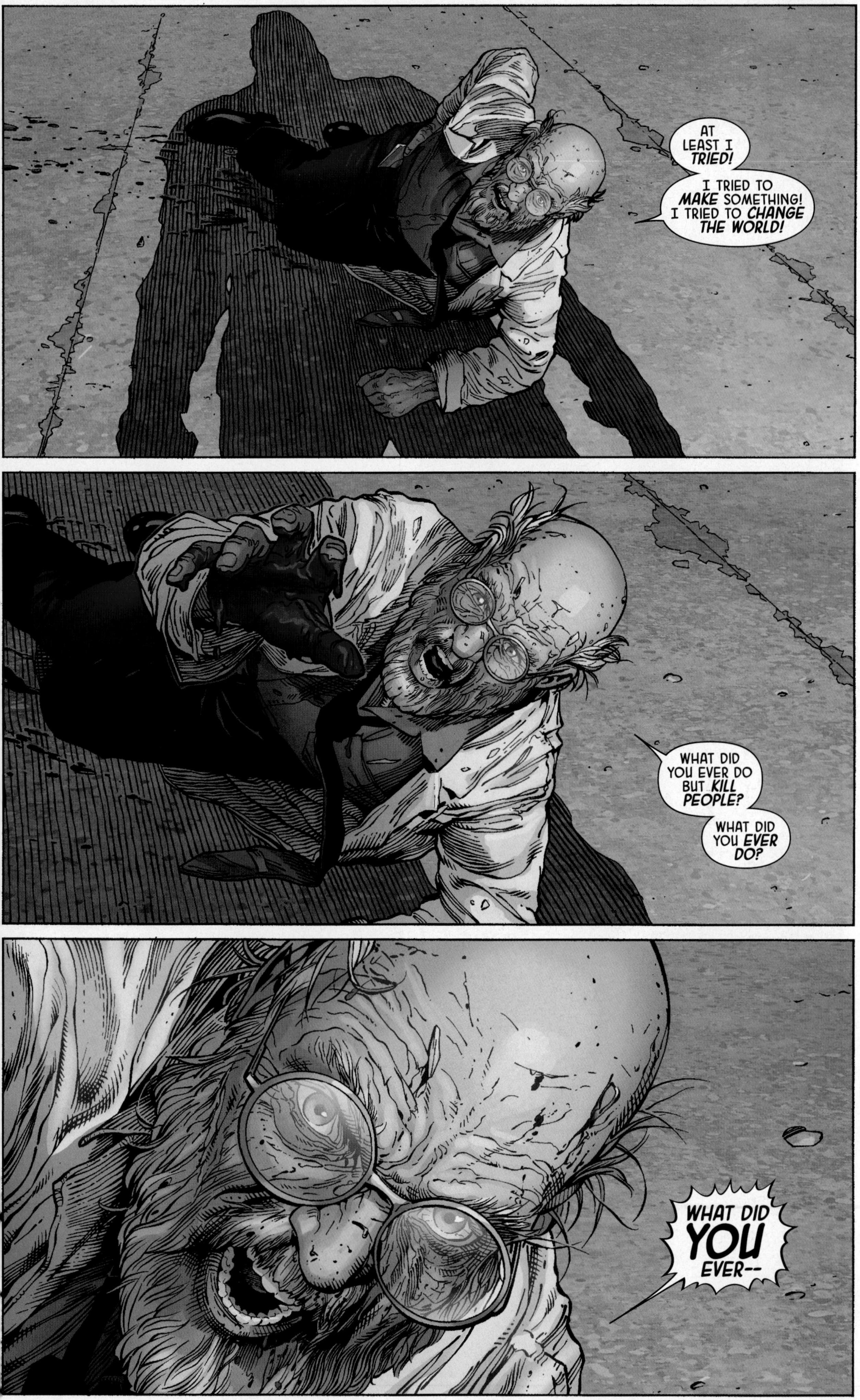
AT LEAST I TRIED!
I TRIED TO MAKE SOMETHING! I TRIED TO CHANGE THE WORLD!
WHAT DID YOU EVER DO BUT KILL PEOPLE?
WHAT DID YOU EVER DO?
WHAT DID YOU EVER--

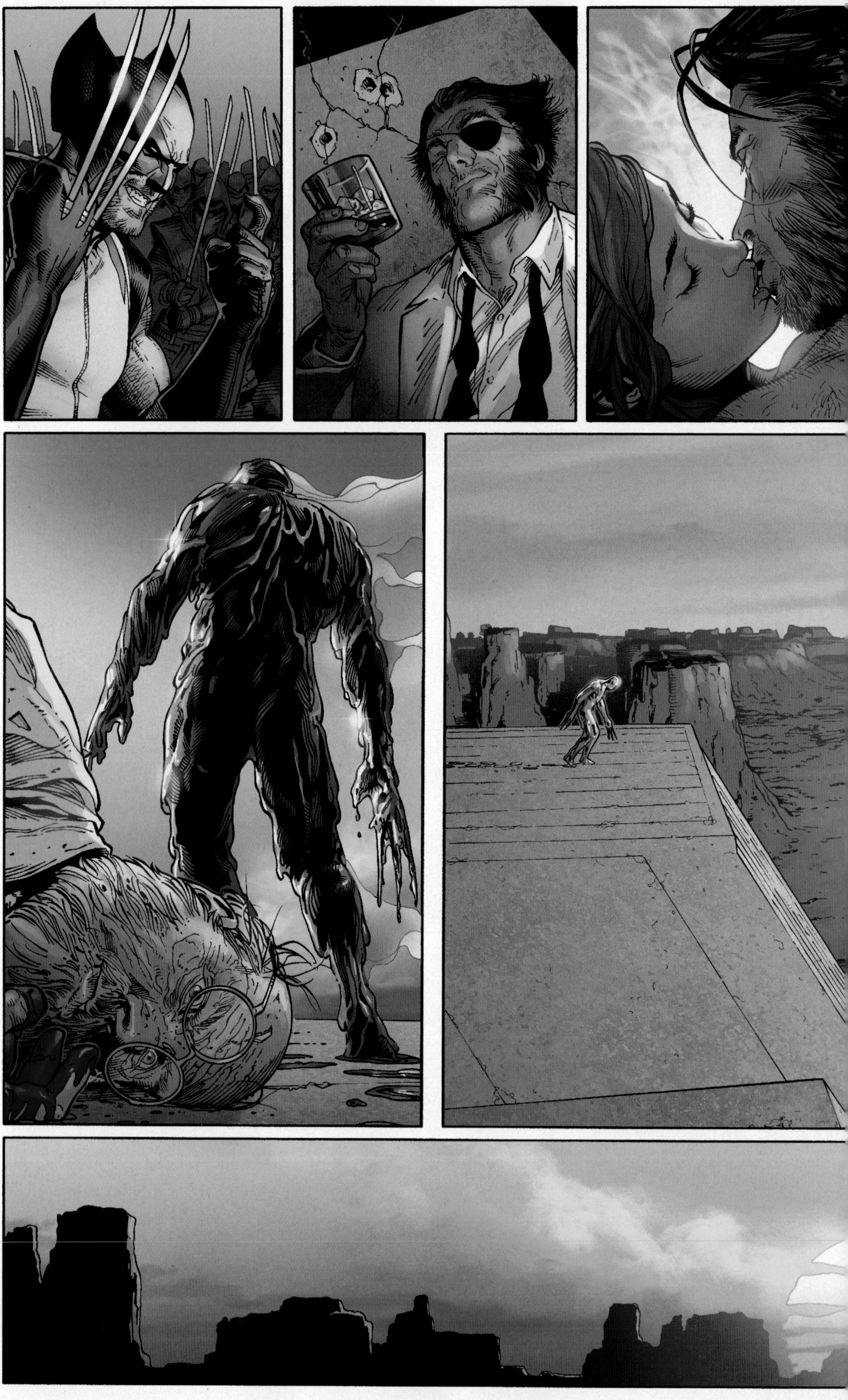

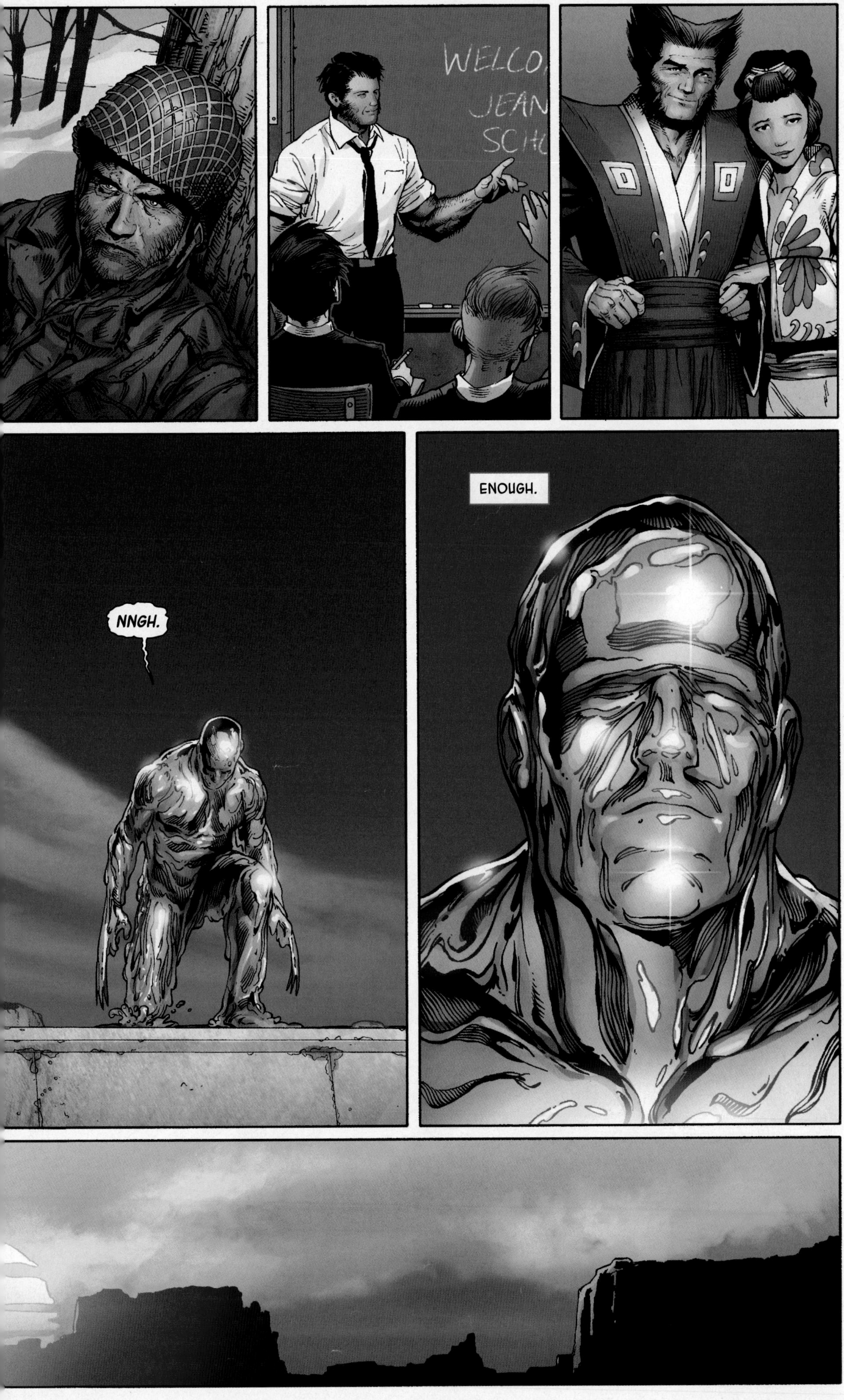
NNGH.
ENOUGH.

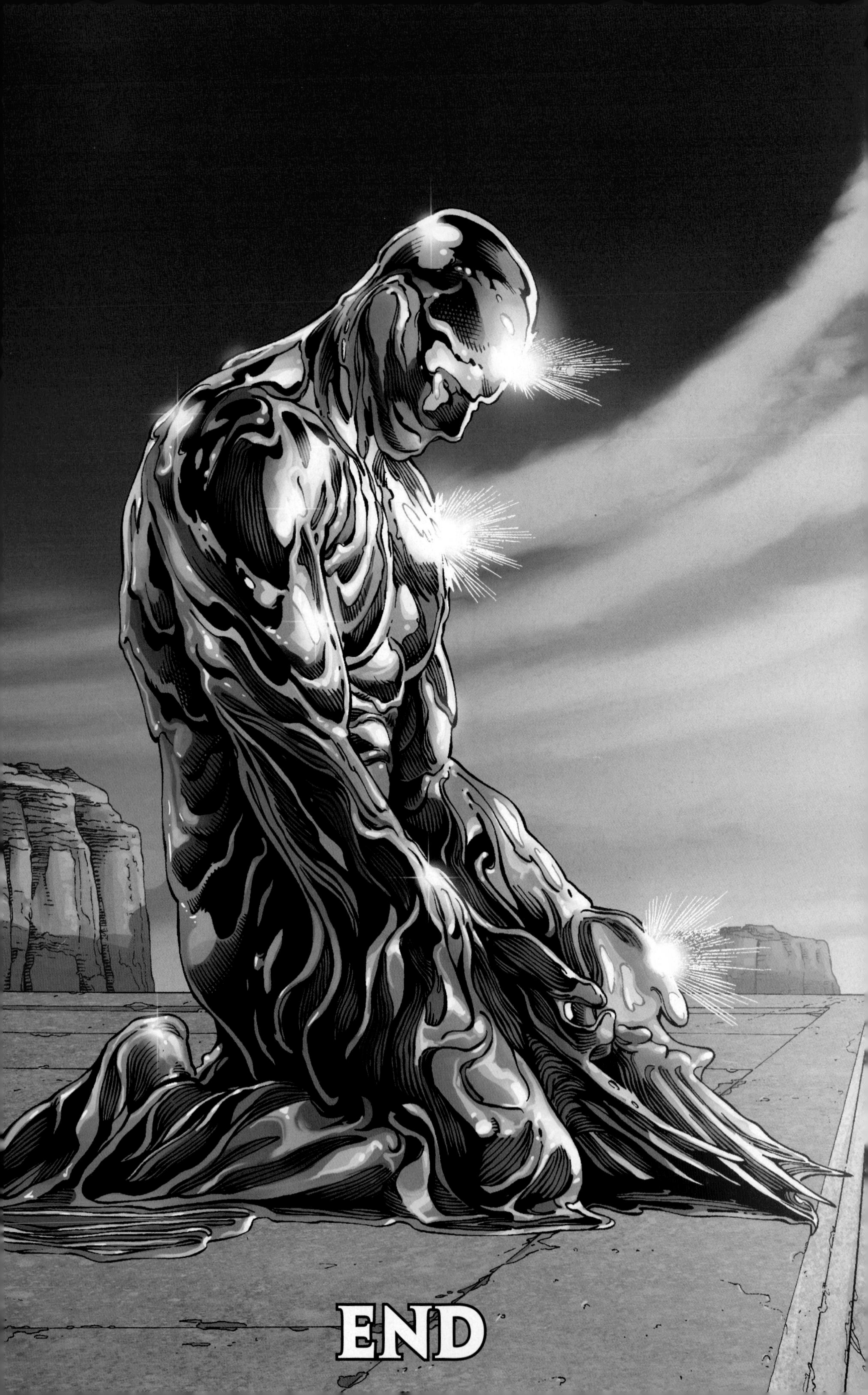
END

VARIANT COVER GALLERY FOR
DEATH OF WOLVERINE #1

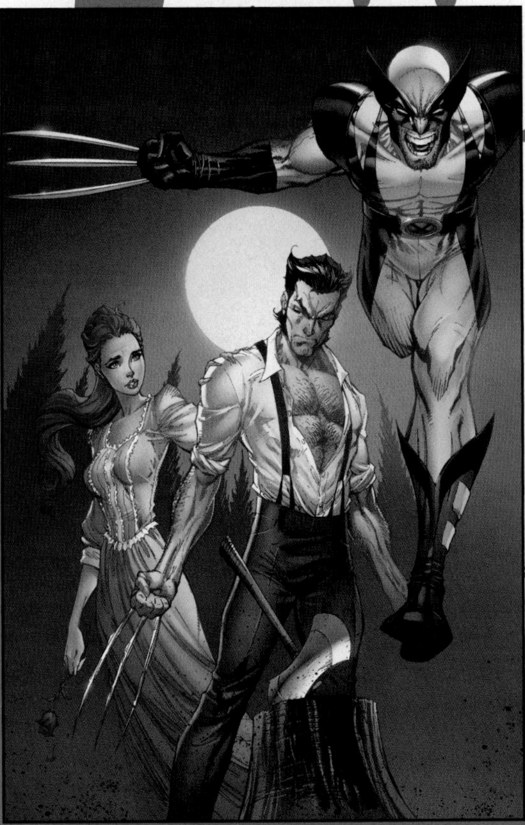

J. SCOTT CAMPBELL & ULA MOSS

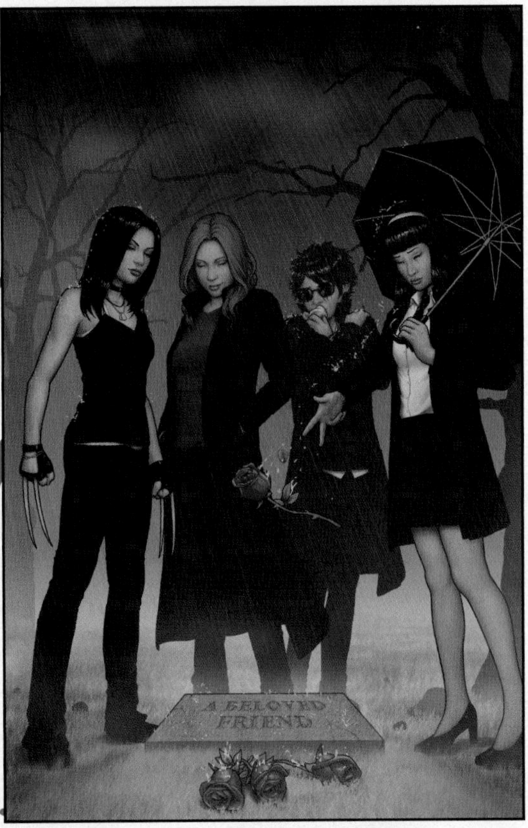
A BELOVED
FRIEND

JOHN TYLER CHRISTOPHER

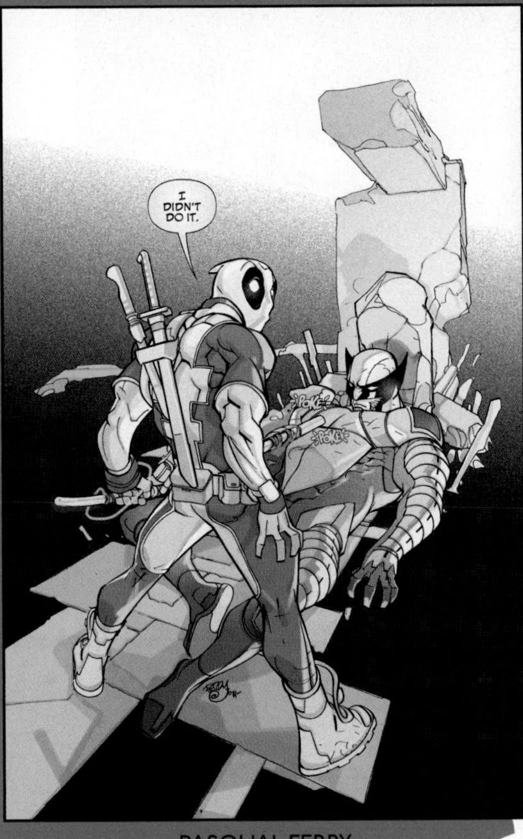
I DIDN'T DO IT.
POKE
POKE

PASQUAL FERRY

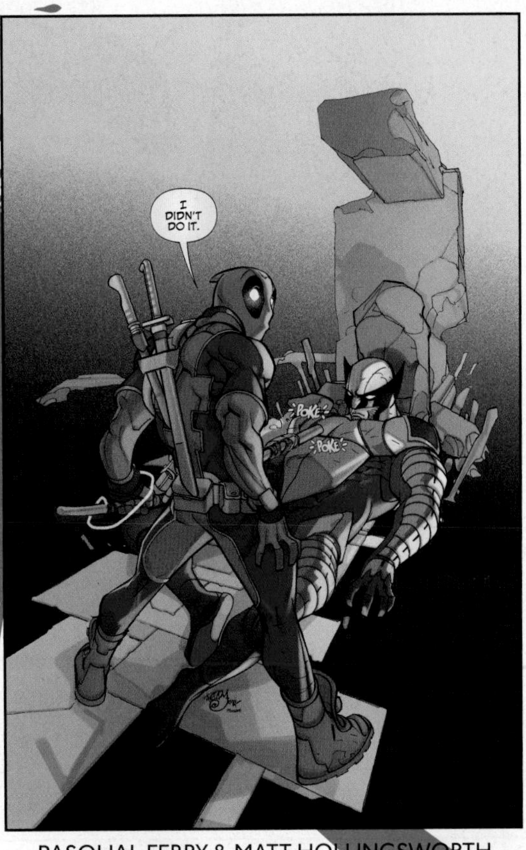
I DIDN'T DO IT.
POKE
POKE

PASQUAL FERRY & MATT HOLLINGSWORTH

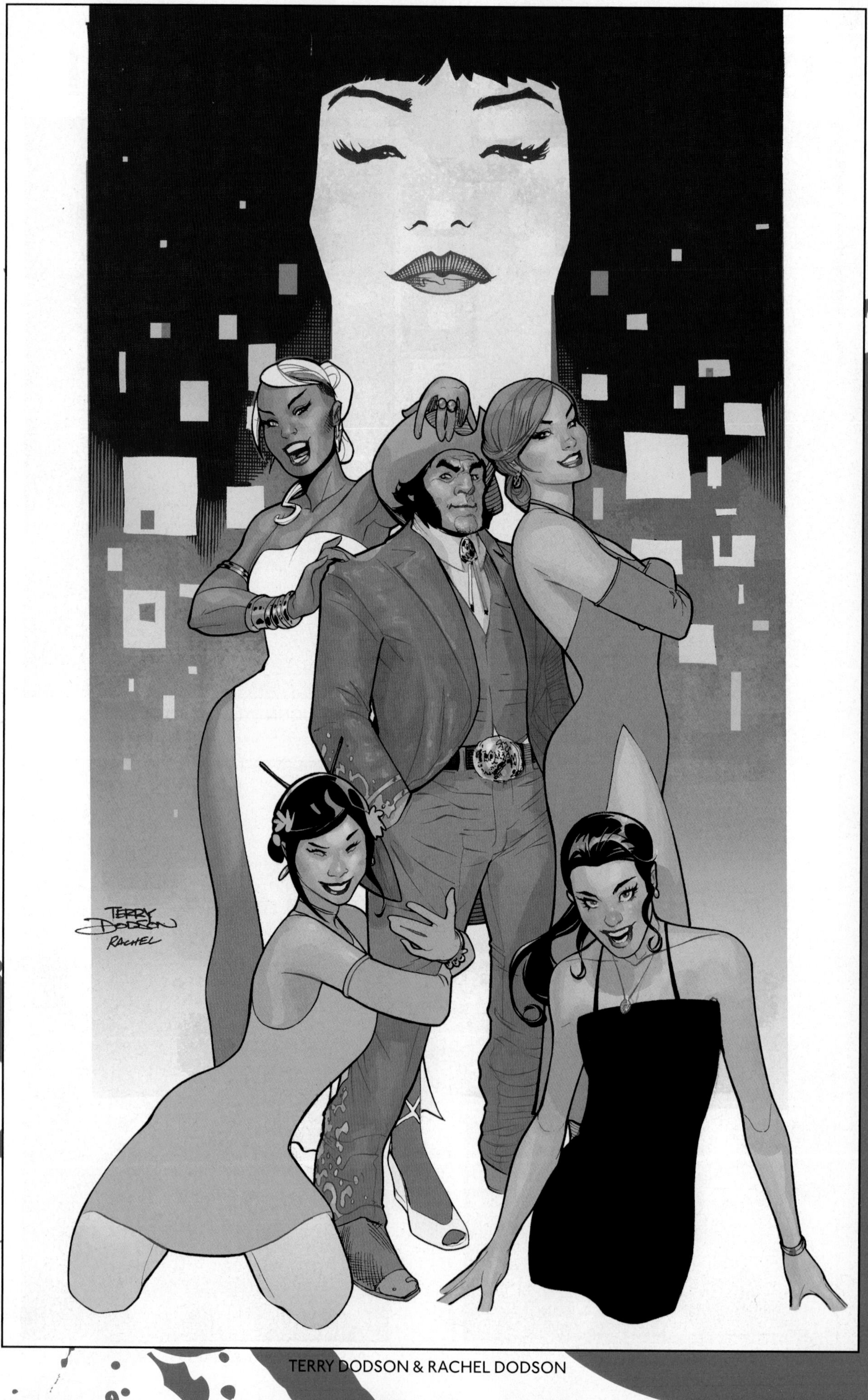
TERRY DODSON
RACHEL

TERRY DODSON & RACHEL DODSON

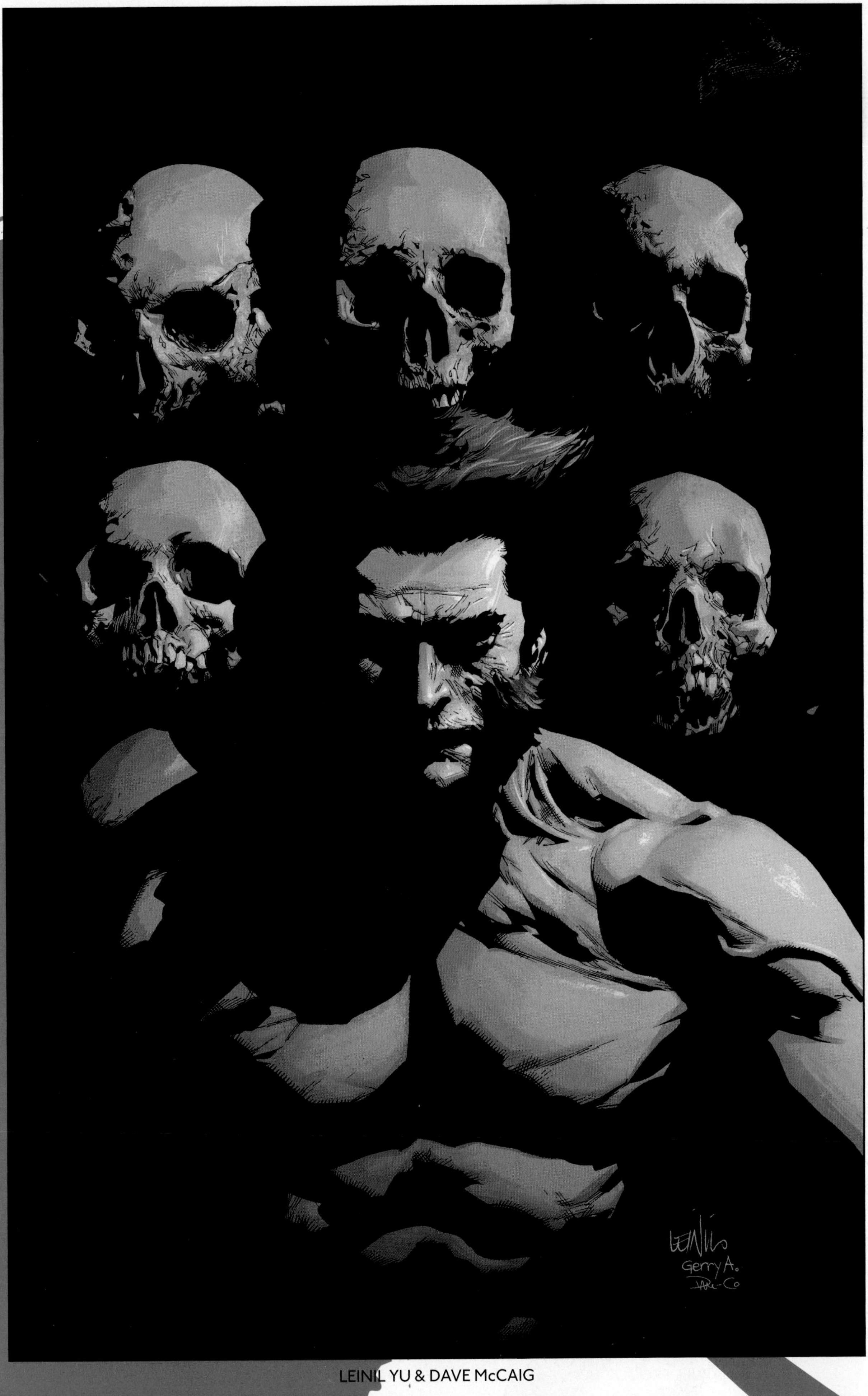

LEINIL YU & DAVE McCAIG

VARIANT COVER GALLERY FOR
DEATH OF WOLVERINE #1

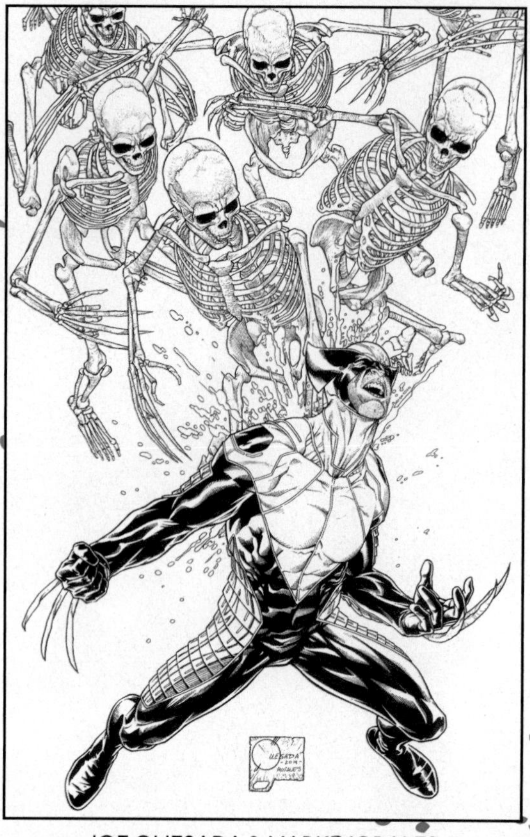

JOE QUESADA & MARK MORALES

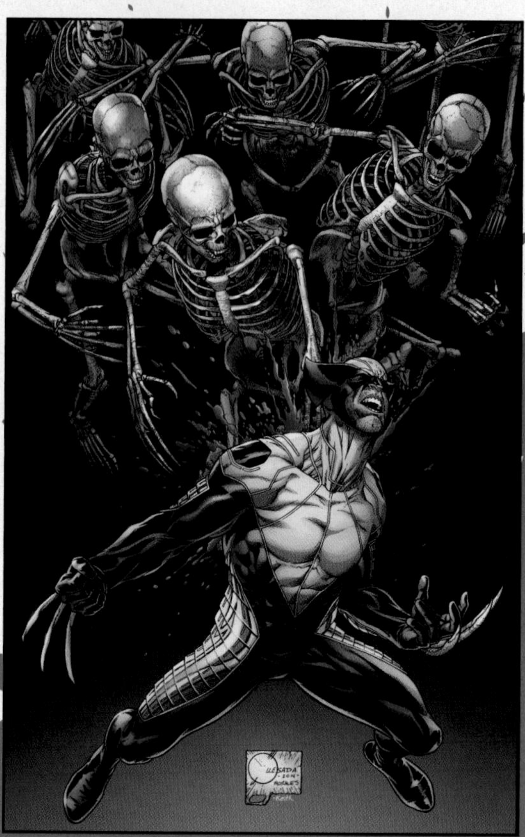

JOE QUESADA, MARK MORALES & JASON KEITH

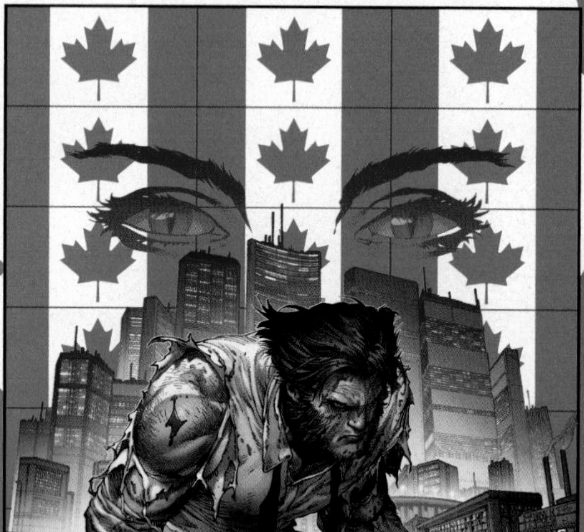

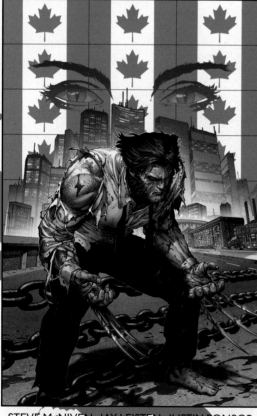

STEVE McNIVEN, JAY LEISTEN, JUSTIN PONSOR
& MARVEL PRODUCTION

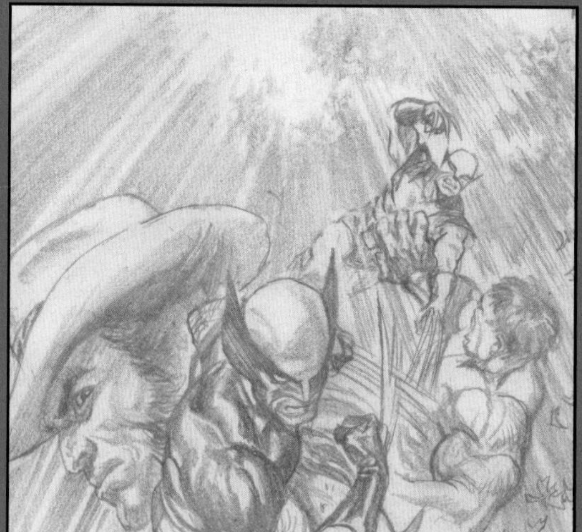

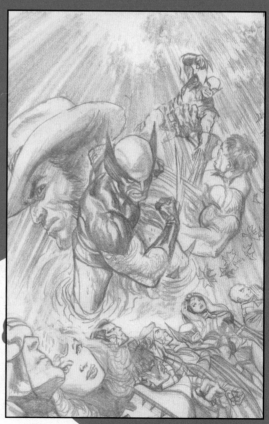

ALEX ROSS

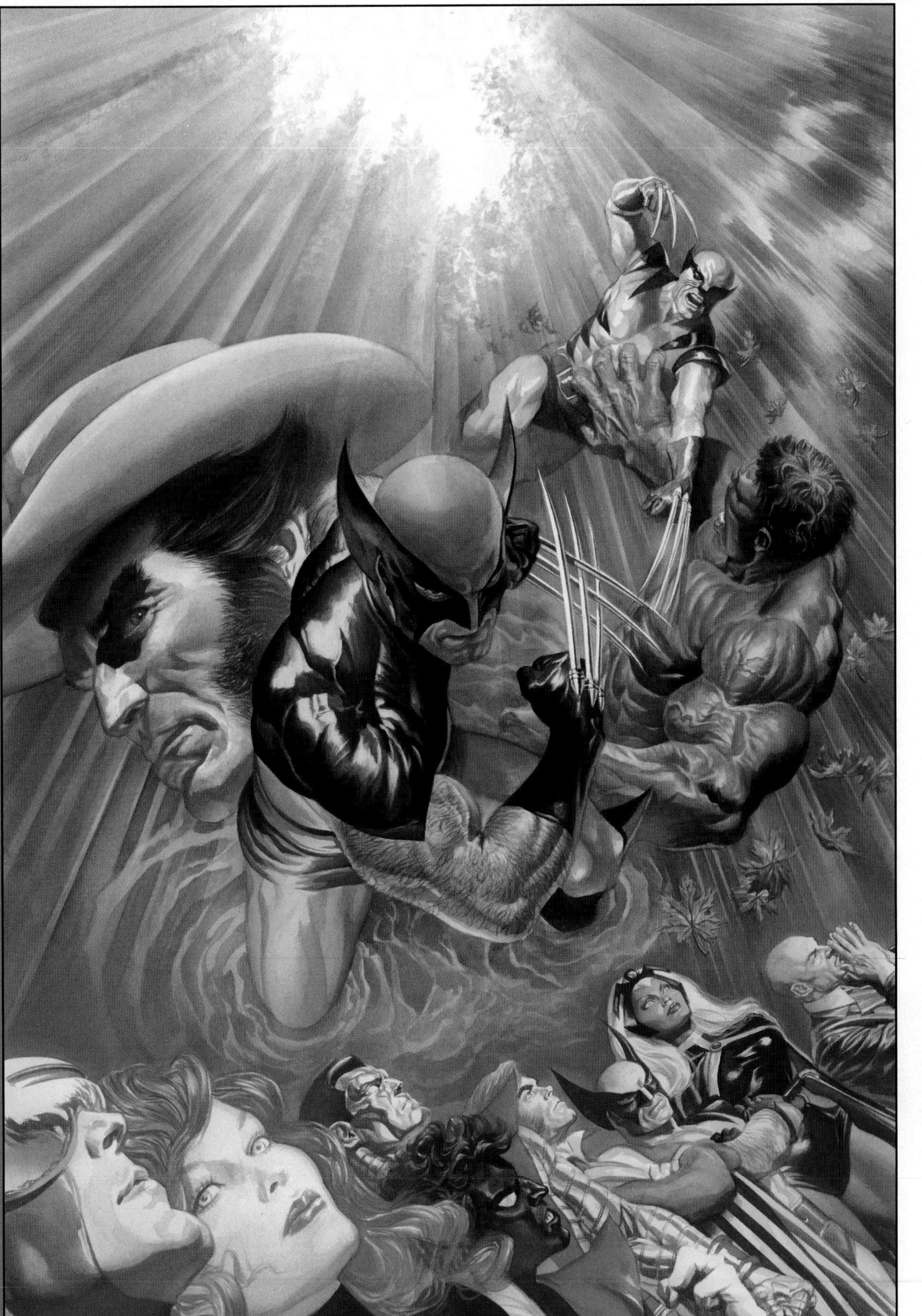

ALEX ROSS

VARIANT COVER GALLERY FOR
DEATH OF WOLVERINE #2

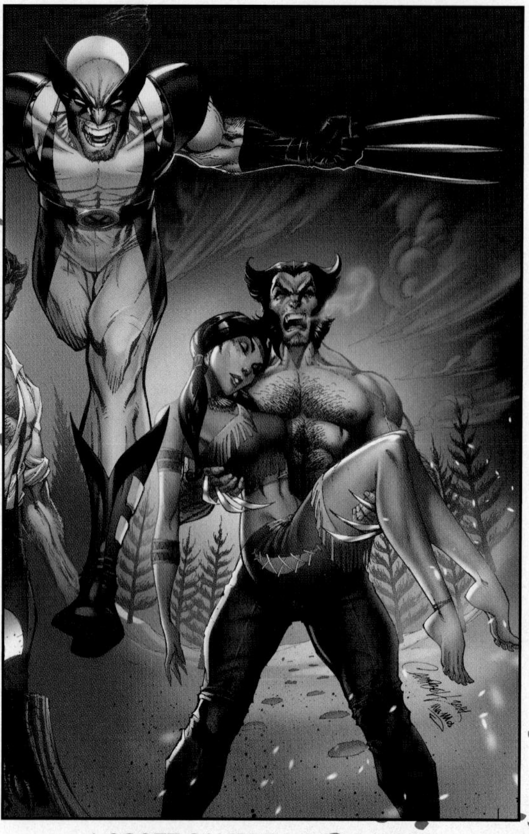

J. SCOTT CAMPBELL & ULA MOSS

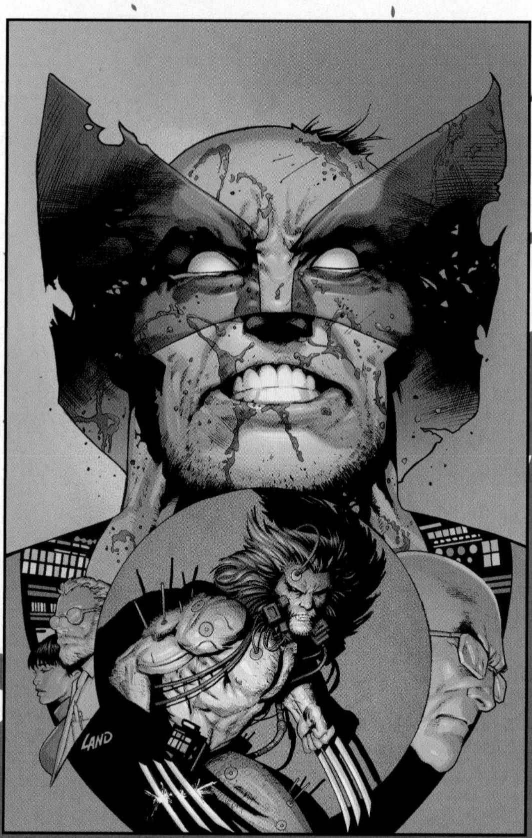
LAND

GREG LAND & DAVE McCAIG

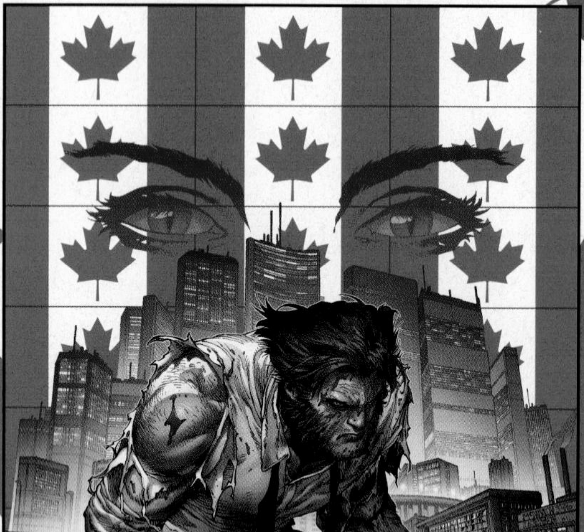

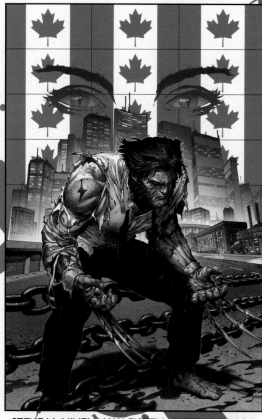

STEVE McNIVEN, JAY LEISTEN, JUSTIN PONSOR
& MARVEL PRODUCTION

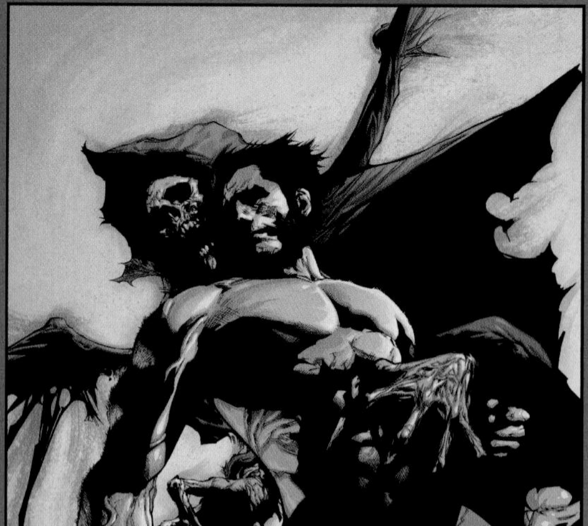

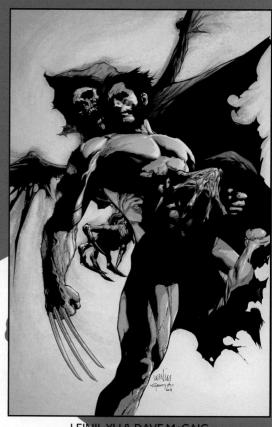

LEINIL YU & DAVE McCAIG

VARIANT COVER GALLERY FOR
DEATH OF WOLVERINE #3

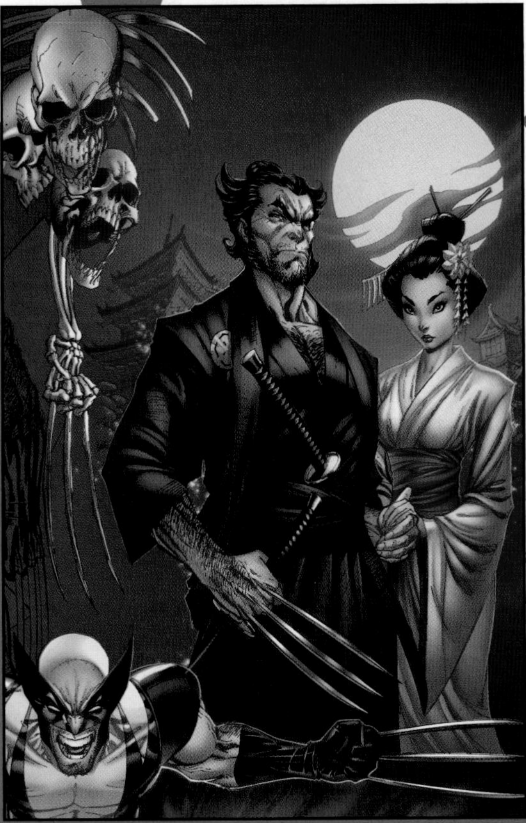

J. SCOTT CAMPBELL & ULA MOSS

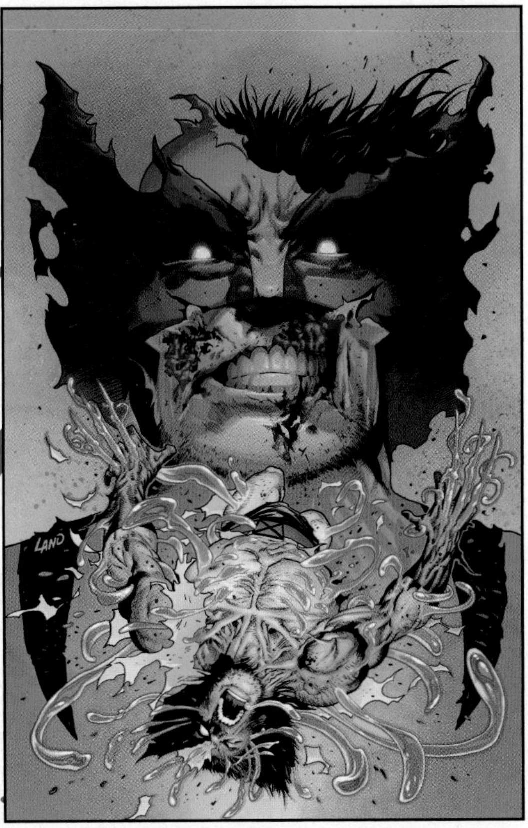

GREG LAND & DAVE McCAIG

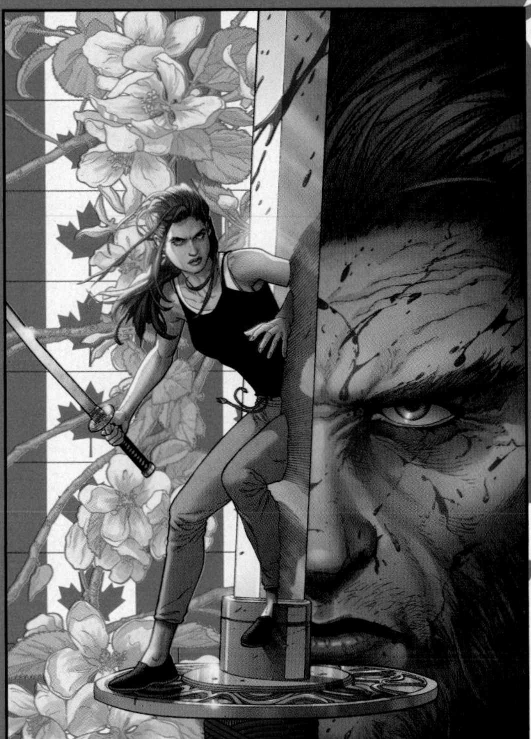

STEVE McNIVEN, JAY LEISTEN, JUSTIN PONSOR
& MARVEL PRODUCTION

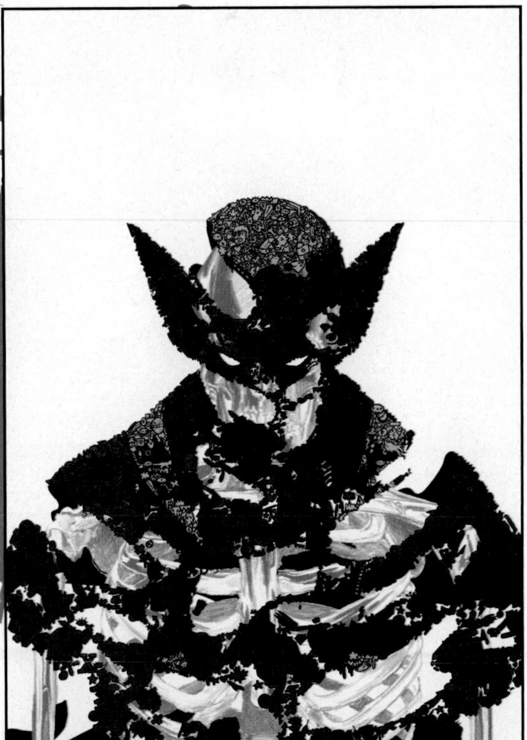

ORLANDO SANTIAGO

VARIANT COVER GALLERY FOR
DEATH OF WOLVERINE #4

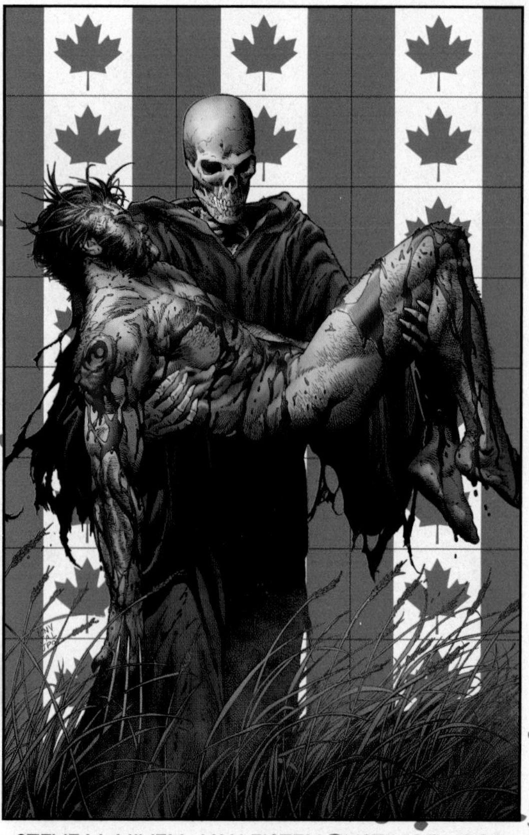

STEVE McNIVEN, JAY LEISTEN, JUSTIN PONSOR
& MARVEL PRODUCTION

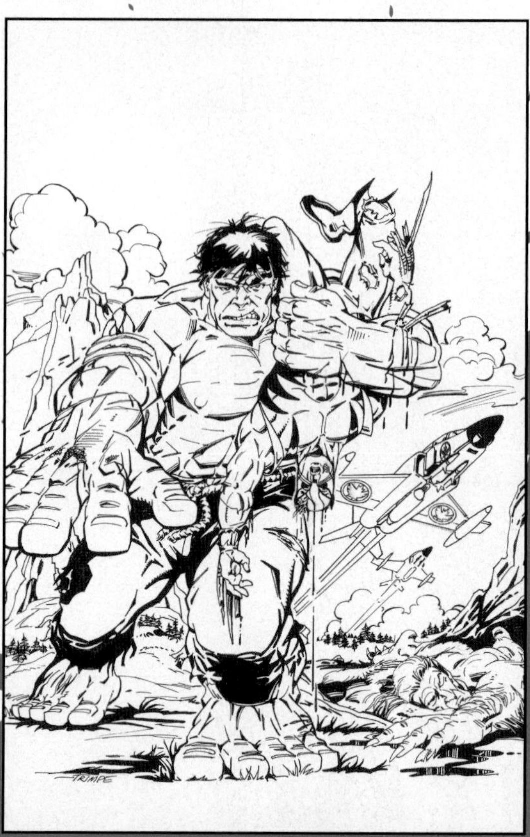

HERB TRIMPE

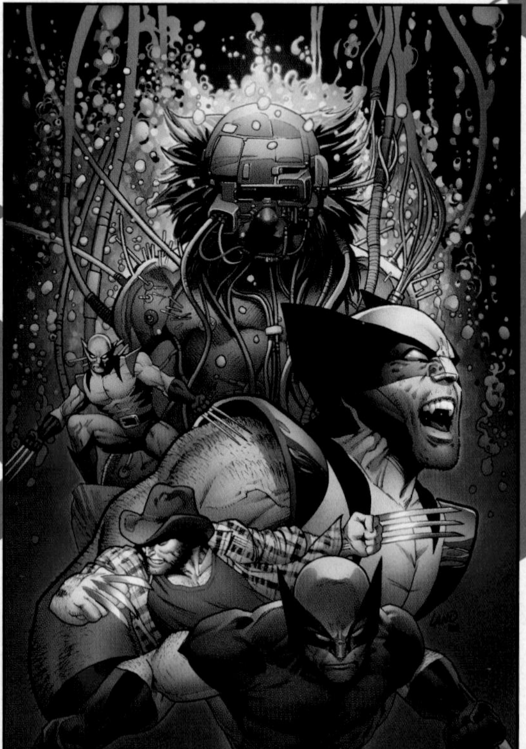

GREG LAND & FRANK D'ARMATA

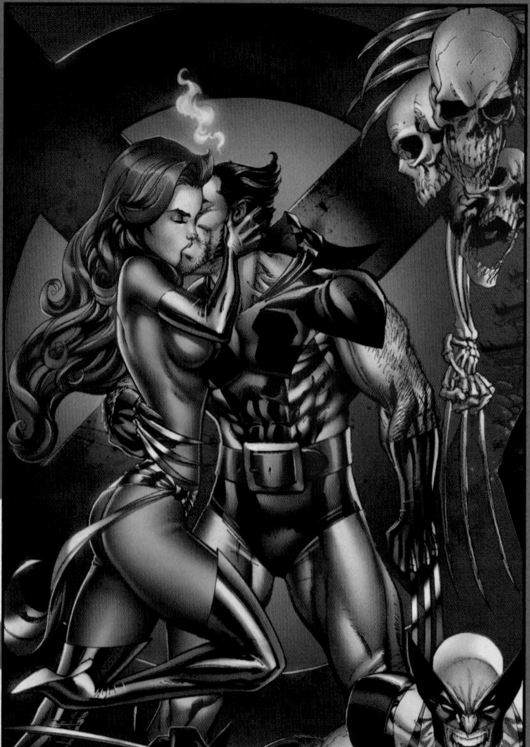

J. SCOTT CAMPBELL & ULA MOSS

INTERIOR SKETCHES FOR ISSUE #1 COMMENTARY BY STEVE McNIVEN

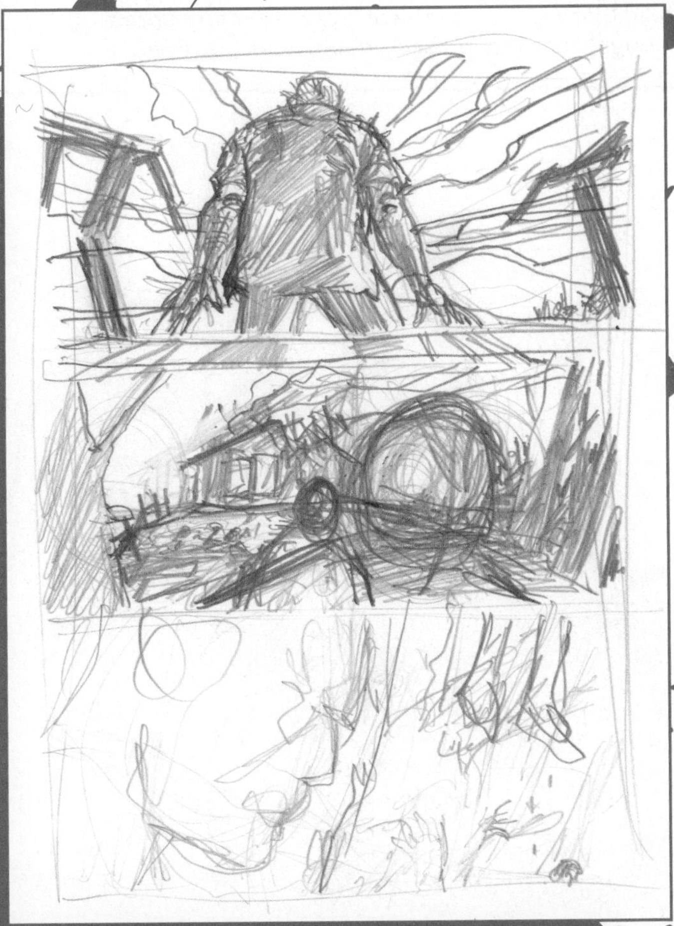

Pg 2: Here's what an initial thumbnail of a page looks like for me. Lotsa scribbles that probably appear to be a mess, but there is a plan in there somewhere.

"This might be a tall order, but I think this would be a nice spot to try to make this look almost elegant. While yes, this is a gory, awful scene, Wolverine is an artist of death. He doesn't cut people twice when once will do."

—Excerpted from *Death of Wolverine #1* script, Charles Soule

Pg 2: This is the next stage after the initial thumbnail, hammering that third panel into shape.

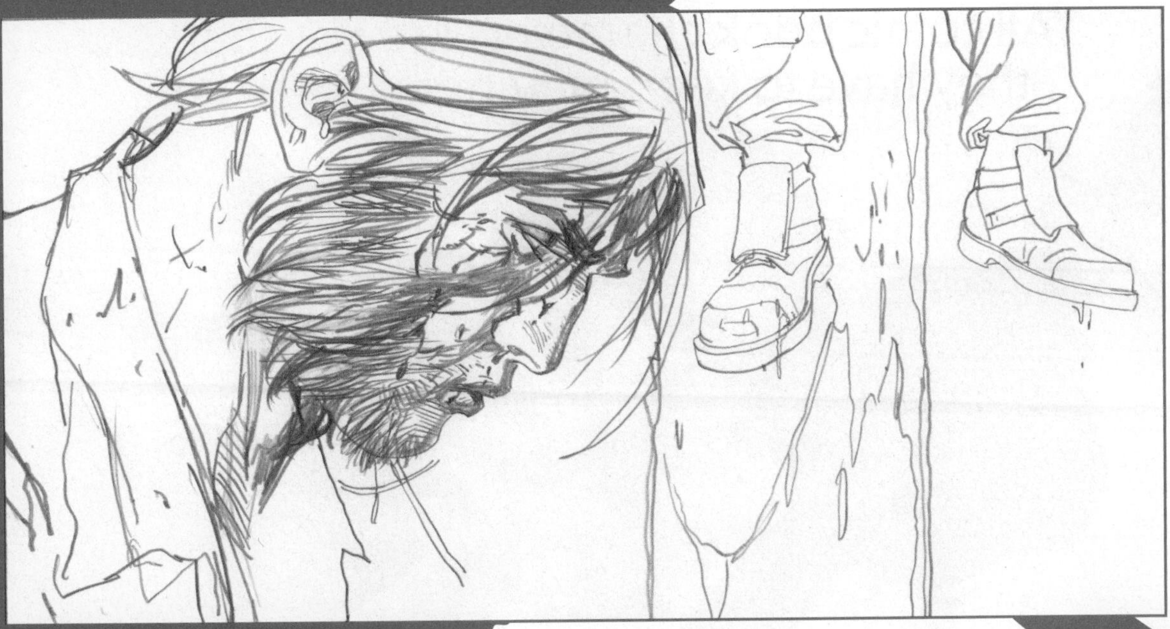

Pg 3-4: Initial study for the double spread that will include the title and credits. I wanted a big broad space to float the title, so I thought that Logan's back would work just fine.

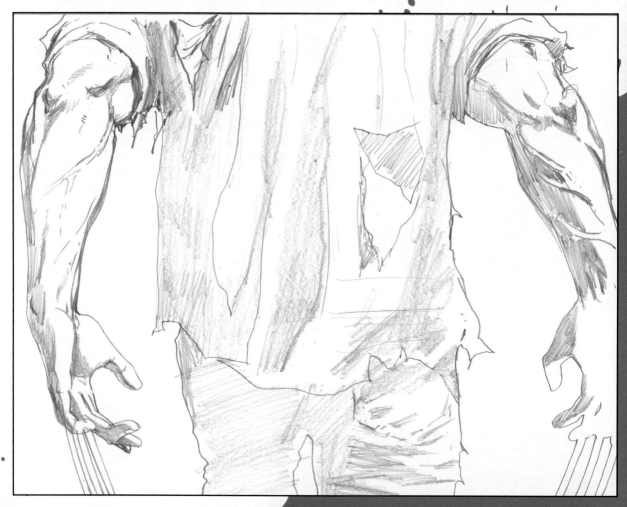

"All comic book characters are like sharks...
they have to keep moving or they die."

—Len Wein

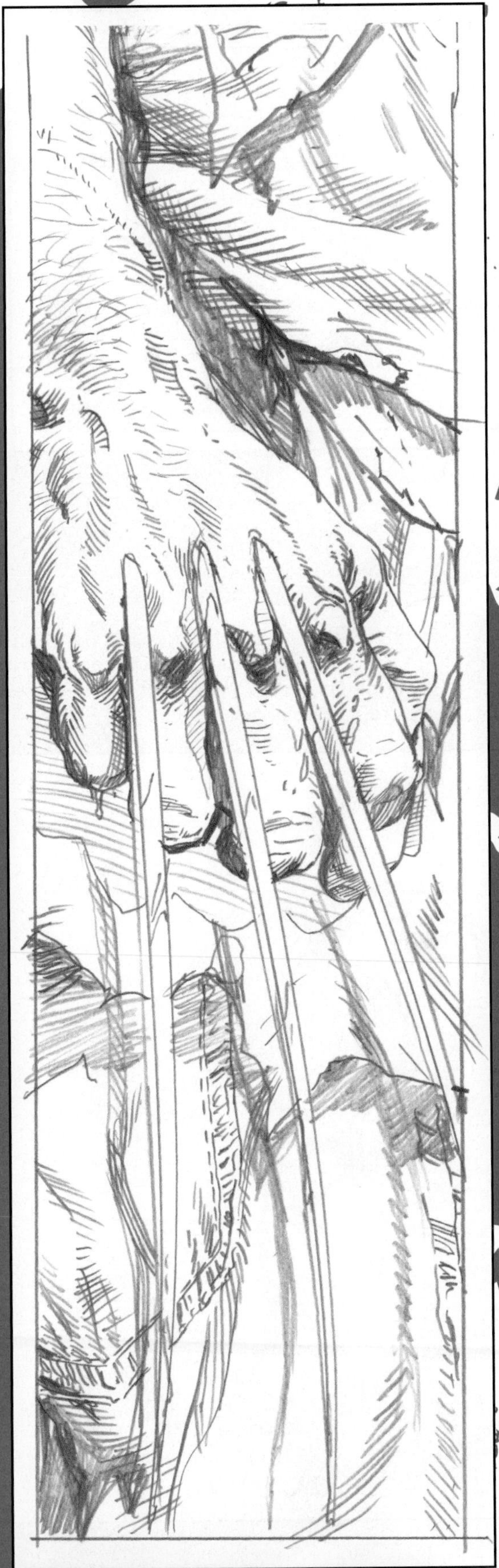

Pg 7: A rough of a close-up of the claws which is, as his healing factor is gone, a messy open wound. I always loved when Barry Windsor-Smith did those wonderful close-ups of Wolverine's hands, and really wanted to give it that flavor.

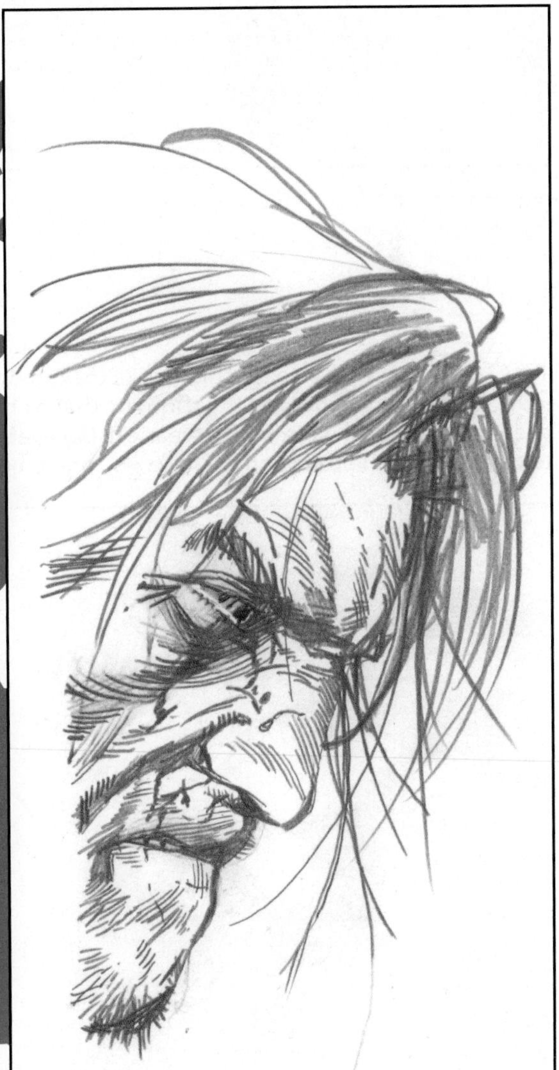

Pg 7: Another angry Logan face rough. He's pulling in his claws, which is a painful thing now, so I wanted to try and get that pain to show through his anger.

Pg 9: Logan with a bottle of Canadian whiskey. What more can be said? I had great fun researching this :)

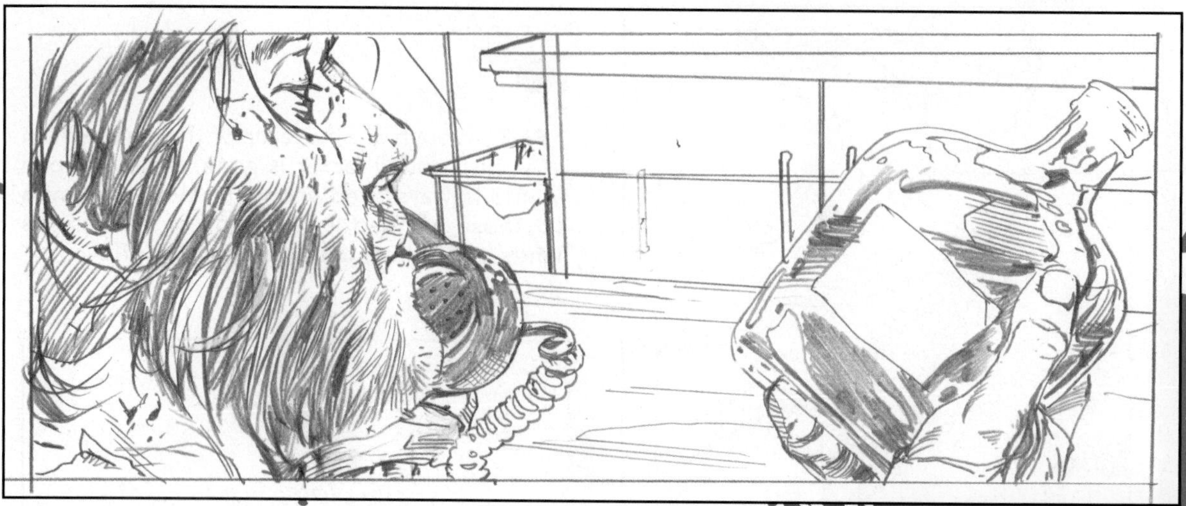

Pg 11: My first real go at getting Nuke locked down. Charles had a great idea of the guy as a gone-to-seed wrestler, so I went with it. I thought that as he has some sort of plastic polymer skin that perhaps, like an old rug, caused his hair to wear off. No eyebrows, no hair whatsoever. Anywhere. Add a beer belly and some fat on the pecs and there ya go...one creepy bad guy ready for a fight.

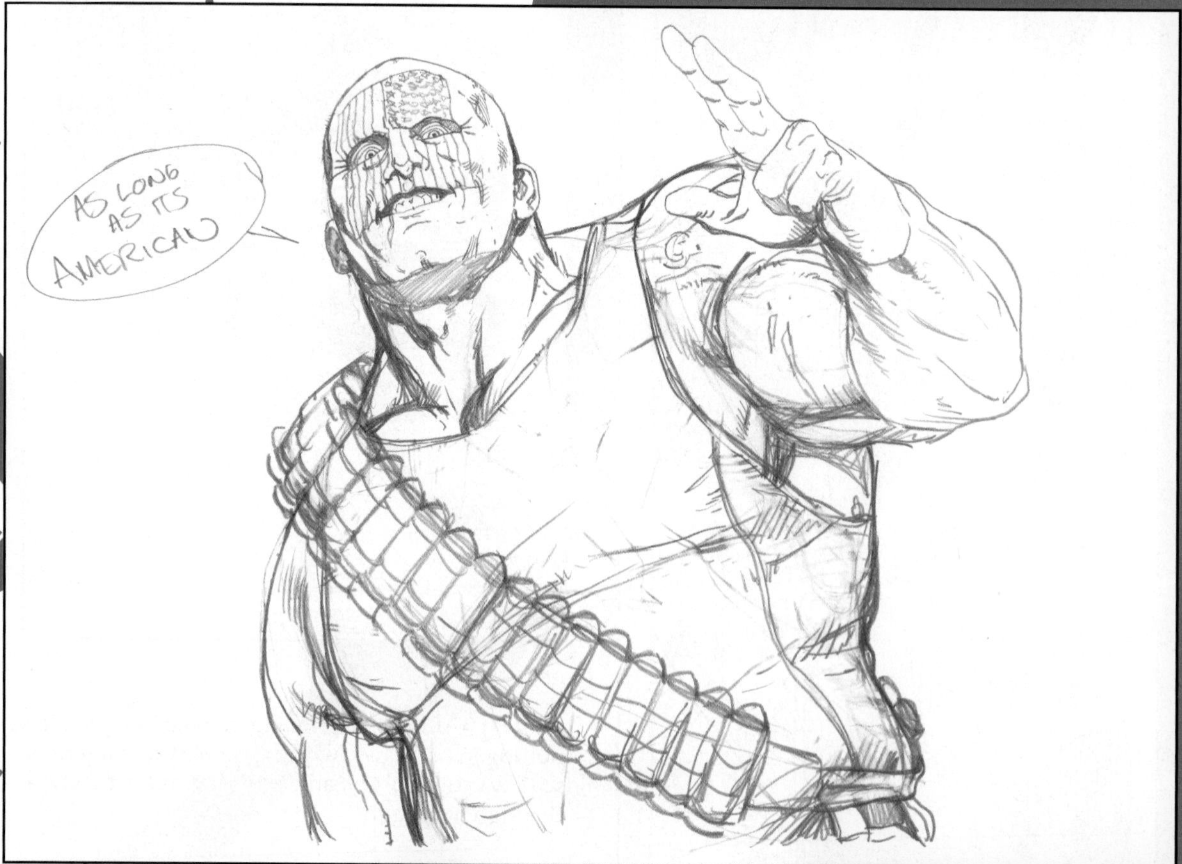
AS LONG AS ITS AMERICAN

Pg 19: This is a rough for the point in the story where Nuke confronts Logan after tossing him onto the rocks. I wanted to get that looming mountain of a man feel from Nuke, who thinks he's in control of the situation.

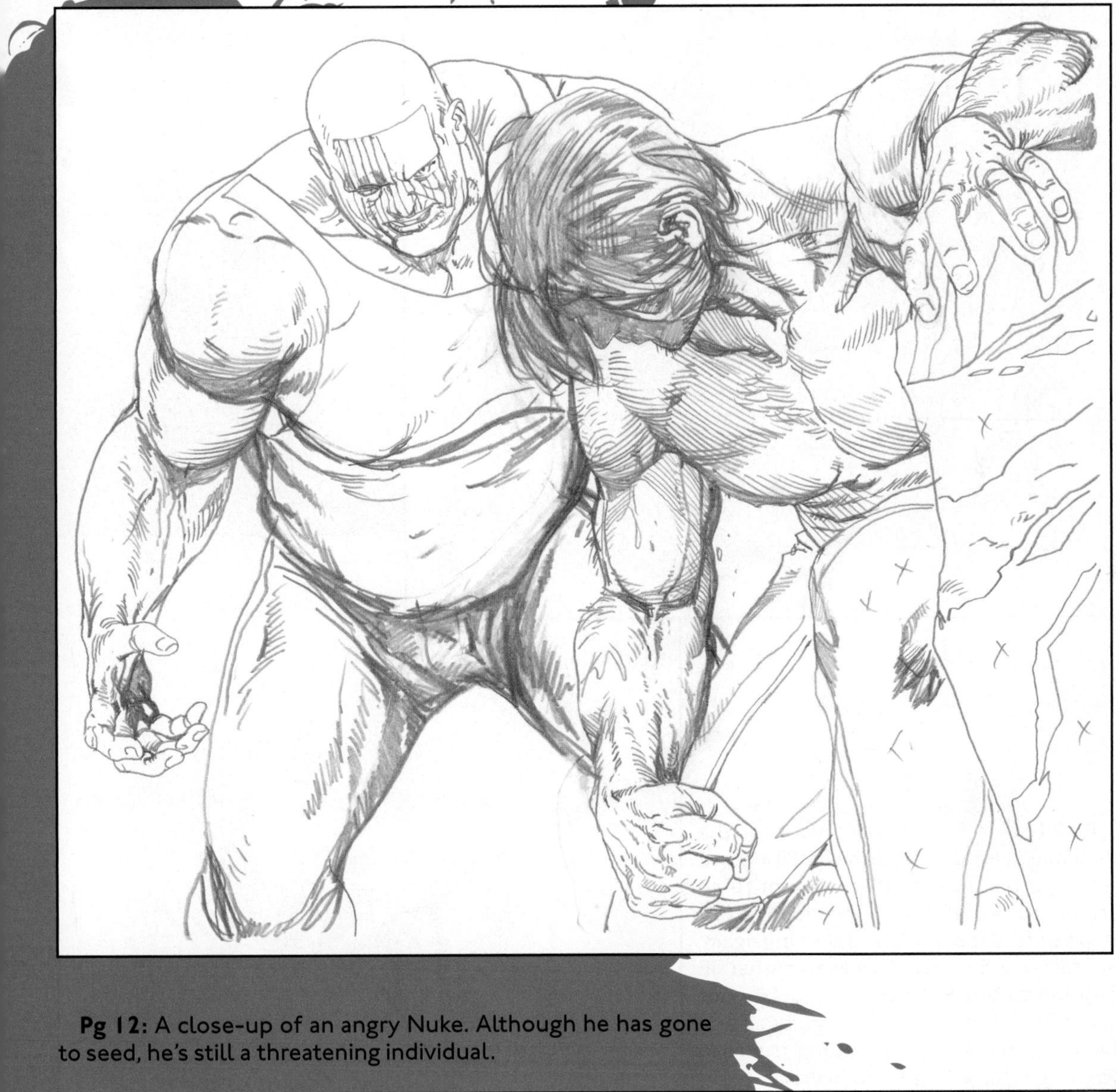

Pg 12: A close-up of an angry Nuke. Although he has gone to seed, he's still a threatening individual.

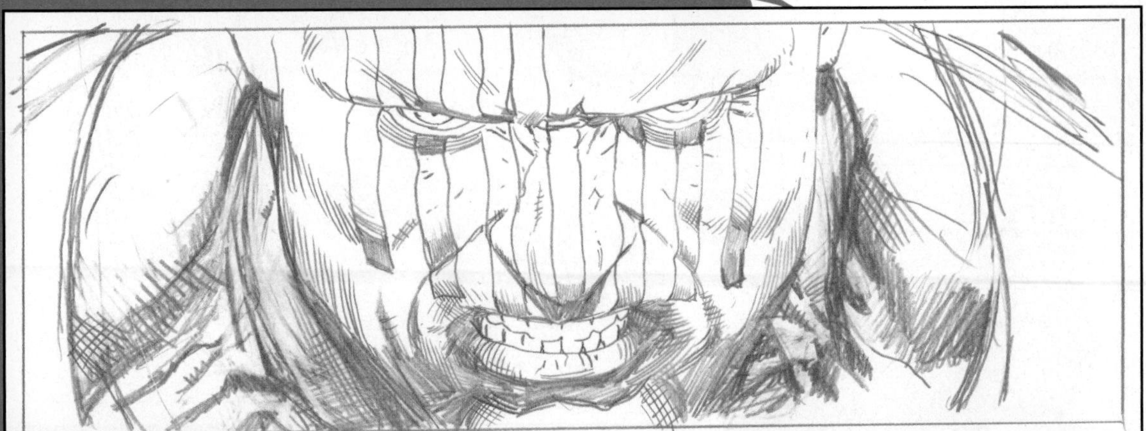

Pg 21: A rough of Logan with no patience left for poor old Nuke. I always feel bad for Jay (my inker) as I cover Logan in hair.

Pg 22: Here is an initial layout for the final page of the book, done 8 x 10 inches, ready to blow up and lightbox onto an art board. Which I did and got mostly done before tossing it and starting again, as I felt that Sabretooth was too small in relation to Viper. It happens, luckily not too often! But you have to go back and fix it, no matter how far along the road you might have wandered in error.

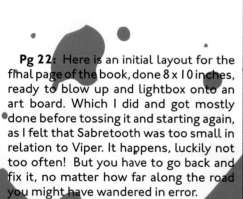

Pg 20: Nuke getting a beat-down at the end of the book. A real brutal fight that has Logan using his head instead of his claws to pound Nuke into submission.

"I mean, you give birth, you try to steer the child in the direction you believe any good person will go, and then they go wherever the hell they want to go, regardless."

—Len Wein

INTERIOR SKETCHES FOR ISSUE #2
COMMENTARY BY STEVE McNIVEN

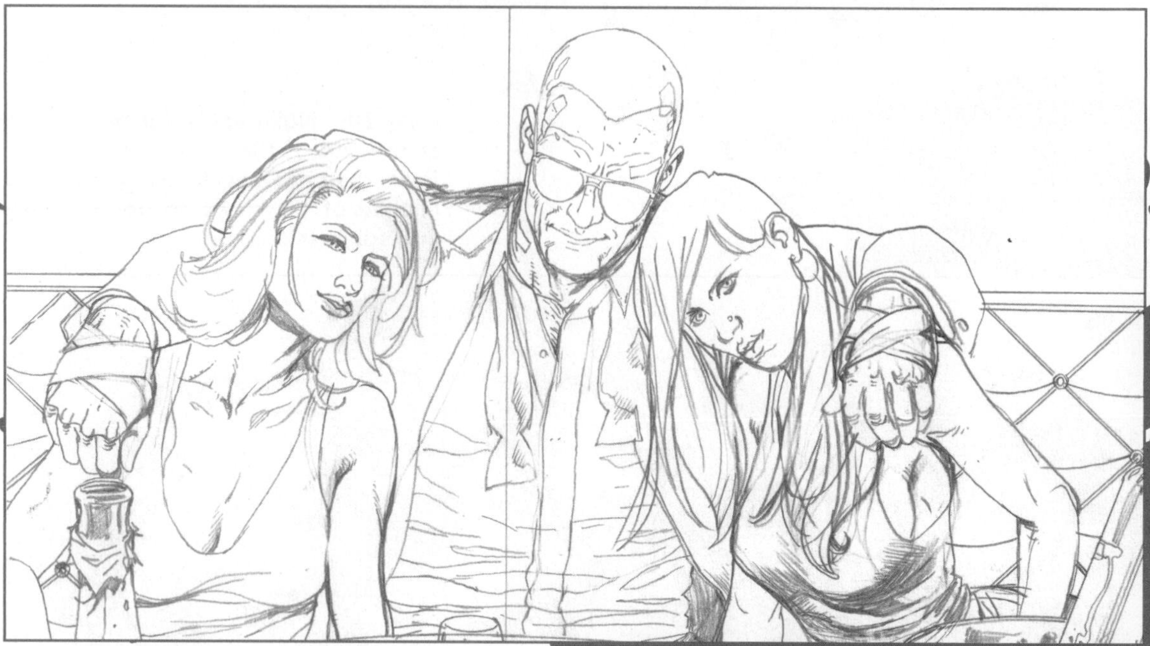

This is the first time we see Logan in disguise and we all kicked around different takes on his look. I started with the close cropped hair, moved to bald with goatee and finally to full beard which we settled on.

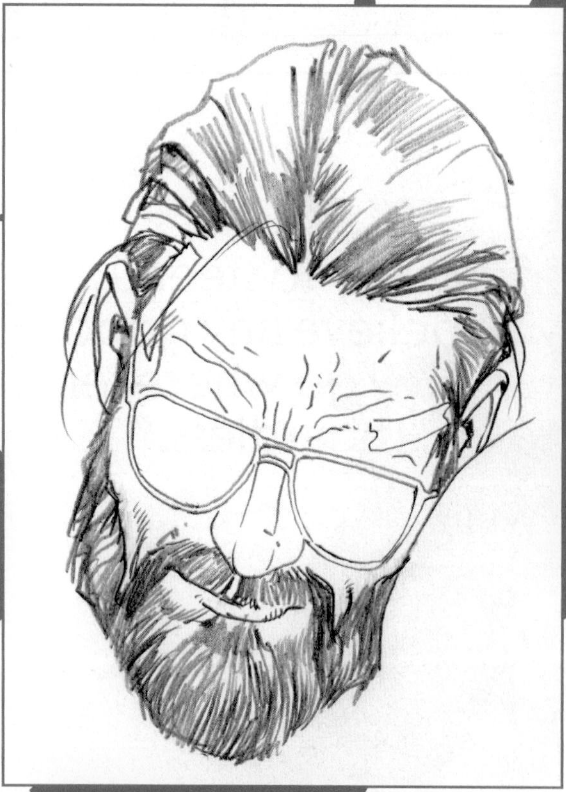

Here's the head that matches up with the above-mentioned spread, with full beard, hipster-style. Forgive me.

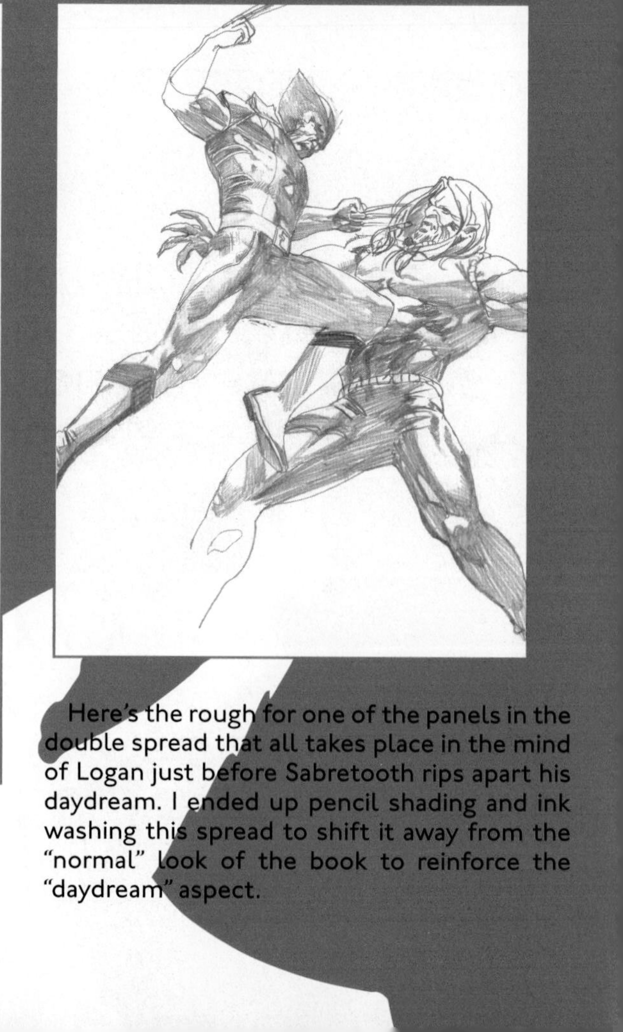

Here's the rough for one of the panels in the double spread that all takes place in the mind of Logan just before Sabretooth rips apart his daydream. I ended up pencil shading and ink washing this spread to shift it away from the "normal" look of the book to reinforce the "daydream" aspect.

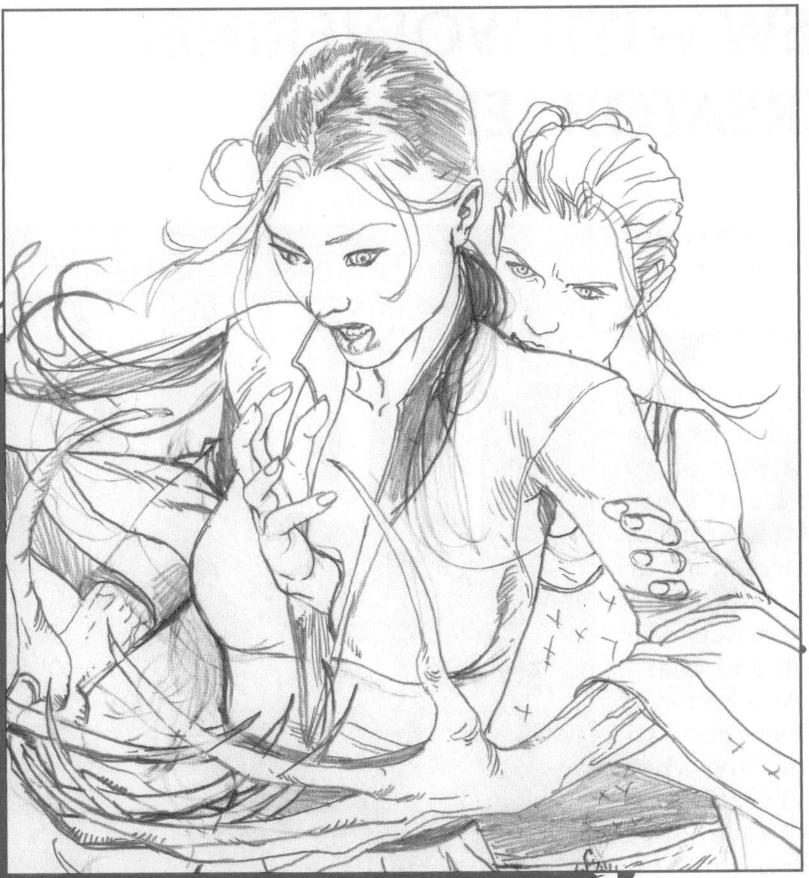

The rough for the final page of the book, a great moment that Charles dreamed up with two of my favorite characters. I love drawing Lady Deathstrike's hands!

Sabretooth's reveal as the captive of Viper. As we have already seen him at the end of issue #1, I wanted a more dramatic pose to get across the notion that Logan might be in a wee bit of trouble...

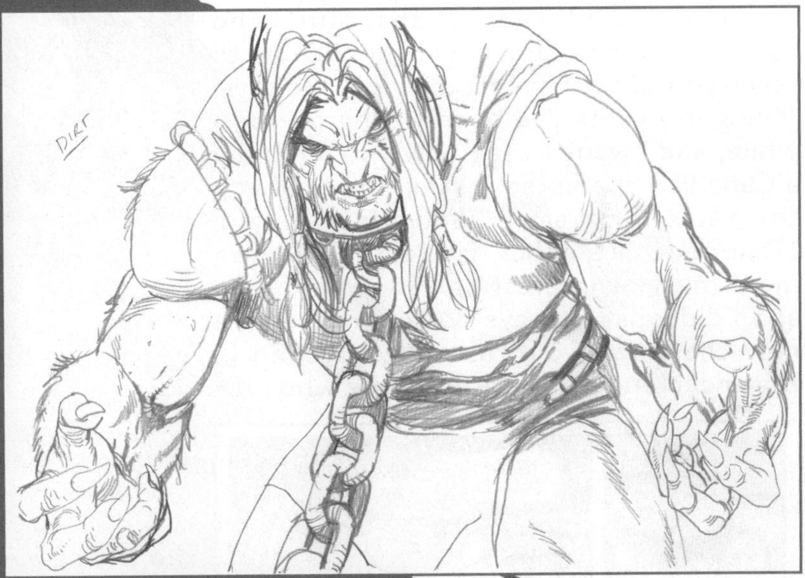

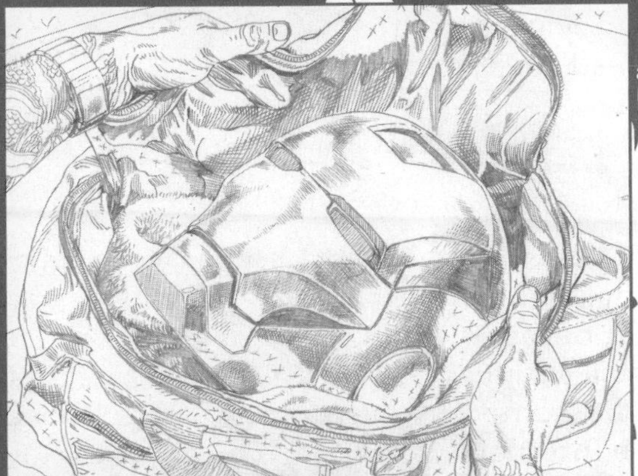

A big reveal of the object that Logan is using to gain access to Viper's lair, a functioning Iron Man helmet! I might have gotten a bit carried away with the rendering here but sometimes I can't help myself, especially when it's something fun to draw, like Iron Man's helmet.

INTERVIEW WITH WOLVERINE CO-CREATOR LEN WEIN

So, starting at the beginning, what are your earliest recollections about the creation of the character? How did that come about and who was involved creatively at that point?

INCREDIBLE HULK
MARVEL COMICS GROUP
25¢ 181 NOV 02456
THE INCREDIBLE HULK
AND NOW... the WOLVERINE!
HE'S HERE! THE WORLD'S FIRST AND GREATEST CANADIAN SUPER-HERO!
AND THE SURVIVOR OF THEIR EPIC BATTLE MUST FACE-- the WENDIGO!

The earliest recollections I have of the character proper start about a year or so before *Giant-Sized X-Men* came out, I was doing a book called *Strange Tales Starring Brother Voodoo*, which you guys may or may not remember, and I got called into Editor in Chief Roy Thomas's office one day and he said, "Let's sit down and chat." And I said, "Sure, what's up?" And he says, "I hate you!" I said, "Oh good. That's good to know from my editor! No, seriously, what do you hate me for?" Roy says, "I can't write accents to save my life. And I love what you're doing with *Brother Voodoo*, with the Caribbean accents, Haitian and Jamaican and whatnot." I love to do that stuff. And I said, "I'm sorry, I don't even know how to teach you to do that sort of thing." He says, "I've got a name I've been sitting on for a while, and I want to see how you'd handle a Canadian character." I said, "Sure, what's the name?" He said, "Wolverine!" I said, "That sounds terrific!" He said, "Go! Make me something interesting." So I went home and I did what I always do when I create a new character, I did research. I looked in the encyclopedia (there are some who may remember what an encyclopedia is) and I did a bunch of research on wolverines. And wolverines, I discovered very quickly, are short, hairy, vicious creatures with razor-sharp claws who are fearless and will take on absolutely anything—animals ten to twelve times their size. And I went, "DONE!"

UNTIL A HARSH VOICE FROM BEHIND THEM MAKES THE TWO BRUTES HESITATE.
A VOICE THAT IS MORE LIKE A SNARL!
ALL RIGHT, YOU FREAKS--JUST HOLD IT!
HUH?
IF YOU REALLY WANT TO TANGLE WITH SOMEONE--
--WHY NOT TRY YOUR LUCK AGAINST--
--THE WOLVERINE!
WELL, NOW YOU KNOW WHAT--ER--WHO WEAPON X IS, FAITHFUL ONE.
HE'S A LIVING, RAGING POWERHOUSE WHO'S BOUND TO KNOCK YOU BACK ON YOUR EMERALD POSTERIOR.
BETTER BE HERE NEXT TIME MARVELITE, SINCE... "The WOLVERINE STRIKES BUT ONCE!"
BUT IN HIS CASE, ONCE IS PLENTY!

So the name came first?

Yes, Roy gave me the name. And I came up with all the rest of it.

And he specifically wanted a Canadian hero?

Yes, that's exactly what it was. I decided to make him a mutant when I was working on it because there had been talk for at least a couple of years at that point about maybe someday reviving the *X-Men* book as an international gang of mutants, as Roy liked to put it, much like DC's equivalent

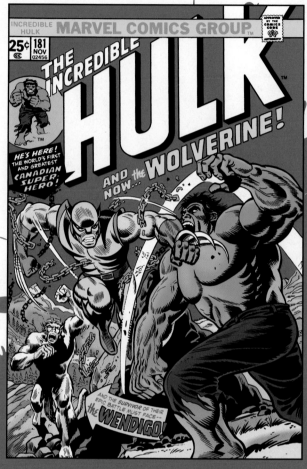

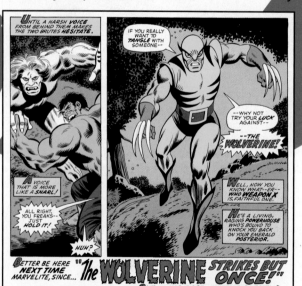

Blackhawk book about the team of pilots from different countries. So I said, "Hey, let's make him a mutant. That way whoever winds up writing that book will have at least one character to pick from if he wants to."

So it was setting the stage for eventually what would become *Giant-Sized X-Men*?

Yes. Well, not knowing I was going to be writing the book when that happened, I thought someone else was going to be writing the book then. But I just figured, "Here's some stuff to pick from if you want."

And at that point, Roy was still Editor in Chief and you were the primary editor?

Yes, I was his assistant editor. There were only two editors at that time—Editor in Chief and the assistant. How the hell we survived I couldn't begin to tell you!

When *Giant-Sized X-Men* came around, and you were writing that, were you Editor in Chief at that point?

Yes, I had just become E-i-C. After six months as Roy's assistant, he said, "Well, I've decided to give up the job and go freelance. So, Ha!, you're now Editor in Chief." And I'm going, "I just turned twenty-five years old and I'm running a company?" And I was!

And that was during the period of time it seemed you guys were taking turns with you, Gerry Conway—

—and Marv Wolfman, Archie Goodwin, yup. It basically was an impossible job. We were supposed to edit something like fifty-four books a month. And now any senior editor has, what, a half-dozen titles?

Yeah, ideally a half dozen. But we're putting close to twelve to fourteen titles a month out at least per editor. It's crazy. But nothing compared to those old days. That sounds fabulous.

That was great fun. I always refer to it as living in the Wild West. We winged it every day!

I bet! Creating new ways of doing things. So with the character, would you say most of the influence for the character came from your research?

Oh, absolutely! With the initial character, I always assumed that if he came back, or if people did stuff with him, or if I myself decided to bring him back or the Hulk or someone else, if no one used him for X-Men, that the character was going to evolve. I mean, any good character has to evolve or die. All comic book characters are like sharks—they have to keep moving or they die. So, it was a one-shot story, I wasn't going to put vast amounts of characterization into the character, because who knew if we'd ever use him again or see him again. But there was enough there to do what I wanted to do. The funny thing was, after what Roy wanted to see, I thought I did the worst Canadian accents in history. I didn't use the "aBOOTs" or things like that. He ended up sounding like he was more Australian than he was Canadian, and the funny thing about it was that in the first cartoon, he WAS Australian!

And you set the stage for the character, but then several creators—Chris Claremont, Frank Miller, Larry Hama—they really took the character and spent so much time with him. What was that like, seeing what the other writers did with the character you created?

I mean, it's always fascinating to me to see how characters evolve once you put something

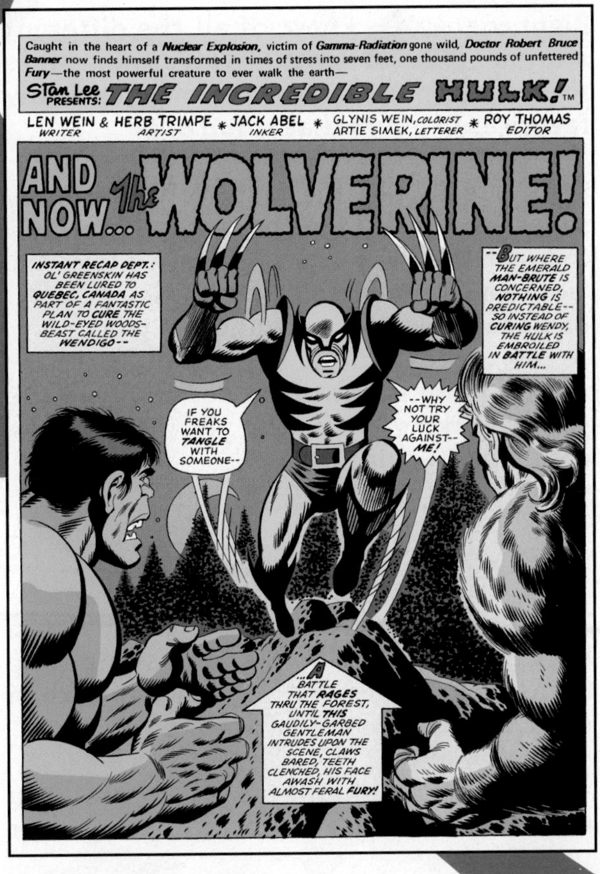

Caught in the heart of a Nuclear Explosion, victim of Gamma-Radiation gone wild, Doctor Robert Bruce Banner now finds himself transformed in times of stress into seven feet, one thousand pounds of unfettered Fury—the most powerful creature to ever walk the earth—
Stan Lee PRESENTS: THE INCREDIBLE HULK! TM
LEN WEIN & HERB TRIMPE WRITER ARTIST * JACK ABEL INKER * GLYNIS WEIN, COLORIST ARTIE SIMEK, LETTERER * ROY THOMAS EDITOR
AND NOW... The WOLVERINE!
INSTANT RECAP DEPT.: OL' GREENSKIN HAS BEEN LURED TO QUEBEC, CANADA AS PART OF A FANTASTIC PLAN TO CURE THE WILD-EYED WOODS-BEAST CALLED THE WENDIGO--
--BUT WHERE THE EMERALD MAN-BRUTE IS CONCERNED, NOTHING IS PREDICTABLE--SO INSTEAD OF CURING WENDY, THE HULK IS EMBROILED IN BATTLE WITH HIM...
IF YOU FREAKS WANT TO TANGLE WITH SOMEONE--
--WHY NOT TRY YOUR LUCK AGAINST--ME!
...A BATTLE THAT RAGES THRU THE FOREST, UNTIL THIS GAUDILY-GARBED GENTLEMAN INTRUDES UPON THE SCENE, CLAWS BARED, TEETH CLENCHED, HIS FACE AWASH WITH ALMOST FERAL FURY!

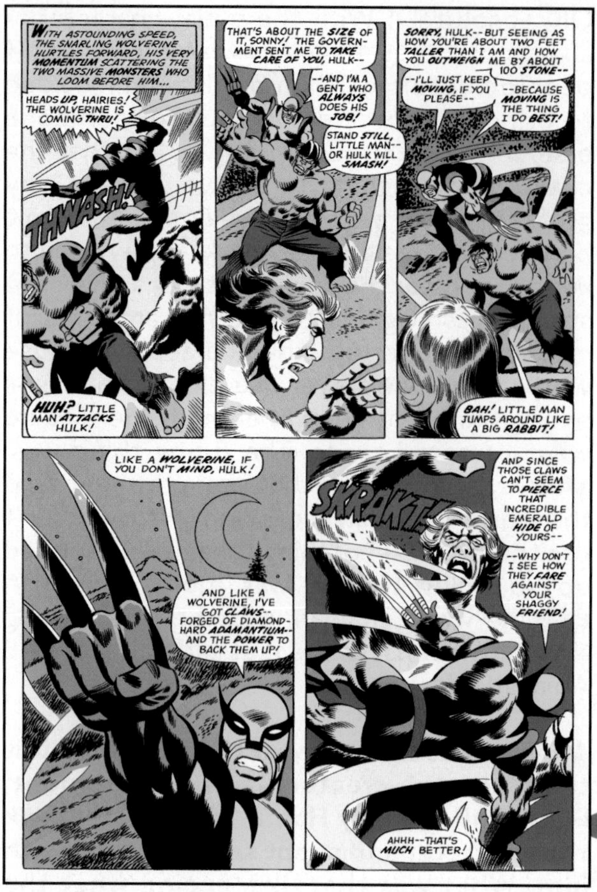
WITH ASTOUNDING SPEED, THE SNARLING WOLVERINE HURTLES FORWARD, HIS VERY MOMENTUM SCATTERING THE TWO MASSIVE MONSTERS WHO LOOM BEFORE HIM...
HEADS UP, HAIRIES! THE WOLVERINE IS COMING THRU!
THWASH!
HUH? LITTLE MAN ATTACKS HULK!
THAT'S ABOUT THE SIZE OF IT, SONNY! THE GOVERNMENT SENT ME TO TAKE CARE OF YOU, HULK--
--AND I'M A GENT WHO ALWAYS DOES HIS JOB!
STAND STILL, LITTLE MAN-- OR HULK WILL SMASH!
SORRY, HULK--BUT SEEING AS HOW YOU'RE ABOUT TWO FEET TALLER THAN I AM AND HOW YOU OUTWEIGH ME BY ABOUT 100 STONE--
--I'LL JUST KEEP MOVING, IF YOU PLEASE--
--BECAUSE MOVING IS THE THING I DO BEST!
BAH! LITTLE MAN JUMPS AROUND LIKE A BIG RABBIT!
LIKE A WOLVERINE, IF YOU DON'T MIND, HULK!
AND LIKE A WOLVERINE, I'VE GOT CLAWS-- FORGED OF DIAMOND-HARD ADAMANTIUM-- AND THE POWER TO BACK THEM UP!
SKRAKT!
AND SINCE THOSE CLAWS CAN'T SEEM TO PIERCE THAT INCREDIBLE EMERALD HIDE OF YOURS--
--WHY DON'T I SEE HOW THEY FARE AGAINST YOUR SHAGGY FRIEND!
AHHH--THAT'S MUCH BETTER!

out in the world—it's almost literally like being a parent. I mean you give birth, you try to steer the child in the direction you believe any good person will go, and then they go wherever the hell they want to go, regardless.

Right, right! You know, of all the different stories created with Wolverine, were there any specific favorites of yours? Any favorites of yours that stood out?

Well, I really like the first Wolverine mini-series—the basis for the second movie. I thought that was a terrific story. I love the fact that Chris and Frank took the character to places you never expected him to go.

And looking at all those stories over the years, looking back, and you created the character back in '74—

Yup, '74. This is his 40th anniversary, in fact, this year!

Yes, it's crazy! At what point did you step back and think, "Wow, we have something here." Something that's much larger than what you and Roy initially talked about.

Well, the audience always tells you that. You never know. I've come up with stories over the years where I've said, "This is going to kick ass. Everyone's going to love this story." And then we find out that people think, "Oh, that was nice." And then I come up with stories and think, "Oh, well I made the deadline. At least it's on time." And I would get huge, wonderful mail and the character would suddenly evolve.

Let me get back to one point about the character—I always thought when I created him that what made Wolverine a hero was that if he did have those bestial instincts—and his inclination was that if you cross him, he guts you. The fact is that he popped the claws and he goes right for your abdomen and then he stops the blade a quarter of an inch from your skin. Because disemboweling people is bad! That's what makes him a hero. And then one issue when they were facing the Hellfire Club during John and Chris's run on the book, Wolverine goes berserk and disembowels a whole bunch of people and suddenly he's the most popular member of the X-Men! So it shows you what the hell I know!

It's amazing that at this point not only is Wolverine such a popular comic character, but he's gone beyond that and become a huge part of pop culture as a whole.

Oh, absolutely! I realized that about five or six years ago when I was looking at a bunch of Marvel products in the outside market—Marvel toys or Marvel clothes or whatever—and I realized here's a little montage of little Marvel characters. And the two foremost characters on every piece of that stuff were Wolverine and Spider-Man. And I went—oh, my God, he's up there! In all probability he's probably superseded Spider-Man as the iconic image of Marvel.

Quite possibly, yeah. And you know, coming back around to the reason why we're here—with the character's long life, did you ever envision him dying? And if so, what were your thoughts on that?

Well, I never imagined him dying or going away. Let me rephrase that: Even at this moment, I never imagine him dying and STAYING away. As opposed to going away. It makes for great story fodder (I haven't read the story but I'm sure it's going to be terrific) but let's be honest—he's not staying away. He's the most lucrative character Marvel has these days. There's no sane way a major corporation is

AND WHEN THE WOLVERINE RISES, HE RISES ALONE!
HAH! LITTLE FRIEND DID GOOD. YOU SMASHED UGLY WENDIGO ONCE--
--AND NOW WENDIGO IS DEAD!
HE SHOULD BE, HULK--BUT HE'S NOT!
APPARENTLY, THE WENDIGO IS AS IMMORTAL AS THE LEGENDS SAY. MY TALONS ONLY RENDERED HIM UNCONSCIOUS!
A STRANGE, UNEASY SILENCE SETTLES OVER THE SCENE THEN. THE THREAT OF THE WENDIGO IS ENDED, OR SO IT SEEMS--
--AND THE HULK PEERS AT HIS PINT-SIZED COMPANION IN QUIET CONFUSION. HE DOES NOT KNOW WHAT TO SAY TO THE WOLVERINE NOW THAT THE BATTLE IS DONE--
--DOES NOT KNOW HOW HE SHOULD RESPOND TO THIS SOMBER LITTLE MAN.
BUT WHEN THE WOLVERINE SUDDENLY LASHES OUT WITH CUSTOMARY SAVAGERY, THE HULK'S RESPONSE BECOMES ALMOST AUTOMATIC!
ALL RIGHT, GREENSKIN-- IT'S YOUR TURN TO TAKE A THRASHING!
HUH?
THRAK
PUNY LITTLE MAN, HULK THOUGHT YOU WERE HULK'S FRIEND! HULK TRUSTED YOU--
--BUT YOU BETRAYED HULK--ATTACKED HULK--JUST LIKE ALL THE OTHER PUNY HUMANS HULK HAS KNOWN!
LITTLE MAN MADE A FOOL OF HULK-- AND FOR THAT, HULK WILL SMASH!
YOU'LL HAVE TO CATCH ME FIRST, UGLY--
--AND NOBODY IS FAST ENOUGH TO DO THAT!

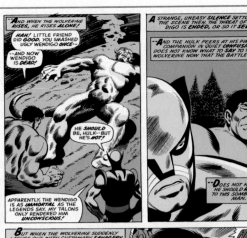

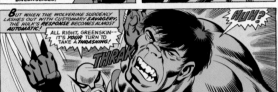

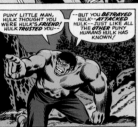

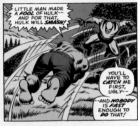

going to decide, "You know, let's knock off the guy who makes us the most money." He'll be back, I don't know how quickly—I don't know what they're going to do with that gap in the Marvel Universe in the interim, I can't wait to find out as a reader—

—the gap is half the fun sometimes.

Yeah, they've done wonderful things with Captain America when he died, especially Dan [Slott] when he did Spider-Man when Doc Ock took over Peter Parker's body, it was brilliant stuff! Those were great comics to read. But you knew, eventually, Peter was going to go jumping back into that body, and Cap was going to get resurrected somehow, partly because they're iconic, and the audience over the long haul wouldn't be able to take not having a Steve Rogers Captain America or a Peter Parker Spider-Man or a Logan Wolverine. I think it's also because when there's a multi-billion-dollar movie coming out in six months where Steve Rogers is Captain America, I guess you've gotta bring him back!

Len, we've covered a lot of topics so far... is there anything we haven't covered?

Well, I don't think anywhere in this conversation have we talked about Dave Cockrum and his contribution, which was considerable to all of the X-Men stuff, not just to Wolverine. I mean, the major things he contributed to Wolverine—three major things, which were critical—were the mask that became the standard mask for the character in his first costume. Because when John Romita, Sr. and I designed him, he had that wolverine-like mask with the tiny ears and the whiskers and the whole dance, and Dave hated that. He said to me, "I hate that mask, I don't want to draw that mask." And I said to him, "You got anything better in mind?" And he came back with that iconic one and I said, "Okay! That's better. We'll use that." But he's also the guy who designed Logan's face without the mask, with the mutton chops and the "someone-please-get-that-man-a-hair-detangler" haircut. I also believe it was Dave's idea for the claws to be organic as opposed to mechanical. I had always envisioned them as mechanical. My thought was you make them out of Adamantium. They can telescope, 'cause they can fit through those little hangers on the back of the glove that the claws come out of, and because Adamantium is indestructible, you can do a telescoping claw that really only needs to be one molecule thick and it's still never going to break off. Then my first thought after that was that if we use the claws on something stainless steel, wouldn't they just rip off the back of the gloves? So I figured the gloves were Adamantium as well, and they're covered with cloth, so that's why they would stay on and he could cut up anything he wanted to. And then after I left the book there was the day where, I don't know if it was Chris or Dave—I believe it was Dave—said, "What if they really come out of his arm?" And it's a great bit—it's utterly illogical because he really wouldn't be able to move his wrists if that's how they worked, but who cares, it's a great bit!

Yeah, exactly, and it's gotten us miles and miles of story out of that great idea.

Exactly! So I want to make sure credit is given to Dave Cockrum, God rest him. He was (a) a brilliant designer and (b) one of the nicest guys I've ever worked with and (c) a great loss to the business.

Yeah, and it's amazing to look at what a fantastic designer Dave was, because so

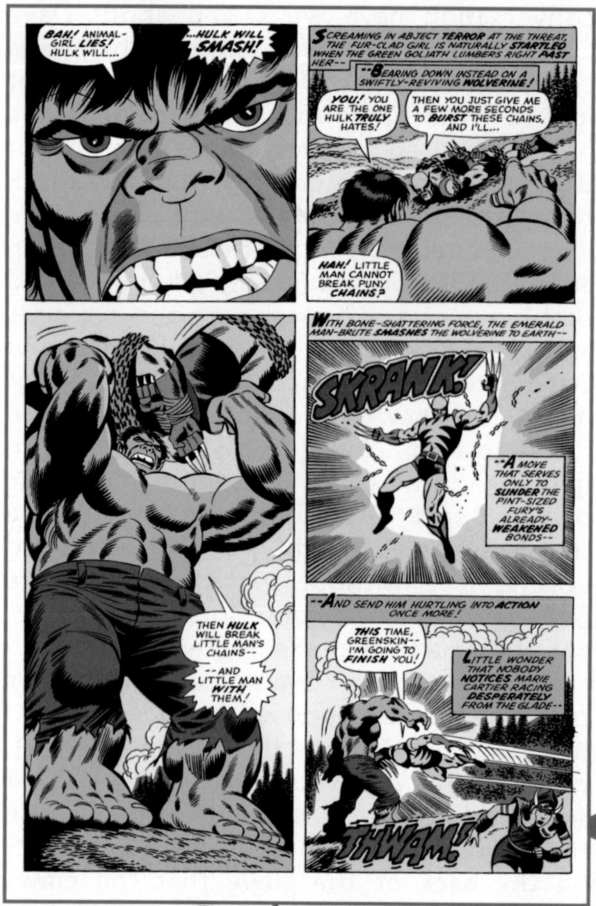
BAH! ANIMAL-GIRL LIES! HULK WILL...
...HULK WILL SMASH!
SCREAMING IN ABJECT TERROR AT THE THREAT, THE FUR-CLAD GIRL IS NATURALLY STARTLED WHEN THE GREEN GOLIATH LUMBERS RIGHT PAST HER--
--BEARING DOWN INSTEAD ON A SWIFTLY-REVIVING WOLVERINE!
YOU! YOU ARE THE ONE HULK TRULY HATES!
THEN YOU JUST GIVE ME A FEW MORE SECONDS TO BURST THESE CHAINS, AND I'LL...
HAH! LITTLE MAN CANNOT BREAK PUNY CHAINS?
THEN HULK WILL BREAK LITTLE MAN'S CHAINS--
--AND LITTLE MAN WITH THEM!
WITH BONE-SHATTERING FORCE, THE EMERALD MAN-BRUTE SMASHES THE WOLVERINE TO EARTH--
SKRANK!
--A MOVE THAT SERVES ONLY TO SUNDER THE PINT-SIZED FURY'S ALREADY-WEAKENED BONDS--
--AND SEND HIM HURTLING INTO ACTION ONCE MORE!
THIS TIME, GREENSKIN--I'M GOING TO FINISH YOU!
LITTLE WONDER THAT NOBODY NOTICES MARIE CARTIER RACING DESPERATELY FROM THE GLADE--
THWAM!

many of the current designs of the X-Men or the Legion of Super-Heroes are either still his designs or based off his designs and haven't changed over the past 30 or 40 years.

Yeah, he was just one of those guys who if John R. wasn't available, or even if John was, and they needed a new character, and Dave was around, they'd go, "Hey, you got ten minutes?" 'Cause they'd use him to design the characters. There's an issue of the Hulk called "You Just Don't Quarrel With The Quintronic Man." Which is one of the dumber villains I ever created—a robot that's so complicated it takes five guys to operate him—a guy in each shoulder joint, a guy in each hip joint and a guy in the head—and it takes the five of them working in coordination to make the robot work. And the robot of course says, "You can't get five guys to agree on everything, not even hamburgers!" It was going to be a throwaway at the beginning of the story, but Dave comes in and designs the character and I say, "Oh, I guess he's going to be in it for the whole issue." Because it was too cool to throw away on a two-page or three-page bit at the beginning of the story. The design was just terrific. That was Dave—everything he did had an extraordinary aesthetic sense to it.

You're absolutely right. And thanks for bringing Dave up, too—he contributed so much to the character over the years.

Oh, absolutely. Dave was that wonderful combination of ultimate fan boy and ultimate professional—you know that whatever he did professionally was stunning to look at, and as a fan boy he kept that enthusiasm and never stopped coming up with ideas. It was always, well, "What if?" Which are the best two words that any comic book writer, or any writer, frankly, can ever use. The stories come from "What if?" "What if he could do this, what if he couldn't? What if he wasn't really this?"

And besides Dave, there's only one other thing I want to cover while we're talking—somehow on the Internet over the past decade or more, some idiot got the idea that the whole original concept of Wolverine was that he WAS a Wolverine—highly evolved by the High Evolutionary—no, no and no.

Yeah, I remember seeing that—that was really strange to me at the time.

That's because it is. It's wrong, it never was the case—I always envisioned him as a human being. That's what I write about—I write about human beings. I don't care what their powers are—unless I suppose I was writing Rocket Raccoon!

Well that's all the rage these days!

It sure is—great movie! I saw it over the weekend—terrific film. The Marvel movie batting average is amazing.

[So happy with it over here,] everyone is just ecstatic. It was so nice to finally see it and have it be such a terrific film, and then getting close to 100 million in the box office, it was just amazing.

Well it deserves it—it was funny, it was fun, it's exciting. And it goes straight to the established Marvel mythos while hanging out on the other side of the universe, and I think it's just fine!

Exactly—just a bunch of flawed people hanging around and trying to do the right thing.

Yeah, which defines the Marvel Universe, really. ⊗

DIRECTOR'S CUT
DEATH OF WOLVERINE #1

PAGE ONE
Splash: We are in British Columbia, up in the mountains near the coast. We're looking at an isolated mountain cabin built up on a crag. Sitting on the front stoop of the cabin, we have Logan. His head is bowed, and his claws are popped. He's spattered with blood, much of it his own. This is the pose of a man who has just lived through the latest in what seems like an endless series of battles. We want to convey that he's a warrior, a fighter, but one who's facing the reality that this could be all that he is.

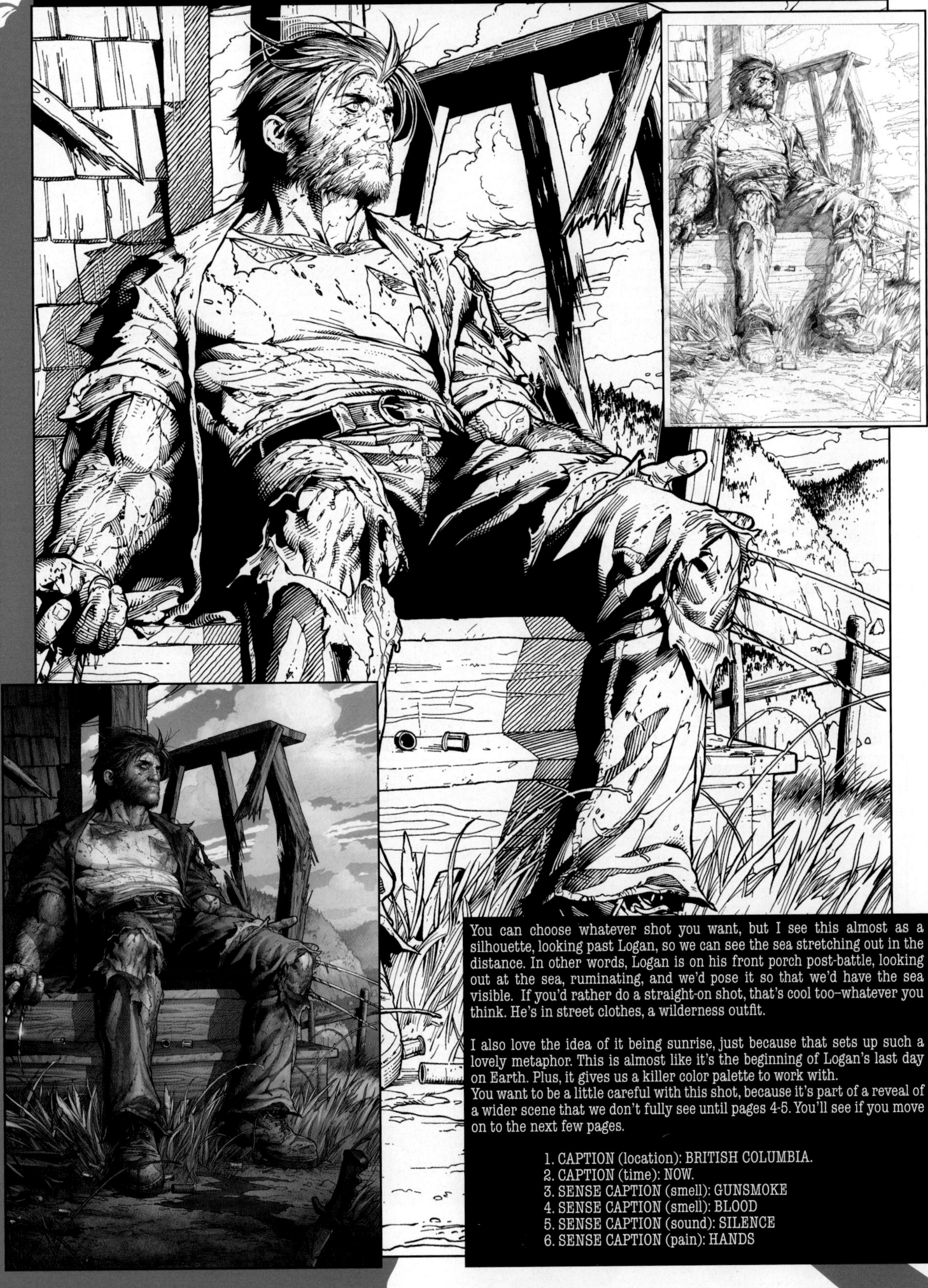

You can choose whatever shot you want, but I see this almost as a silhouette, looking past Logan, so we can see the sea stretching out in the distance. In other words, Logan is on his front porch post-battle, looking out at the sea, ruminating, and we'd pose it so that we'd have the sea visible. If you'd rather do a straight-on shot, that's cool too–whatever you think. He's in street clothes, a wilderness outfit.

I also love the idea of it being sunrise, just because that sets up such a lovely metaphor. This is almost like it's the beginning of Logan's last day on Earth. Plus, it gives us a killer color palette to work with.
You want to be a little careful with this shot, because it's part of a reveal of a wider scene that we don't fully see until pages 4-5. You'll see if you move on to the next few pages.

1. CAPTION (location): BRITISH COLUMBIA.
2. CAPTION (time): NOW.
3. SENSE CAPTION (smell): GUNSMOKE
4. SENSE CAPTION (smell): BLOOD
5. SENSE CAPTION (sound): SILENCE
6. SENSE CAPTION (pain): HANDS

PAGE TWO

Panel 1: Wolverine is standing up from the porch. We've gone a bit wider here, but we still can't see much around him.

NO DIALOGUE.

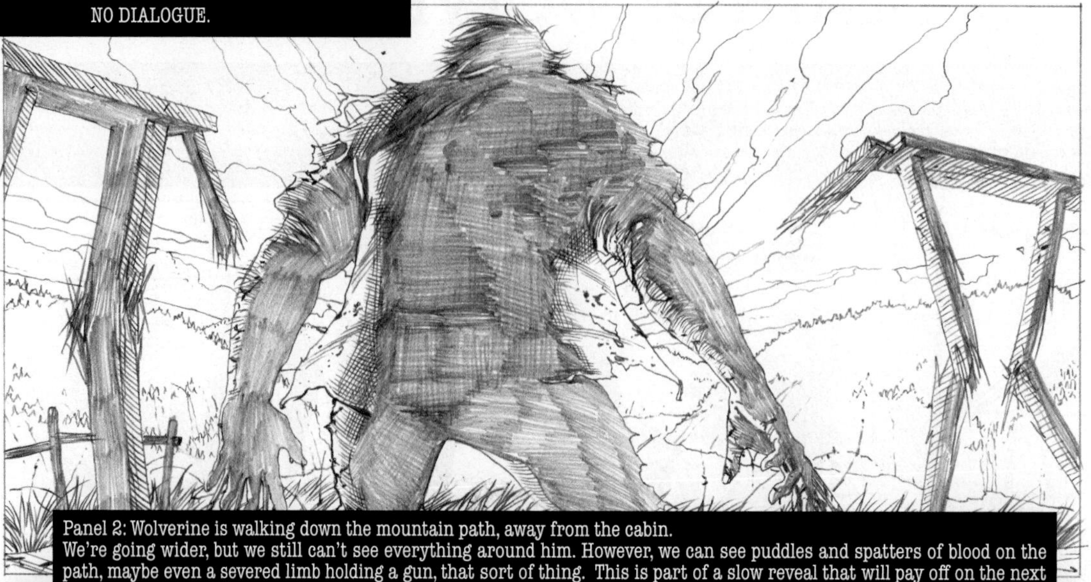

Panel 2: Wolverine is walking down the mountain path, away from the cabin.
We're going wider, but we still can't see everything around him. However, we can see puddles and spatters of blood on the path, maybe even a severed limb holding a gun, that sort of thing. This is part of a slow reveal that will pay off on the next page–we're getting the sense that Logan was just involved in something pretty violent.

Note–his claws are still out here. Blood is dripping off them, much of it Logan's.

NO DIALOGUE.

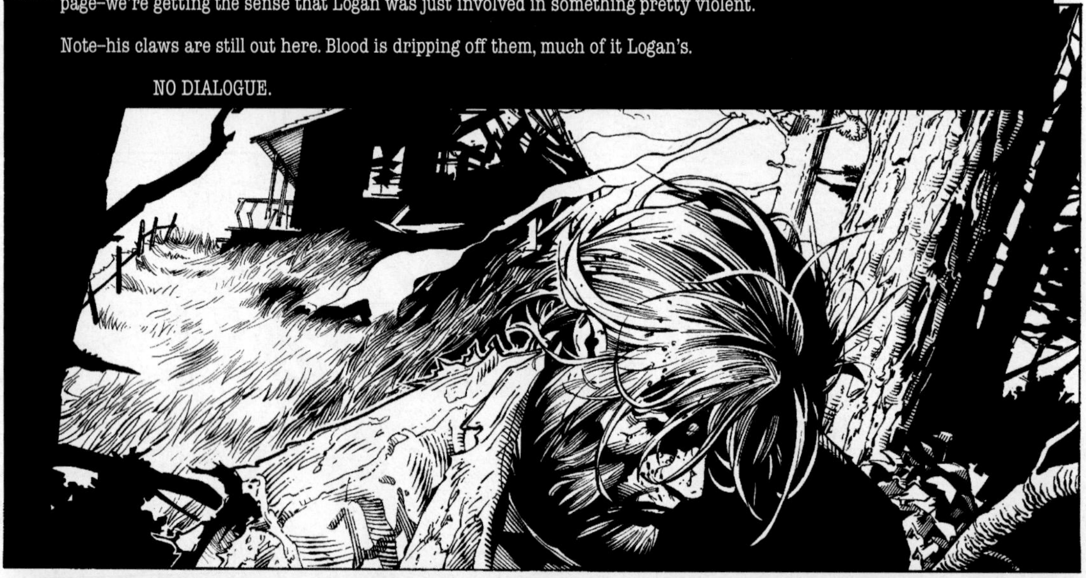

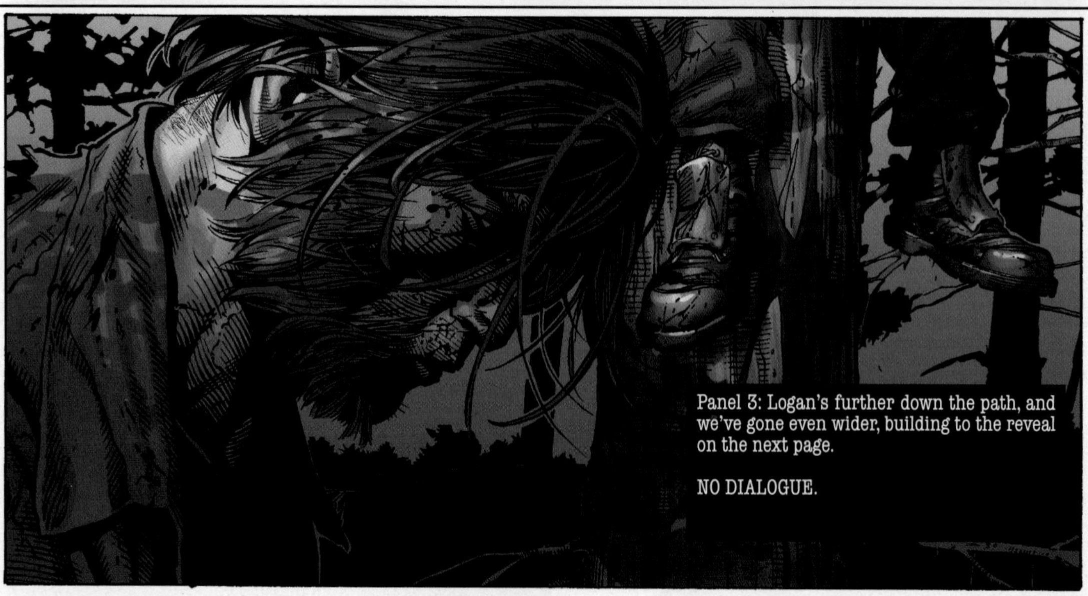

Panel 3: Logan's further down the path, and we've gone even wider, building to the reveal on the next page.

NO DIALOGUE.

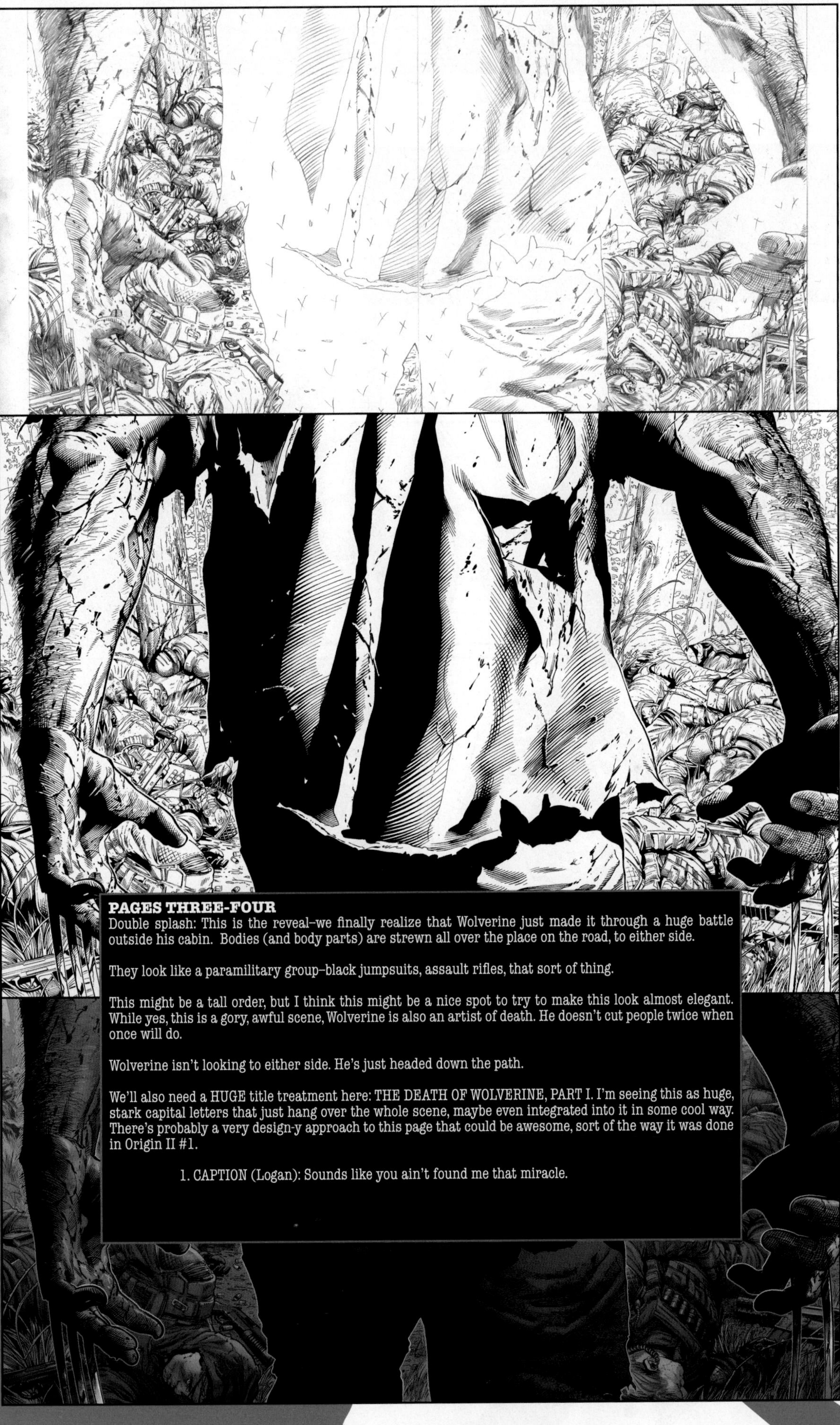

PAGES THREE-FOUR

Double splash: This is the reveal–we finally realize that Wolverine just made it through a huge battle outside his cabin. Bodies (and body parts) are strewn all over the place on the road, to either side.

They look like a paramilitary group–black jumpsuits, assault rifles, that sort of thing.

This might be a tall order, but I think this might be a nice spot to try to make this look almost elegant. While yes, this is a gory, awful scene, Wolverine is also an artist of death. He doesn't cut people twice when once will do.

Wolverine isn't looking to either side. He's just headed down the path.

We'll also need a HUGE title treatment here: THE DEATH OF WOLVERINE, PART I. I'm seeing this as huge, stark capital letters that just hang over the whole scene, maybe even integrated into it in some cool way. There's probably a very design-y approach to this page that could be awesome, sort of the way it was done in Origin II #1.

1. CAPTION (Logan): Sounds like you ain't found me that miracle.

Panel 1: We have changed location–we are now in a lab in the Baxter Building in New York City.

Reed Richards, Mr. Fantastic, is holding up an X-ray of Logan's head to a light source. Both his arm and his neck are stretching a bit, so he can get the X-ray closer to the light, and his eyes closer to the X-ray. Behind him, Wolverine is leaning against a piece of gear — a lab table or something like that. He's not in any sort of costume — it's street-level clothing. Reed seems concerned — whatever the X-ray is showing him, he doesn't like it.

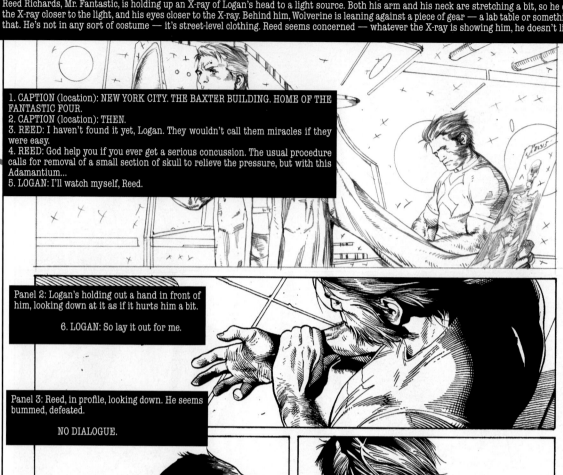

1. CAPTION (location): NEW YORK CITY. THE BAXTER BUILDING. HOME OF THE FANTASTIC FOUR.
2. CAPTION (location): THEN.
3. REED: I haven't found it yet, Logan. They wouldn't call them miracles if they were easy.
4. REED: God help you if you ever get a serious concussion. The usual procedure calls for removal of a small section of skull to relieve the pressure, but with this Adamantium...
5. LOGAN: I'll watch myself, Reed.

Panel 2: Logan's holding out a hand in front of him, looking down at it as if it hurts him a bit.

6. LOGAN: So lay it out for me.

Panel 3: Reed, in profile, looking down. He seems bummed, defeated.

NO DIALOGUE.

Panel 4: Same shot, except Reed has turned to face Logan. He's looking up, straight at him.

9. REED: All right. Listen.
10. REED: You have lost your healing factor. The problem is that everything you do–your entire physical structure–is built around the fact that you can rapidly heal from almost any injury.
11. REED: Or... you could.

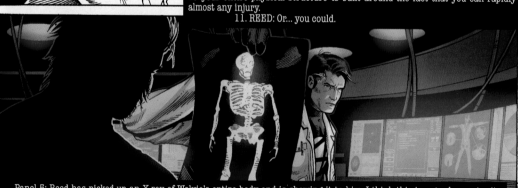

Panel 5: Reed has picked up an X-ray of Wolvie's entire body and is showing it to him–I think this is a good opportunity to showcase Reed's stretchy powers again–he's stretching his arm across the room a bit to show the X-ray to Wolverine. Logan's metal skeleton is clearly visible in white.

12. REED: You still have your strength, your speed. That's good–otherwise you wouldn't be able to move with this much metal inside you.
13. REED: But that's the only good news.
14. REED: Your bones are mildly radioactive from various exposures over the decades. Didn't you tell me once you were present at Nagasaki?

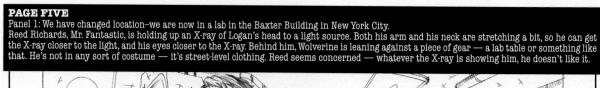

PAGE SIX

Panel 1: Panel of Logan being incinerated–the idea is that he's remembering back to Nagasaki, when he survived the blast in World War II. If you want to make this more of a wide shot, with the mushroom cloud, the harbor, etc., I'd be totally into that. This is our one chance to refer to Logan's WW2 history, so I'd love to make it cool.

NO DIALOGUE.

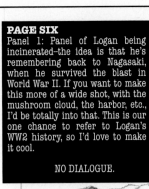

Panel 2: Logan, tight on his face. Cool as a cucumber.

1. LOGAN: Yeah.

Panel 3: Back to a wider shot.

2. REED: Yes, well. The upshot is that you're a prime candidate for heavy-metal related leukemia.
3. REED: That's assuming you don't get endocarditis from all the bacteria you keep pulling into yourself every time you use your claws.

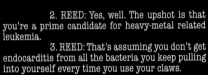
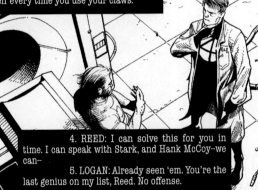

4. REED: I can solve this for you in time. I can speak with Stark, and Hank McCoy–we can–
5. LOGAN: Already seen 'em. You're the last genius on my list, Reed. No offense.

Panel 4: Reed.

6. REED: None taken. We've never been close.
7. REED: But that doesn't mean I want to see you die. You're important, Logan. The things you've accomplished in your life... the world needs you.
8. REED: I can reactivate your healing factor. I know I can. But I need time. You have to stop fighting. Stay out of things for a while. Find a place to hole up.

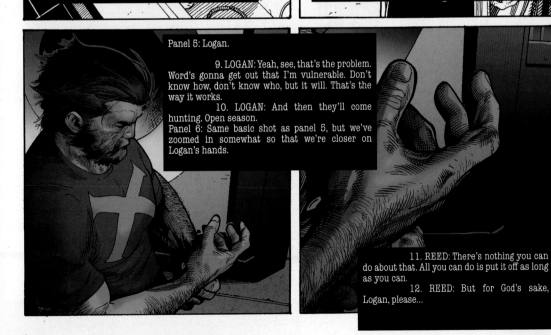

Panel 5: Logan.

9. LOGAN: Yeah, see, that's the problem. Word's gonna get out that I'm vulnerable. Don't know how, don't know who, but it will. That's the way it works.
10. LOGAN: And then they'll come hunting. Open season.

Panel 6: Same basic shot as panel 5, but we've zoomed in somewhat so that we're closer on Logan's hands.

11. REED: There's nothing you can do about that. All you can do is put it off as long as you can.
12. REED: But for God's sake, Logan, please...

PAGE SEVEN

Panel 1: Large, close-up panel of the backs of Wolverine's hands, which look horribly lacerated, bruised, etc. They look, in other words, how a person's hands might look if six incredibly sharp knives were shoved through them. The claws are still out.

The idea here, hopefully, is that it will feel something like a continuation of the last panel on page 5, like a jump cut from his uninjured hands to his wrecked ones.

We're back in British Columbia, in the scene we last saw on page 1.

1. CAPTION (Reed): ...do not use your claws.

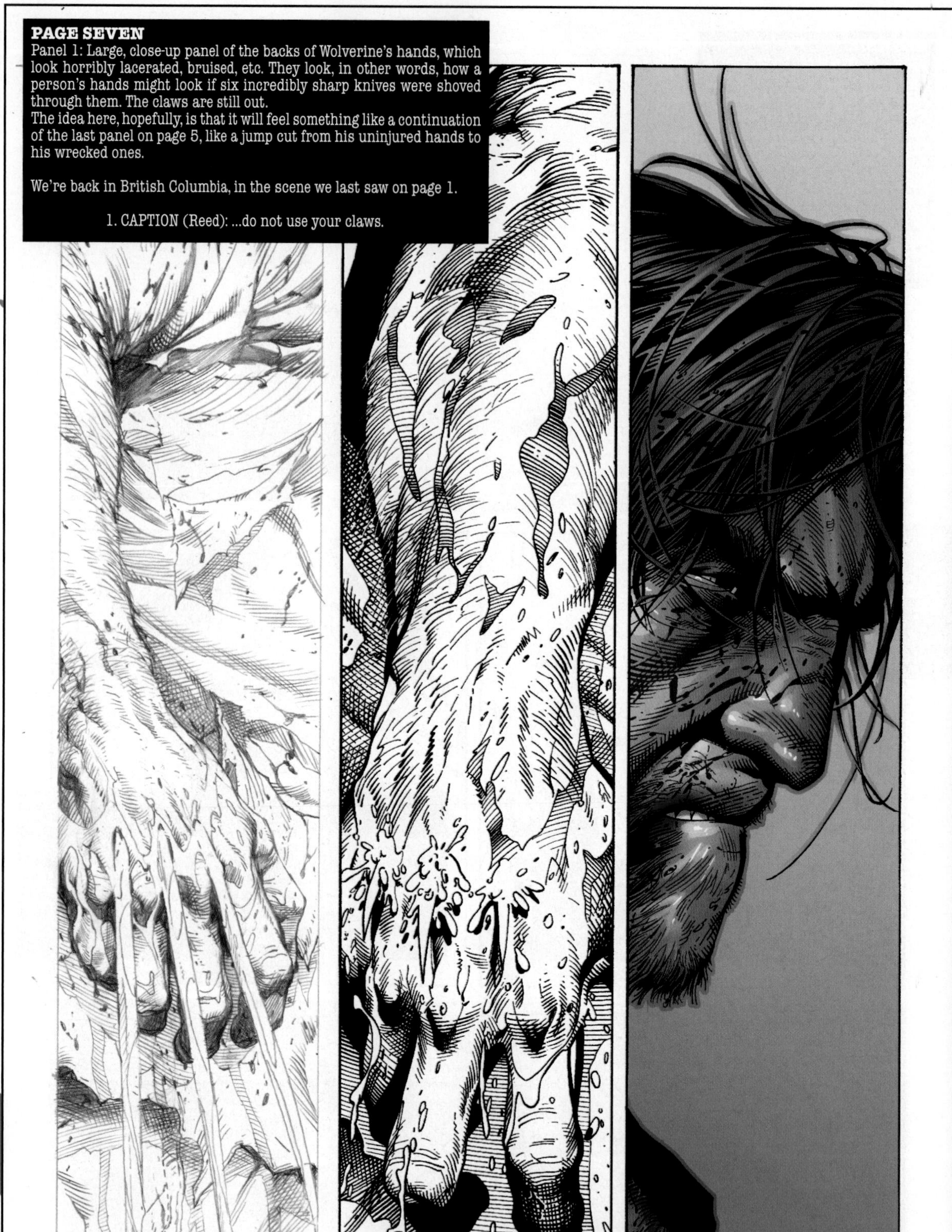

Panel 2: Wolverine is retracting his claws. Blood is spraying out - it seems painful, gory, and gross.

SFX: SHKK

1. SENSE CAPTION (Pain): HANDS (let's make this bigger and more intense than the one on page one–the idea should be to convey that this hurts like hell.)

Panel 3: Tight on Wolverine's face, or even just his jaw–his mouth has tightened, and his face is clenched–we want to suggest that this hurt him. He's vulnerable. We'll hit that note again and again.

NO DIALOGUE.

Panel 1: Wolverine has entered a small fishing town on the coast. Not much to it, just a main street, a few side streets, very small. This is essentially an establishing shot–if you prefer, you can get this into the splash on page 7, by showing Logan from behind looking down towards this town.

Logan is entering a bar on the main street, just a total dive, pretty much home base for a guy like Logan. He should have rags wrapped around his hands–ripped-off pieces of shirt, just temporary bandages.

NO DIALOGUE.

Panel 2: We're now just inside, looking at the bar from Logan's POV. This is a FLASHBACK to let's say 80 years before. The bar should look appropriate for the 1930s, and should be colored differently than present-day stuff. (Sepia-toned? Greyscale? Sort of misty?) A few scattered drinkers are sitting at the bar, but not too many. Again, all dressed in 1930s-appropriate wear.
The bartender, a stout-but-strong fellow with grey muttonchops, is polishing a glass and calling out to Logan.

      1. BARTENDER: Hey, Logan. Been–

Panel 3: The same exact shot as panel 2, but now it is present day — the flashback is over. The bartender is in the same place, doing the same thing, but he looks younger–this is the original bartender's great-grandson. I'd still include some drinkers, but put them in different spots.

A television is mounted above the bar, where a talking head news broadcast is playing. The little inset on the TV screen next to the guy's head has a photo (headshot) of a handsome, blonde young man (20s) on it.

      1. SENSE CAPTION (smell): BAR
      2. BARTENDER: –a little while since you've been in. You want one?
      3. LOGAN: Sure. Actually, give me the whole bottle, no glass, and a couple clean bar rags, if you got 'em. And your phone. That all right?
      4. BARTENDER: Sounds like a solid afternoon. Comin' up.
      5. TV (radio balloon): –the missing plane containing the French Olympians is just the latest in a string of disappearances of high-profile athletes. At this point–

Panel 4: Logan is seated at the bar. He's got the bottle of whiskey in one hand, and some bar rags in the other. He's pouring the whiskey into the rags, soaking them. A rotary-style phone is on the bar next to him, the cord extending back behind the bar. He has removed the dirty temp bandages from his hands–they look raw and awful.

      6. SENSE CAPTION (smell): ROTGUT

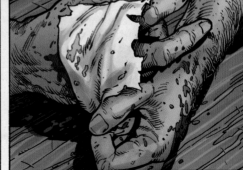

Panel 5: Logan is wrapping the bandages around his hands. He's wincing, gritting his teeth a little — even for Logan, this hurts. You could do this as a tight shot of his hands if you prefer–whatever you think works.

      7. SENSE CAPTION (pain): HANDS

PAGE NINE

Panel 1: Logan is now talking on the phone. His hands are now "bandaged," more or less. As a subtle thing, let's have them be in the shape of an 'X' across the back of his hands.

1. PHONE (radio bubble): Logan! My god. I was just thinking about you.
2. LOGAN: Yeah?
3. PHONE: Yeah. You know Battlestar?
4. LOGAN: Battlest- Cap's guy?
5. PHONE: Yeah. His shield was stolen, I guess. It's made of Adamantium. Made me think of you.

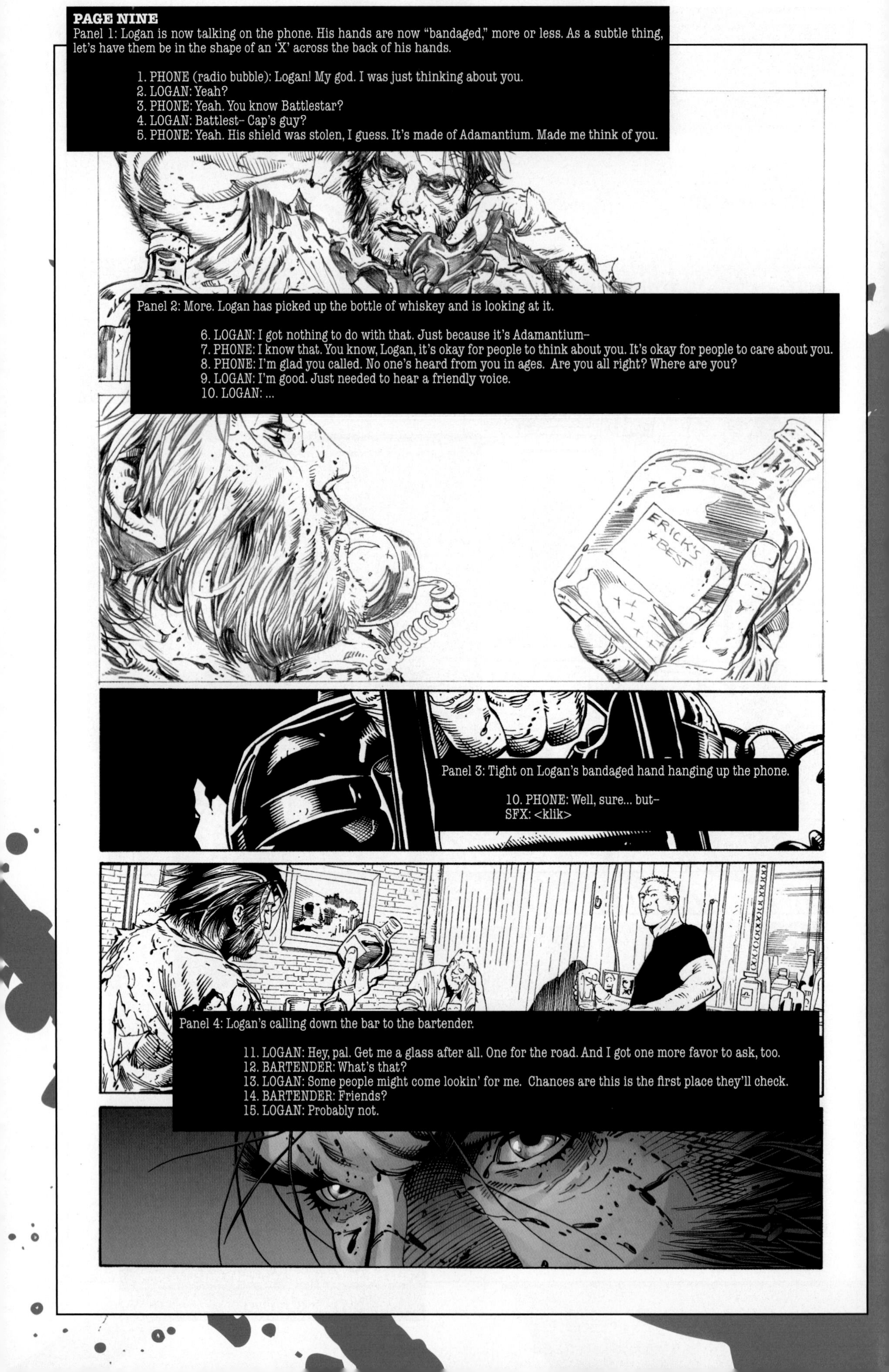
ERICK'S
*BEST

Panel 2: More. Logan has picked up the bottle of whiskey and is looking at it.

6. LOGAN: I got nothing to do with that. Just because it's Adamantium–
7. PHONE: I know that. You know, Logan, it's okay for people to think about you. It's okay for people to care about you.
8. PHONE: I'm glad you called. No one's heard from you in ages. Are you all right? Where are you?
9. LOGAN: I'm good. Just needed to hear a friendly voice.
10. LOGAN: ...

Panel 3: Tight on Logan's bandaged hand hanging up the phone.

10. PHONE: Well, sure... but–
SFX: <klik>

Panel 4: Logan's calling down the bar to the bartender.

11. LOGAN: Hey, pal. Get me a glass after all. One for the road. And I got one more favor to ask, too.
12. BARTENDER: What's that?
13. LOGAN: Some people might come lookin' for me. Chances are this is the first place they'll check.
14. BARTENDER: Friends?
15. LOGAN: Probably not.

PAGE TEN (The point of this page is to suggest that some time is passing--it's all basically the same shot, but you can arrange as you like.)
Panel 1: Shot looking down the bar past the bartender, towards the front door. Wolverine is leaving. Still day, visible through the window.

NO DIALOGUE.

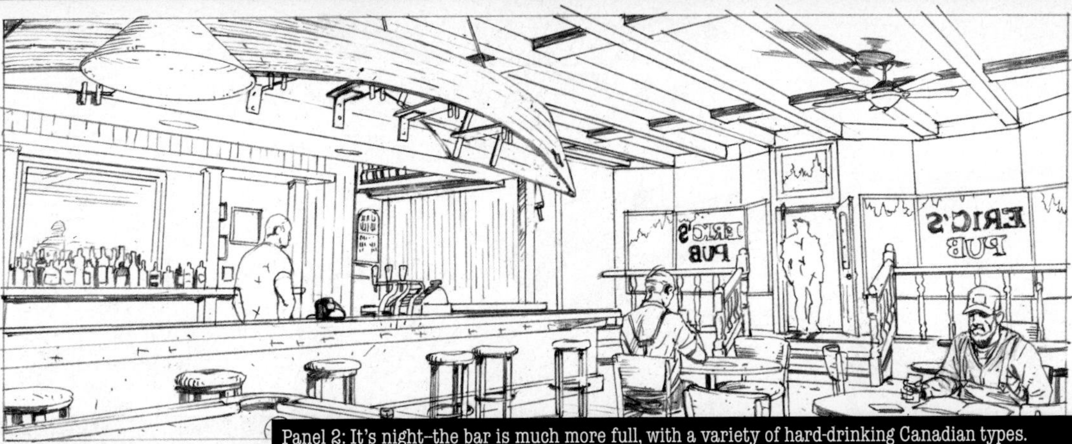
MORNING
ERIC'S PUB
ERIC'S PUB
FILL IN ERIC'S PUB LETTERS

Panel 2: It's night–the bar is much more full, with a variety of hard-drinking Canadian types.

NO DIALOGUE.

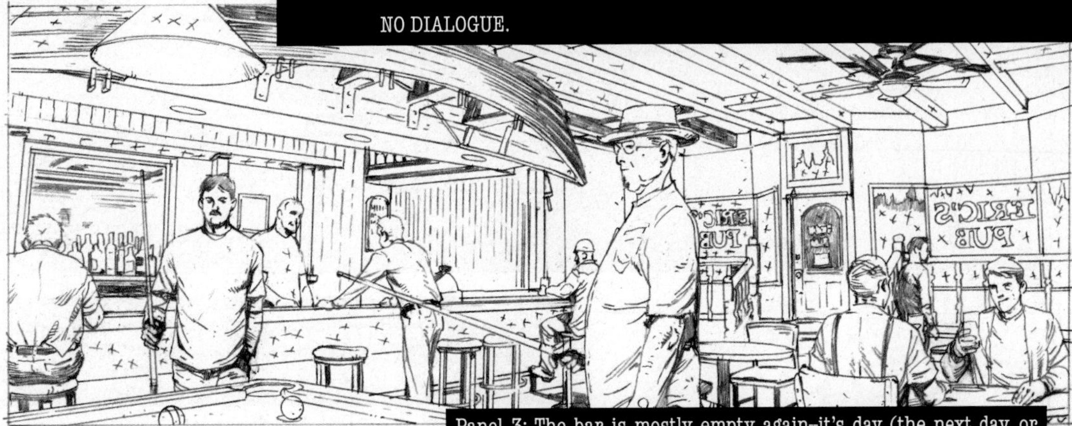
NIGHT
ERIC'S PUB
ERIC'S PUB
DON'T FILL IN

Panel 3: The bar is mostly empty again–it's day (the next day, or so). The bartender is polishing the bar with a cloth or something like that.

NO DIALOGUE.

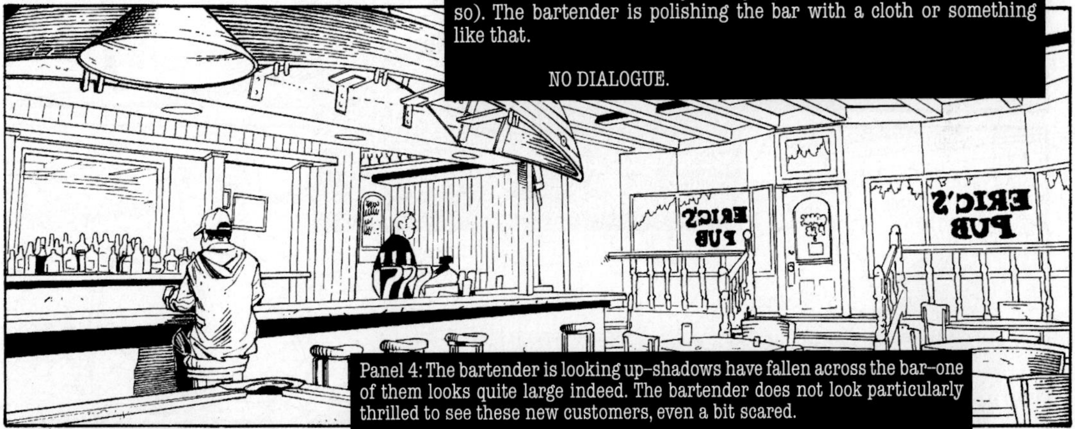
ERIC'S PUB
ERIC'S PUB

Panel 4: The bartender is looking up–shadows have fallen across the bar–one of them looks quite large indeed. The bartender does not look particularly thrilled to see these new customers, even a bit scared.

1. VOICE (O.S.): Hello there. Four beers, please.
2. BARTENDER: You... you want anything in particular?
3. VOICE (O.S.): Doesn't really matter–

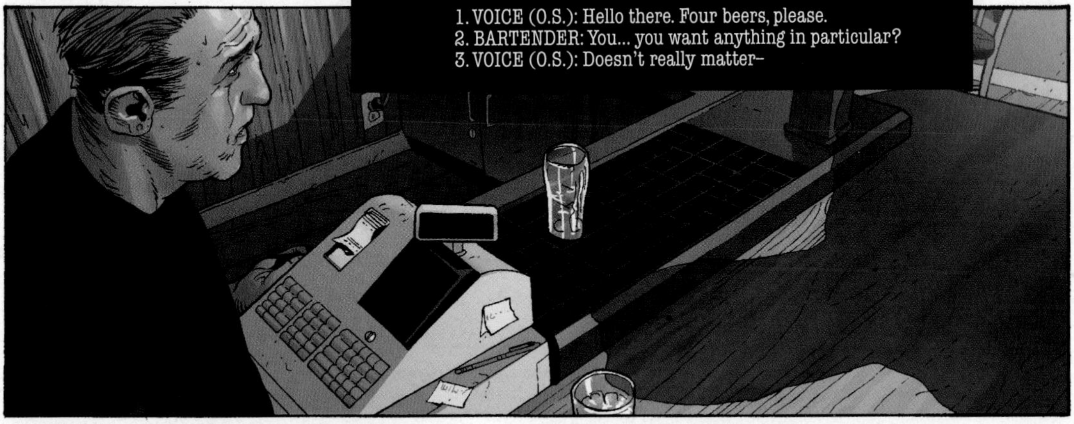

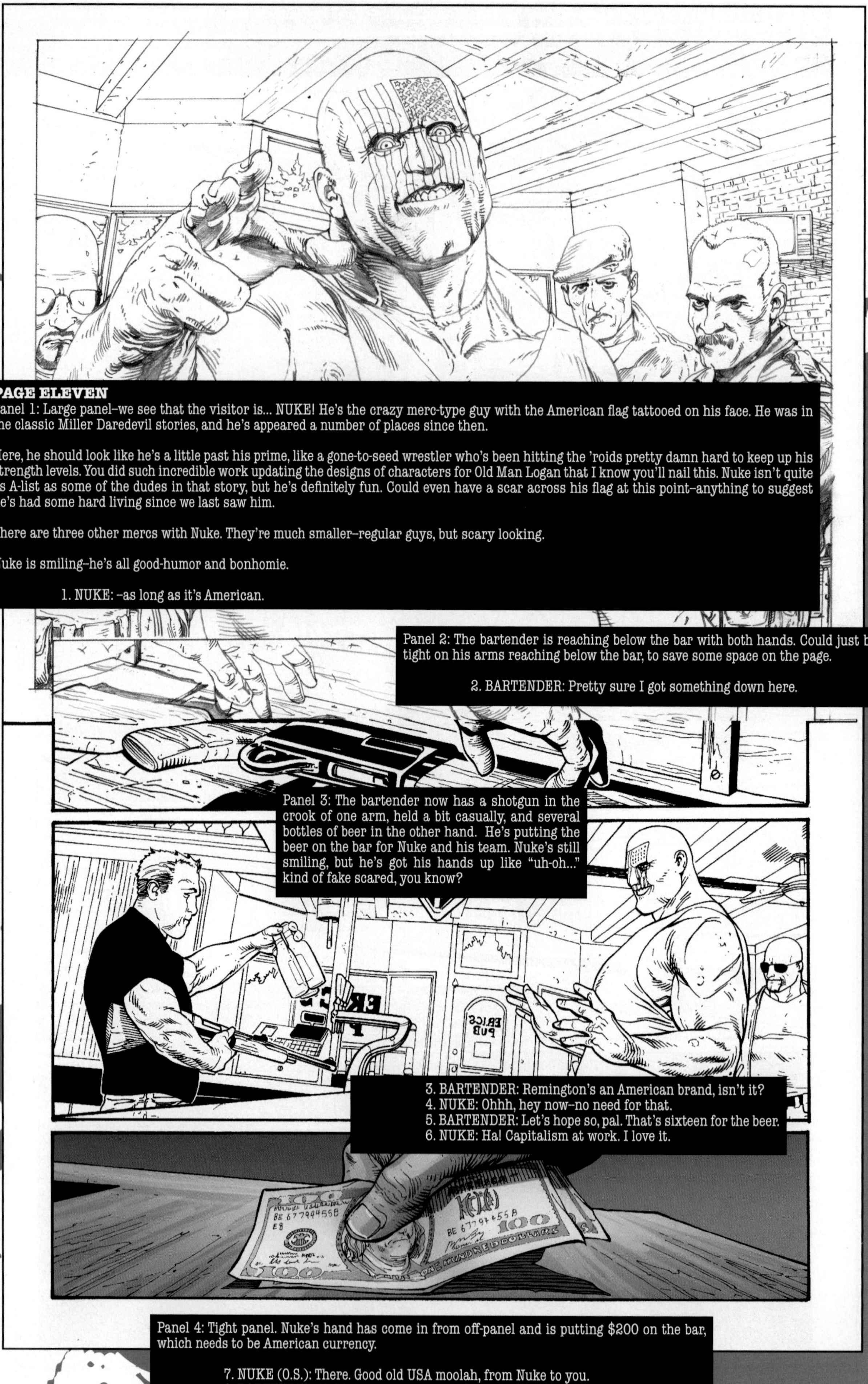

PAGE ELEVEN

Panel 1: Large panel–we see that the visitor is... NUKE! He's the crazy merc-type guy with the American flag tattooed on his face. He was in the classic Miller Daredevil stories, and he's appeared a number of places since then.

Here, he should look like he's a little past his prime, like a gone-to-seed wrestler who's been hitting the 'roids pretty damn hard to keep up his strength levels. You did such incredible work updating the designs of characters for Old Man Logan that I know you'll nail this. Nuke isn't quite as A-list as some of the dudes in that story, but he's definitely fun. Could even have a scar across his flag at this point–anything to suggest he's had some hard living since we last saw him.

There are three other mercs with Nuke. They're much smaller–regular guys, but scary looking.

Nuke is smiling–he's all good-humor and bonhomie.

1. NUKE: –as long as it's American.

Panel 2: The bartender is reaching below the bar with both hands. Could just be tight on his arms reaching below the bar, to save some space on the page.

2. BARTENDER: Pretty sure I got something down here.

Panel 3: The bartender now has a shotgun in the crook of one arm, held a bit casually, and several bottles of beer in the other hand. He's putting the beer on the bar for Nuke and his team. Nuke's still smiling, but he's got his hands up like "uh-oh..." kind of fake scared, you know?

3. BARTENDER: Remington's an American brand, isn't it?
4. NUKE: Ohhh, hey now–no need for that.
5. BARTENDER: Let's hope so, pal. That's sixteen for the beer.
6. NUKE: Ha! Capitalism at work. I love it.

Panel 4: Tight panel. Nuke's hand has come in from off-panel and is putting $200 on the bar, which needs to be American currency.

7. NUKE (O.S.): There. Good old USA moolah, from Nuke to you.
8. BARTENDER (O.S.): I said sixteen. What's the rest for?

DIRECTOR'S CUT
DEATH OF WOLVERINE #2

PAGES THREE-FOUR

Splash: WOLVERINE! Our boy is lounging back in the booth–total VIP stuff. He has each arm around a gorgeous lady, and the remains of what appears to be an amazing evening litter the table.

Logan himself is rocking a pretty amazing look. For one thing, he's in a tuxedo, with the bow tie untied and his collar unbuttoned. For another, his head is shaved. (The idea being that he doesn't want to be recognized, and his hairstyle is, after all, pretty recognizable.) He's wearing a pair of dark sunglasses, and he's grinning, totally relaxed. In case you're curious, he does not have a patch over his eye here.
He should have some bruises on his face — these are remnants of the injuries he took in the fight with Nuke back in Issue 1. He should still have the bandages on his hands, too–the X-shaped wraps–but these are clean, not the filthy rags he used back then.

Basically, it's a total Ocean's 11 / James Bond look, and it is amazing.

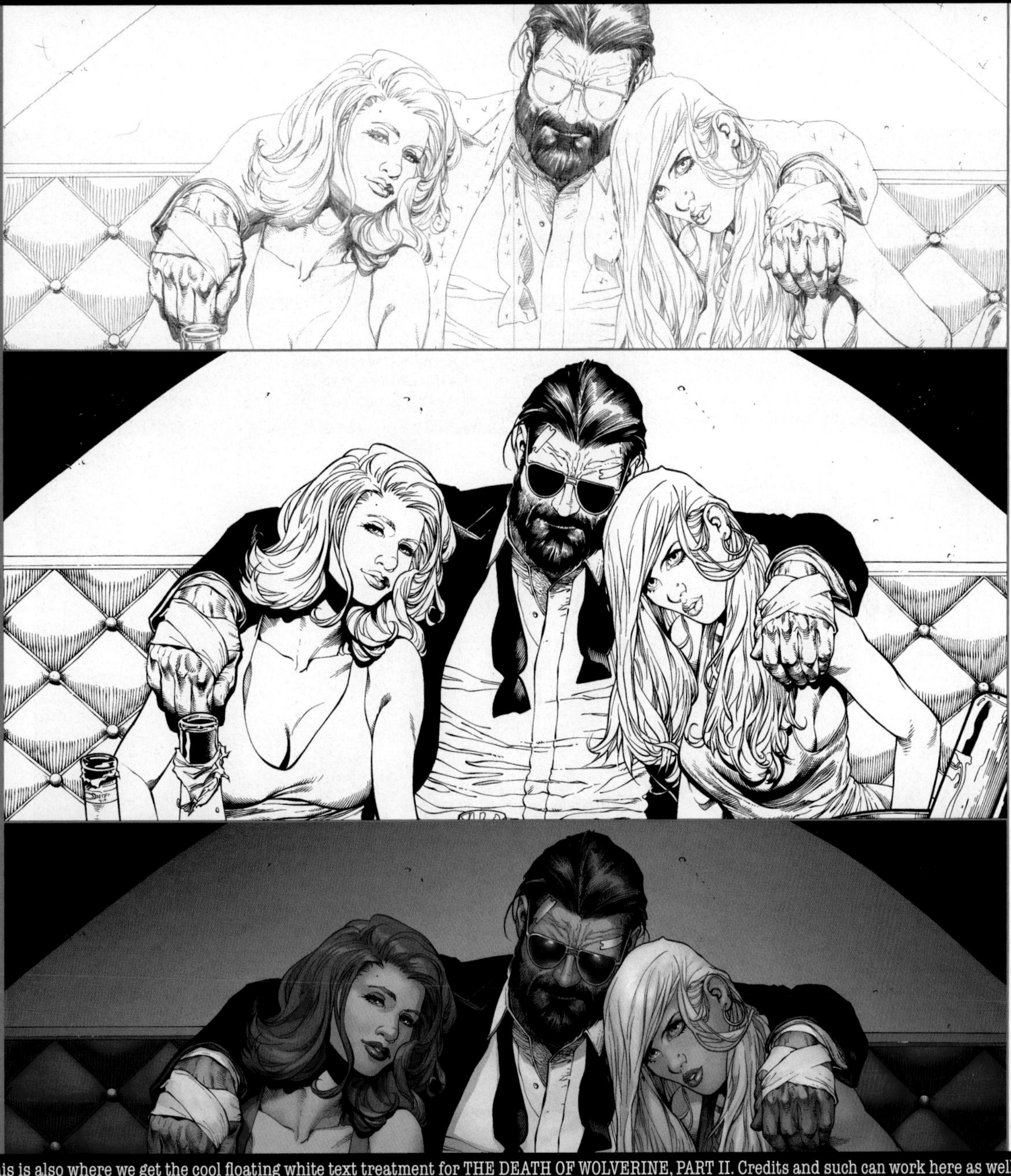

This is also where we get the cool floating white text treatment for THE DEATH OF WOLVERINE, PART II. Credits and such can work here as well.

1. LOGAN: Hey, man.
2. LOGAN: Have a seat.

TITLE & CREDITS:
THE DEATH OF WOLVERINE, PART II

PAGE SEVEN

Panel 1: Koro peering through the curtain.

1. LOGAN (O.S.): Real enough for you?

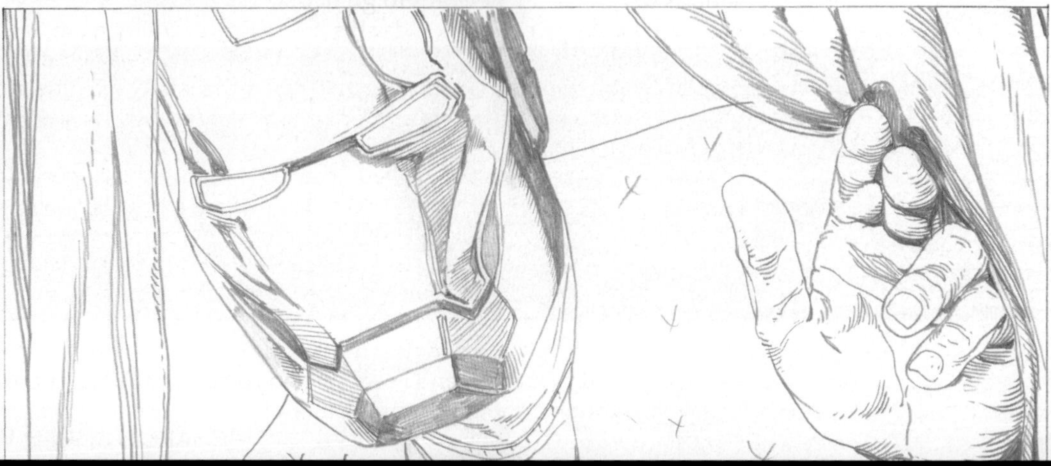

Panel 2: Awesome shot of the bar, as seen through the Iron Man helmet's interface. What we're seeing is that at least half the people in the bar have weapons strapped to themselves under their clothes, even (especially) the hot young ladies in cocktail dresses. Shotguns are stashed under the bar, bags are filled with cash, certain people have dossiers popping up next to them (actually, one thing that would be super cool would be to have one of the people be a Marvel U villain–can we have one of these fellows be Kristoff Vernard, the son of Dr. Doom? I'm trying to establish him as a total Eurotrash party guy in some of the other stuff I'm writing, and this is exactly the kind of scene where he'd hang out.

2. CAPTION (Koro, quotes): "This is...incredible. The tactical advantage something like this could convey... What is your price?"
3. CAPTION (Logan): "No offense, Koro, but I didn't come here to deal with an underling.
4. CAPTION (Logan): "If Viper wants this, she'll have to deal with me in person."
5. CAPTION (Koro): "...
6. CAPTION (Koro): "You may come to regret your insistence. But very well...
7. CAPTION (Koro): "...I will take you to the Lady."

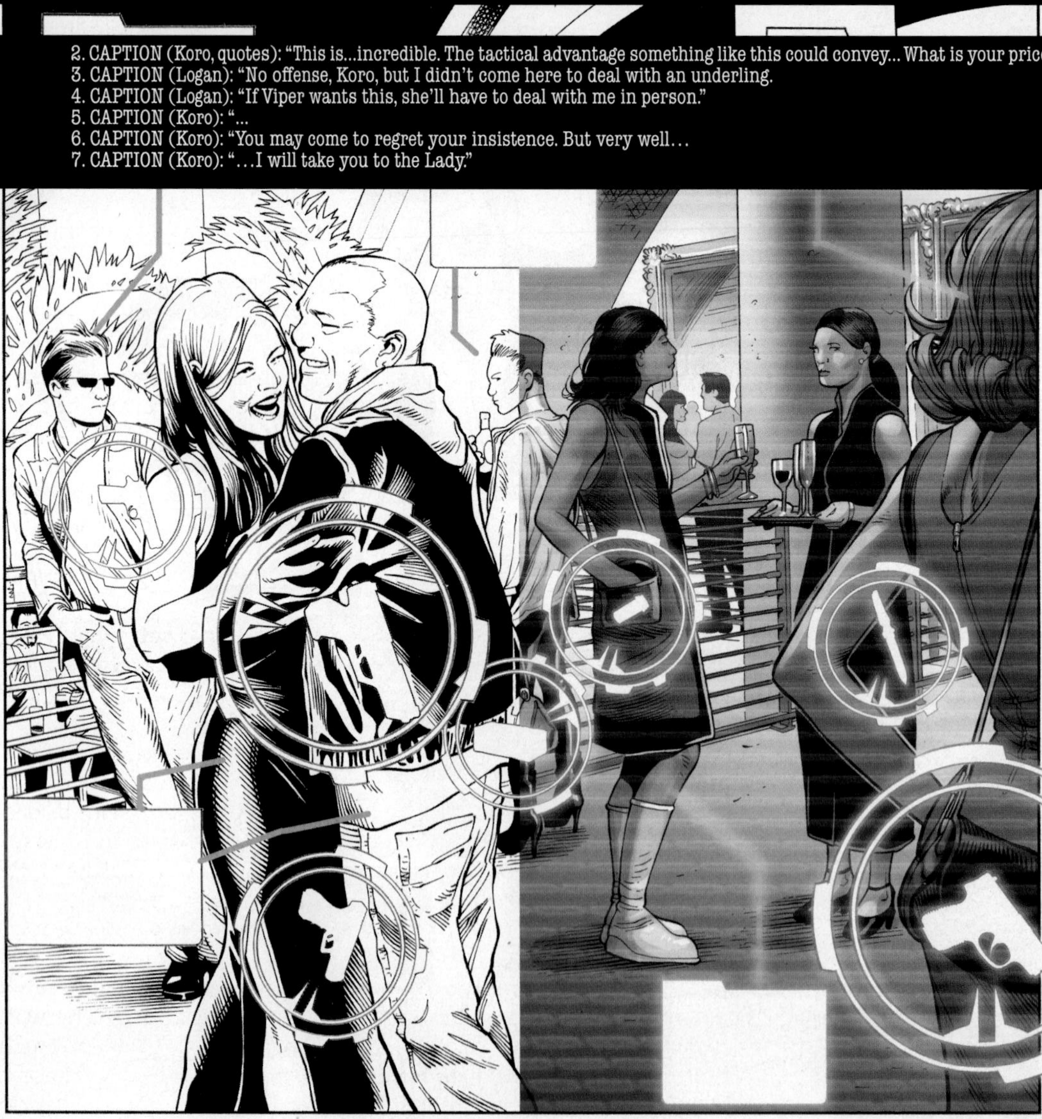

REFLECTIONS FROM THE CREATORS

Being asked to write this book was all the things you would probably expect it to be, and since a quote about that wouldn't be all that revelatory, I'd rather talk about the experience of making it. I kicked around a few metaphors, and after some serious deliberation, decided to go nautical. I've never been a sailor on a 19th century ship, but I've read a lot of books about those intrepid folks. Every one of them, from the captain on down, had to know their job perfectly while also relying completely on the idea that everyone else knew their job perfectly, or their little speck of livable environment would sink into the bottom of the distinctly unlivable environment surrounding them. The invention and operation of tall ships always strikes me as one of the most incredible achievements of human ingenuity.

Was *Death of Wolverine* quite as amazing as inventing a schooner and sailing it around the world? No. It's a comic, albeit a comic which attempts to provide a noble, fitting end to an extraordinarily well-known pop culture figure. No one would die if we screwed up (except Logan, obviously), but here's the thing — everyone on the team acted as if we would. A level of professionalism and dedication to craft that doesn't always show up in entertainment products appeared, and stuck around to the very last page. Everyone wanted to make something special, and A-games were brought all around. McNiven, Leisten, Ponsor, Eliopolous, Alonso, Marts, Kubert and Jarowey (not to mention all the behind-the-scenes folks who had their hands on this project in one way or another) — that's a hell of a crew, and I was so glad to be a part of it. Thank you to all of them, and to every reader who gave this book a try. On to the next one!

—CHARLES SOULE, WRITER

What can I say? This has been an amazing time for me, working on the book with such a talented group of folks during such a pivotal moment in a character's history.

I can only hope that I did justice to Charles' wonderful scripts, and that I didn't cause too many headaches for Jay and Justin over the course of putting this series together.

I jumped at the chance to do this book when Mike offered it to me, as Wolverine is one of those characters that I love to draw, and I gotta say this has been one of those times when I relished every moment of drawing these pages.

Those last few pages, though, difficult stuff to draw, but I hope it connects to some of the readers of this series and fans of Wolverine. May he rest in peace.

—STEVE McNIVEN, PENCILLER

In my early teens I met a character that would change my life, Logan, or Patch, as he was called on the rough streets of Madripoor. Before then I had been aware of comics and a fan of many characters in the genre, but something about him and the way he was drawn was different. At the time, Marc Silvestri was drawing *Uncanny X-men* and there was a real power in his drawings, especially Wolverine. He made him so intense, with a darkness to his outward appearance. When Marc moved over to draw the Wolverine solo title, I was sold immediately! The energy he brought, along with inker Dan Green, was so intense! That run with him and Sabretooth (42-45? 1991) is some of my favorite comics. It's all fur, teeth and visceral passion, with this great artwork that flipped a switch for me. I wondered what it would take to do the art in the books I was seeing every week. Now 20 years later here I am working on the characters that started it all, with a group of friends and co-workers who are all trying to give another generation that same kind of story that will ignite the passion in them to create an experience much the same as this. *Death of Wolverine* is exactly the kind of project I'd hoped it would be. A fond farewell, to a friend, from people who loved him. Your furry arms and hair wings will be missed, my friend.

—JAY LEISTEN, INKER

Here is the project that makes me wish for a time machine to show my 15-year-old self what I'd be doing a couple decades on. Even among all the fantastic projects in which I've been fortunate enough to participate, Wolverine's swan song would undoubtedly excite that young Patch fan most — especially if I could show the level of craftsmanship involved.

I tried to figure out a way to praise my colleagues that won't sound like the effusive, actor-in-a-press-junket gushing. But really, everyone turned in performances at the tops of their respective games. We managed to squeeze so much into a short tale that was world-hopping in scope, full of villains and violence, yet reflective, personal and steeped in the character's history. So much credit should go to the captains of the ship for its success. I'm just happy to have been invited. This is a book I will be able to look back upon with pride, knowing no corner was cut in presenting the best possible series for Logan's curtain call.

—JUSTIN PONSOR, COLORIST

I've always found Wolverine to be a really cool character. The mysterious loner who can barely control his dark side, but always striving to do what's right. To be better than what people thought he was. When I was on staff at Marvel many years ago, I had the joy of doing lettering corrections as well as the logo for the Weapon X series. So, I've been there for his birth and now his death…and, who knows, perhaps beyond. Wolverine and Puck, my two favorite characters in the Marvel Universe. Both are short, mysterious and Canadian. Strangely, just like me…except the mysterious and Canadian part.

—CHRIS ELIOPOULOS, LETTERER